MW00565080

WORKSHOPPING THE CANON

NCTE Editorial Board

Steven Bickmore

Catherine Compton-Lilly

Deborah Dean

Bruce McComiskey

Jennifer Ochoa

Duane Roen

Anne Elrod Whitney

Vivian Yenika-Agbaw

Kurt Austin, chair (ex officio)

Emily Kirkpatrick (ex officio)

Workshopping the Canon

Mary E. Styslinger
University of South Carolina

NATIONAL COUNCIL OF TEACHERS OF ENGLISH
1111 W. KENYON ROAD, URBANA, ILLINOIS 61801-1096
WWW.NCTE.ORG

Staff Editor: Bonny Graham

Production Editor: The Charlesworth Group

Interior Design: Jenny Jensen Greenleaf

Cover Design: Pat Mayer

Portions of this text and student work were previously published in NCTE journals, including *English Journal, Talking Points,* and *Voices from the Middle.* Used with permission.

NCTE Stock Number: 58470; eStock Number: 58494
ISBN 978-0-8141-5847-0; eISBN 978-0-8141-5849-4

©2017 by the National Council of Teachers of English.

All rights reserved. No part of this publication may be reproduced or transmitted in any form or by any means, electronic or mechanical, including photocopy, or any information storage and retrieval system, without permission from the copyright holder. Printed in the United States of America.

It is the policy of NCTE in its journals and other publications to provide a forum for the open discussion of ideas concerning the content and the teaching of English and the language arts. Publicity accorded to any particular point of view does not imply endorsement by the Executive Committee, the Board of Directors, or the membership at large, except in announcements of policy, where such endorsement is clearly specified.

NCTE provides equal employment opportunity (EEO) to all staff members and applicants for employment without regard to race, color, religion, sex, national origin, age, physical, mental or perceived handicap/disability, sexual orientation including gender identity or expression, ancestry, genetic information, marital status, military status, unfavorable discharge from military service, pregnancy, citizenship status, personal appearance, matriculation or political affiliation, or any other protected status under applicable federal, state, and local laws.

Every effort has been made to provide current URLs and email addresses, but because of the rapidly changing nature of the Web, some sites and addresses may no longer be accessible.

Library of Congress Cataloging-in-Publication Data

Names: Styslinger, Mary E., 1966- author.
Title: Workshopping the canon / Mary E. Styslinger.
Description: Urbana, Illinois : National Council of Teachers of English, 2017. | Includes bibliographical references and index. |
Identifiers: LCCN 2017028801 (print) | LCCN 2017047562 (ebook) | ISBN 9780814158494 () | ISBN 9780814158470 (pbk.)
Subjects: LCSH: Language arts (Middle school) | Language arts (Secondary) | Canon (Literature)—Study and teaching (Middle school) | Canon (Literature)—Study and teaching (Secondary)
Classification: LCC LB1631 (ebook) | LCC LB1631 .S838 2017 (print) | DDC 428.0071/2—dc23
LC record available at https://lccn.loc.gov/2017028801

For my husband, John Clothiaux, who has always believed in me; for my daughters, Sophie and Anabelle, who now know that anything is possible with hard work; for my mother and father, who would have loved to have read this book.

Contents

Acknowledgments

This book could not have been written without the inspiration and guidance of the many teachers I have known in Alabama, Ohio, and South Carolina. They have whispered in my ear during this long writing process, offering words, ideas, and encouragement. Professors and classmates from Auburn and Kent State University; teachers from St. Vincent-St. Mary and Coventry High School; teacher-consultants from the Midlands Writing Project; literacy coaches in the South Carolina Reading Initiative; and the many students, teachers, and colleagues I have come to know at the University of South Carolina.

I would especially like to acknowledge and thank those teachers who shared their classroom experiences in the pages of this book: Jesse Barrett, Charles Bell, Tempie Bowers, Angela Byrd, Jenn Doyle, Emily Langdon Eberlin, Kayla Hyatt Hostetler, Lamar Johnson, Jessica Overstreet, Timothy Pollock, Nicole Walker, Julianne Oliver Ware, and Alison Whisenant. I also want to recognize the following graduate students: Kayla Finn, Erin McCarthy, Brittany Porter, and Amber Snelgrove. You all amaze me with your passion, talent, and commitment to the profession. Thank you for lending your voice and sharing your models and ideas. Schools are better places because of you.

And last, I would like to thank the editorial team at the National Council of Teachers of English, especially Samantha MacDonald and Bonny Graham, for believing this book into being. None of this would be possible without your professional commitment and expertise.

Introduction

Thought must be divided against itself before it can come to any knowledge of itself.

—ALDOUS HUXLEY, *Brave New World*

*I*t's a Tuesday morning, around 9:45, in a nondescript high school classroom. A teacher sits on a stool, ready to introduce twelfth graders to Macbeth. Joaquin puts his head down. Steve is more direct and asks, "Ms. S., I still don't get why we gotta read this stuff. It don't got nothing to do with me, and it's too hard to understand."

Ready to defend Shakespeare, I respond, "What about the idea of ambition? You're on the basketball team, right? How far would you go if some witches, or recruiters, predicted you could play for the NBA someday? How far would *you* go to make this happen? Even though this play is really old, the ideas in it are relevant to your life today. Give it a chance." I hold up three articles—one about a mother who attempted to hire a hitman to kill her daughter's cheerleading rival, another about an attack on a figure skater instigated by a competitor, and a third about songwriters accused of copying a Marvin Gaye song. "I want each of you to choose one of these short articles to read in class today. Either while reading or after reading—whatever is easiest—write down at least two things you learned from your reading and one question you have about your article. Then we are going to talk about what we read in small groups. At the end of class, I'm going to play you a song called "I Want It All.'" I gesture to a stack of six different young adult novels, then continue, "And tomorrow, you are going to get to pick out to read one of these other books, not so old, that deal with ambition." Joaquin opens one eye.

Are you a teacher who sometimes feels divided? On the one hand, I love literature, and I mean Literature with a capital *L*. It is one of the reasons I became an English teacher. I want to inspire others to love *Macbeth*, *To Kill a Mockingbird*, *Beowulf*, *The Canterbury Tales*, *Lord of the Flies*, *Hamlet*, *1984*, *The Odyssey*, *Romeo* and *Juliet*, *Animal Farm*, *The Crucible*, *The Great Gatsby*, and even *The Scarlet Letter* as much as I do.

On the other hand, I am passionate about literacy, too often spelled with a small *l*. I want to inspire a generation of lifelong readers and recognize that not every student is going to be excited by or ready to read about a Scottish thane's obsession for power, a knight's pilgrimage to Canterbury, or a bunch of talking pigs. Many teachers and students struggle with the readability and relatability of classical literary works that school districts and national standards often expect us to teach. We know that each reader's interests, strengths, and challenges are unique, and no single text is appropriate for every student in a middle or high school English classroom.

So, should we teach canonical works or not? There are those of us who keep trying, and there are those of us who jump at the chance to teach other texts, such as young adult novels, nonfiction works, graphic novels, picture books, and other genres and media such as music and art. And there are those of us who bounce back and forth, teaching a classic novel, followed by a young adult novel, with an essay squeezed in between, who end up feeling a bit schizophrenic in our efforts to satisfy the expectations of districts, standards, parents, students, and ourselves.

It has taken me more than twenty-five years of teaching, a whole lot of reading and listening, not to mention a bunch of teacher trial and error, to figure out a way to interweave literature with literacy. This book suggests a process for planning and teaching called "workshopping the canon." In this book, *workshop* is used as a verb (i.e., to workshop) because it involves action on the part of teachers. When we workshop the canon, we actively and purposefully partner classical texts with a variety of high-interest, multiple genres within a reading and writing workshop structure, aligning the teaching of literature with what we have come to recognize as best practices in the teaching of literacy.

No longer do we have to feel divided between a longtime love for literature and a high regard for literacy. When we "workshop the canon," we can still teach *Beowulf*, but within a focused unit that includes other genres such as young adult novels, short stories, informational texts, picture books, music, art, and movies. We can explore heroes, past and present, through a variety of reading workshop structures, including read-alouds, independent reading, shared reading, close reading, readers theater, response engagements, Socratic circles, book clubs, mini-lessons (e.g., how-to, reading, literary, craft, vocabulary, and critical), and writing workshop structures such as mentor texts, writing plans, mini-lessons (e.g., how-to and craft), independent writing, conferences, writing circles, and publishing opportunities. If we workshop the canon, we can be both a teacher of literacy and a teacher of literature. One does not have to preclude the other.

Workshopping the Canon is a practical text. Aligned with College and Career Readiness anchor standards for reading, writing, language, speaking and listening, and designed to meet other state standards as well, this book introduces foundational reading and writing workshop structures in the context of middle and secondary classrooms and curricula. Along with providing detailed suggestions for implementing workshop structures and strategies, it includes authentic teacher vignettes and examples of student work. Many teachers share resources, engagements, and ideas from their workshopping classrooms across chapters. Whereas much has already been written about reading and writing workshops, it is important to reconsider and reimagine these ideas for middle and high school classrooms, in the context of classical works of literature.

In writing this book, I draw on my experiences as a classroom teacher, as a teaching team member for a statewide reading initiative, as a director of a National Writing Project site, as an educator of new teachers at a state university, and as a colleague of so many inspirational teachers who surround me at the university, secondary, middle, and elementary levels. It is written, I hope, like those professional resources I like to read. It is filled with teacher voices, useful models, and helpful ideas. It is written to enrich and transform practice.

My hope in writing *Workshopping the Canon* is to provide middle and high school English teachers with ideas for "workshopping" their own classrooms and curricula. The teachers who write alongside me detail their classroom experiences to encourage colleagues. While this book does provide specific suggestions for "workshopping" certain canonical texts, the ideas are shared to prompt independent, creative, and critical thinking. The suggestions offered are not meant to be prescriptive but descriptive. This book endeavors to make the often invisible and always messy processes of workshop planning visible. It is written to show teachers a way to teach reading, writing, language, speaking and listening using familiar classical texts. It is a book to help bridge the divide between literature and literacy. It is a book for those teachers wanting to workshop. It is a book to help you through the process.

Why and How to Workshop

"What'll we do with ourselves this afternoon?" cried Daisy,
"and the day after that, and the next thirty years?"

—F. SCOTT FITZGERALD, *The Great Gatsby*

I will never forget the first time I walked into an elementary classroom and saw a workshop taking place. Several students were on the floor reading independently; others were gathered in a circle, with a teacher guiding their reading; pairs were reading to each other; some were writing in notebooks and typing on computers; three students were trying to select new books from a classroom library; one was listening to a book on headphones. All students were engaged in reading or writing, as was the teacher. I was stunned. I was envious. I wanted that sort of literacy experience for my students.

Workshopping is a great idea in theory, but it isn't so simple to put into practice, especially with older students. Translating what I saw into middle and high school classroom contexts and curricula was not easy. So many questions initially overwhelmed me. Could I teach Shakespeare and still have authentic and engaging workshop structures such as read-alouds, book clubs, and independent reading and writing? How could I include other kinds of text such as young adult (YA) novels, short stories, newspaper articles, informational and argumentative essays, and poetry? When could I teach literary elements? What kinds of writing would students create? What about close reading? Where was the place for literary theory? How would it all fit together?

While I had read a wide variety of inspiring professional texts about establishing reading and writing workshops, most were set in elementary classrooms or featured far less complicated and complex texts. I wanted rich descriptions and detailed procedures that could help me establish a reading and writing

What if the "how" isn't as important as the "what"

workshop with literature most frequently taught at the middle and high school levels.

Workshopping the Canon is a book written to show teachers how to create and conduct a workshop with and around frequently taught texts in middle and secondary classrooms. It offers a straightforward process for "workshopping" those works of literature traditionally accepted as important and influential in shaping Western culture. But, before we can consider *how* to workshop the canon, let's start with *why*. Why is it important to workshop the canon?

Why Workshop the Canon?

We need to workshop the canon in order to better support and motivate readers and writers in middle and high school classrooms. The supporting statistics are startling and scary. According to recent National Assessment of Educational Progress results, more than 60 percent of middle and high school students scored below the *proficient* level in reading achievement. Twenty-three percent of eighth-grade students and 25 percent of twelfth-grade students scored below the *basic* level in reading (National Center for Education Statistics, 2013). American fifteen-year-olds rank seventeenth in reading among developed nations, lagging behind countries such as Estonia, Lichtenstein, and Poland (Organisation for Economic Co-operation and Development, 2013, p. 1). As for writing, the National Council of Teachers of English has reported that 40 percent of high school seniors never or rarely write a paper of three or more pages, and the scores of twelfth graders show no significant changes in writing (National Council of Teachers of English, 2007). So, what can teachers do about it?

In the past decade, we have come to know more and more about out-of-school literacies (Hull & Schultz, 2001). We have discovered that many of our students possess secret literacy lives, not always evident or valued in schools. They are reading YA novels, contributing to a 21 percent increase in young adult readership (National Endowment for the Arts, 2009). Our challenge is to integrate out-of-school literacies into the school curriculum. We want to bring more authentic reading and writing processes into classrooms. This is one reason why we should workshop the canon.

There are books students are more likely to read in English class, and there are books they are more likely to read out of English class. They read *1984* in class, Veronica Roth's *Divergent* out of class; *Romeo and Juliet* in class, John Green's *The Fault in Our Stars* out of class; *Lord of the Flies* in class, Suzanne Collins's *The Hunger Games* out of class; *The Scarlet Letter* in, Laurie Halse Anderson's *Speak* out; *Julius Caesar* in, Gail Giles's *Shattering Glass* out; *The Great Gatsby* in, Gordon Korman's *Jake, Reinvented* out. The Drama High, Perfect Chemistry, Runaways, Bone, and Kimani TRU series are devoured by students, but out, out, out, outside of class.

So, what are we reading in class? Same old, same old. Applebee (1993) first shared this fact in his foundational and comprehensive study of the content used in the teaching of literature in American high schools. Included in his still staggeringly relevant 1988 listing of literary works required in 30 percent or more of public schools, grades 7–12, are *Romeo and Juliet*, *Macbeth*, *The Adventures of Huckleberry Finn*, *To Kill a Mockingbird*, *Julius Caesar*, *The Pearl*, and *The Scarlet Letter*. More recently, Beers and Probst (2013) conducted an extensive survey of 2,300 teachers in 2008 and 2010 to determine the most frequently taught books in grades 4–10, and their listing for grades 9–10 includes *The Adventures of Huckleberry Finn*, *Romeo and Juliet*, *The Scarlet Letter*, and *To Kill a Mockingbird*. Sound familiar? The century has changed, but many of the texts taught in English classrooms have not.

There are valid arguments for and against teaching canonical works. There are those (Bloom, 1994) who support the canon and use these texts as a basis for comparison, and there are those who challenge these texts for their Eurocentric, masculine representations of experience—those who note the absence of female, African American, Native American, Asian American, and Latinx representation in terms of author or understanding (Baker, 1980; Barker, 1989; Bruchac, 1987; Ling, 1990).

No matter your position, if we want students to read more often and subsequently improve their reading performance, we need to provide high-interest and more accessible text. We need to better incorporate what students are more likely to read out of school into the school. We need to surround students with all kinds of relatable genres. At the same time, some teachers or districts may find it hard to let go of a number of great works of literature. Luckily, the workshopping classroom encourages both, broadening our view of classical texts.

Workshopping structures and strategies enable teachers to interweave other genres as a means of providing students with more accessible text and diverse cultural representations, bridging the gap between out-of-school and in-school reading. We partner those texts students are expected to read with those they are more willing and ready to read, and everybody wins. When we create a workshopping classroom, we simultaneously introduce students to literature and relate it to the kinds of reading completed outside of class. We do so through a variety of workshop structures, to be detailed in the following chapters.

Another reason why we want to workshop the canon is to increase student comprehension and motivation. When I first began teaching, I taught differently than I do today. Like many English teachers before me, I taught *Macbeth*, *Frankenstein*, *Of Mice and Men*, and the *Scarlet Letter*; I lectured on King James and

Romanticism, the Great Depression and Puritan values. Students wrote essays, created monsters and scarlet *A*s, and took tests, listing Romantic elements and drawing Freytag's pyramid.

Even though students were busy around these works of mostly British and American literature, generating lots of literary products, I have to ask myself, did they really "read" any of these texts? Or did I read for them? Did I, with the very best of intentions, foster a classroom environment that provided students with all of the information necessary to write essays, create projects, and take tests without ever having to make meaning of or transact with the text? Was literature something I did to students, rather than something they figured out for themselves? Did I enable students not to comprehend? It all depends on how we define *reading*.

"What's in a name?" Juliet asks. Well, a lot, if we are talking about reading. How we choose to define it lays the foundation for all English language arts teaching. In my old classroom described above, reading is defined by products (e.g., essays, projects, tests). Attention is placed on that which follows reading; *reading* is best defined as "after the fact." While we might have called aloud some of the text together, the majority of class time was spent, after the fact, explaining and analyzing the assigned text. Students were then enabled to create the products of reading necessary to succeed in class, perhaps with little to no understanding of the assigned text.

Quite a while ago, Harste (1978) claimed the theoretical orientations teachers hold about reading significantly affect their expectations, goals, behaviors, and outcomes. What we believe reading is (and is not) greatly impacts what we do (with literature) in classrooms. If we associate reading with after-the-fact products, then we structure classrooms that lead to greater productivity; if we consider reading a meaning-making process and emphasize comprehension, then we organize classrooms that emphasize individual processes. Whether we are aware of this or not, our classrooms reveal deeply held beliefs about literacy.

Students' definitions of reading are shaped by teachers' definitions of reading. The definition of reading we employ in class, the instructional approaches we use when teaching literature, mold students as readers (Weaver, 2002). Does reading mean identifying words, listing characteristics, or matching characters? Or is reading constructing meaning, connecting with vocabulary, making inferences about plot, and predicting actions of characters? If we spend time emphasizing parts of literature, students will conclude reading is parts—disassociated vocabulary or stems, grammar or daily oral language, attributes of the author or qualities of characterization.

As teachers, we shape readers—and not always for the better. When I first read Atwell's (1998) foundational text on workshopping, I was struck by her

"Twenty-One Lessons Teachers Demonstrate about Reading" (pp. 28–29). Was I unintentionally teaching students the following?

- Reading is a serious, painful business.
- Literature is even more serious and painful, not to mention boring.
- Reading is a performance for an audience of one: the teacher.
- There is one interpretation of a text: the teacher's (or that of the teacher's manual).
- Reading requires memorization and mastery of information, terms, definitions, and theories.
- Reading is followed by a test.
- You learn about literature by listening to teachers talk about it.
- Teachers talk a lot about literature, but teachers don't read.
- Reading is a waste of English class time.

The ramifications of these lessons are troubling.

Jobe and Dayton-Sakari (1999) described a variety of student stances toward reading that occur in today's classrooms, offering four different labels: the "I can't" readers may choose not to read, or truly don't know how to read; "I don't know how" readers aren't sure what reading is, and may have become dependent on teachers telling them what the text means; "I'd rather" readers prefer to do something other than reading; "I don't care" readers really don't want to be in the classroom. What role do teachers play in supporting these labels? How can we tell if a student cannot make meaning if we explain everything that is read and fail to allow time and support for the actual processes of reading? Do we motivate students to read with texts and practices? Do we create literacy environments students want to be a part of?

Reading and writing workshop structures and strategies increase reading comprehension and motivation (Gaughan, 2003; Keene & Zimmerman, 2013; Lause, 2004; Swift, 1993). To deepen student understanding and counter negative attitudes, we can stop teaching in product-oriented, text-centered, top-down ways. When we provide students with choice and foster responsive classroom environments with connections to real-life experiences, we help students stay engaged. In a workshop, students take responsibility for making sense of texts. Teachers support the processes of individual readers and are concerned with how readers make meaning from their experiences with text, implementing structures, strategies, and technologies that facilitate sharing of these responses.

The processes of reading, writing, and talking about literature are valued as much as the substance of what is read, written, or spoken.

Yet another reason to workshop the canon is to reach diverse learners and foster diverse perspectives. Monocultural approaches to teaching increase the achievement gap and augment adolescents' disengagement with literacy (National Council of Teachers of English, 2007). When we teach one text at a time, we limit perspectives. Only one voice is heard. So much of English language arts education is departmentalized and compartmentalized, resulting in too-limited points of view. Literature is detached from literacy. Reading is separated from writing. Grammar is disconnected from both reading and writing. We break apart genres like crackers and study poetry, memoir, short stories, then plays. Classical literary works are split from YA novels. We have also been known to celebrate, albeit isolate, works by women, African American, Latinx, Native American, and Asian authors. Time periods and literary movements further sever texts into smaller pieces. When we workshop the canon, we increase multicultural perspectives through students' multiple and varied engagements with texts and one another.

The schools in which we teach are increasingly academically, economically, socially, culturally, and linguistically diverse. To foster students' interactions with a range of ideas and ways of being, teachers need to provide different representations of peoples, societies, mores, backgrounds, traditions, ethnicities, and customs through texts, and encourage engagement with cultural issues in literature, literacy, and the world. Workshopping classrooms are places in which students think critically and honor different perspectives—necessary qualities for living within a democratic society.

When we workshop the canon, we immerse students in a wide assortment of texts, providing multiple viewpoints and an array of representations gathered around a unit focus. Whereas the Common Core State Standards (CCSS) might encourage the teaching of more expository and less narrative texts, there are important reasons for still teaching fiction. Oately (2011) reminded us that stories help us understand not only characters in books but human character as well. Reading stories prompts better understanding of other human beings as we take on varied points of view within fictional settings, helping us make sense of one another and the wider world. When we workshop the canon, we bring together classic texts and contemporary texts; fiction and nonfiction; and, especially, a wide array of texts representing a range of world literatures, historical traditions, and genres and texts representing the experiences of different genders, ethnicities, and social classes.

The workshopping classroom encourages transaction with multiple texts through a variety of workshop structures and strategies. Sustained experience with diverse texts across a range of genres that offer multiple perspectives enhances motivation in students (Greenleaf, Schoenbach, Cziko, & Mueller, 2001). We want students to enjoy what they read, respond to it, and leave classrooms thinking about it. We encourage them to discover more about themselves, others, and the world around them. Social and collaborative experiences reaffirm the idea that no single reading of a text is definitive. The student, not the work, remains at the heart of each day's lesson as we foster transactions within each reader through writing, talking, listening, and other workshopping means.

When we workshop the canon, we can better meet the diverse needs of students because workshop structures and strategies are accessible to all learners. We can better differentiate learning and meet individual needs in a reading and writing workshop environment. If there are more texts, there are more choices. Students can make guided selections for independent reading across levels and languages while the reading of a core canonical text is supported and shared.

How to Workshop the Canon

Now that we have a shared understanding of reasons for workshopping the canon, we can begin to discover how to do it. A *workshop* is a metaphor for a particular kind of learning environment that organizes reading and writing experiences in meaningful ways. Richly described and detailed by Atwell (1998), a reading and writing workshop creates authentic and sustained literacy experiences in classrooms. Students spend time engaged in real reading and writing. A workshop is learning and learner centered, social and collaborative. Students have some choices regarding what they read and write. There is access to varied texts and time allocated for reading, writing, talking, and sharing. The schedule is predictable, and blocks of time are allotted for each literacy experience. Teachers teach focused mini-lessons designed to guide students through reading and writing processes. Expectations are high, but there is room for reflection and confusion as long as a safe learning environment is established, which teachers ensure through structured management.

To foster lifelong literacies, reach diverse learners, and increase comprehension and motivation, workshop teachers create genuine reading and writing environments, immersing students in language-rich, high-quality experiences through literature. When designing a workshopping classroom, we provide opportunities for immersion, demonstration, expectation, responsibility, approximation, employment, and feedback (Cambourne, 1984). As we workshop the canon, we immerse students in a wide variety of genres and provide sustained opportunities for reading and writing. The teacher demonstrates how he or she reads and writes, and utilizes his or her own processes of reading and writing as a model for students. In turn, the teacher expects students to read, write, talk, and listen, and encourages them to take responsibility for many of their own assignments. Students have time during class to read and write with, and talk and listen to, one another; the teacher and other students provide feedback on literacy experiences.

Along with the above, when structuring reading and writing workshops around classical works in middle and high school classrooms, it is important to keep in mind the stages of reading literature suggested by Milner, Milner, and Mitchell (2012). They proposed four stages of reading literature: (1) reader response, (2) interpretive community, (3) formal analysis, and (4) critical synthesis. This four-stage construct moves student readers from responding personally to sharing and deepening these responses within an interpretive community, to illuminating them through formal analysis, and toward synthesizing critical perspectives into their own interpretation. Milner et al. (2012) explained the teacher's role during the initial stage of reading as nurturing unmediated, unencumbered, felt responses to the text. Once students have responded to the text personally, they are ready to move into an interpretive community, as teachers facilitate engagements that bring students together to unravel the text. During formal analysis, we help students explore the craft of the text read, noting such elements as plot, character, setting, point of view, tone, style, themes, or symbols. In the final stage of reading literature, critical synthesis, the text is considered from the perspectives of varied schools of literary criticism, such as historical/biographical, moral/philosophical, archetypal, feminist, Marxist, or Freudian.

These recursive stages of reading literature are already recognizable in most middle and high school English language arts classrooms. On any given day in any given classroom, we might observe students responding to what they have read, talking about what they have read in a group, analyzing formal elements of the text, or delving into schools of literary criticism. What we see may depend on the day of the week, the work of literature, or the objectives for that particular lesson. As teachers, we often have favorite stages; some of us preferring reader response, others eager for more formal analysis. While Milner et al. (2012) indicated movement through these stages is not linear, a workshopping classroom provides initial opportunities for students to engage in reader response that helps to establish the interpretive community. There is certainly formal analysis and critical synthesis in a workshopping classroom, but not until students have had the opportunity to transact with the text and interact with one another. Personal response, formal analysis, and critical synthesis are all facilitated through workshop structures and strategies.

Becoming a workshop teacher requires a move away from traditional toward workshop teaching. In a traditional classroom, students engage more in formal analysis and critical synthesis, with less regard for personal response or the interpretive community. Students may practice skills and memorize facts, content is broken down into discrete sequential units, products are of primary importance, test performance is valued highly, and expectations are the same for all. Characteristics of traditional English language arts teaching are easily recognizable as students read chronologically through the textbook, listing facts about the authors and elements of a tragedy, perhaps memorizing soliloquies along the way. Learning is discrete and separate, as literature is isolated from composition and word study. There is little room for personal responses to literature here.

In a workshop classroom, students actively construct concepts and meanings; content is represented in whole, meaningful contexts; processes are as valued as products; students are assessed through performance on meaningful tasks; and learning is individualized. A workshop classroom environment provides and supports opportunities for students to read, write, talk, and listen in authentic and sustained ways around a wide variety of literature. Students respond personally, interpret collaboratively, analyze formally, and think critically through a variety of workshop structures and strategies.

So, what are the reading and writing workshop structures teachers use to prompt students' personal responses, foster the interpretive community, engage in formal analysis, and embark on critical synthesis? To be detailed in the following chapters, our reading workshop includes time and opportunity for the following: read-alouds, independent reading, shared reading, close reading, readers theater, response engagements, book clubs, Socratic circles, and a variety of mini-lessons (e.g., how-to, reading, literary, craft, vocabulary, and critical). Our writing workshop evolves from and interweaves with the reading workshop, as students write in response to the unit focus, mentor/model texts, or other texts introduced throughout the unit. The writing process is supported through workshop structures including writing plans, mini-lessons (e.g., how-to and craft), independent writing, conferences and/or writing circles, and publishing opportunities. While each of these reading and writing workshop structures is detailed in the following chapters, we begin workshopping the canon by first finding a unit focus.

Find a Unit Focus

Workshopping the canon begins when teachers find a unit focus. So often, we begin and end our planning as middle and high school English teachers with a classical literary work. *Romeo and Juliet, To Kill a Mockingbird, Animal Farm, The Great Gatsby,* or *1984,* for example, provide the inspiration. We spend so much time and effort exploring the single literary work, pondering its allusions, foreshadowing, foils, imagery, and irony. When we workshop the canon, rather than planning around a single text, we select a unit focus that allows for multiple texts, voices, ideas, and perspectives to be explored within an array of reading and writing workshop structures.

A unit focus originates from the core canonical text. Think about the common novels, plays, or memoirs that you teach. *Beowulf* comes to mind when teaching British literature. How I love those Anglo Saxons, their scops and mead. My mind wanders to the gory details of the fight between Grendel and Beowulf—how the monster twists in pain as the sinews deep in his shoulder snap. And when Grendel's mother returns and carries off her son's claw . . . well, everyone loves a good sequel. I think about the timeless qualities of this epic and the characteristics of an epic hero. I recall the writing style, the kennings, alliteration, allusions, and the poem's rhythm. However, workshopping requires a move from pieces to a whole, from content to process. So, while I may begin with literature as a focus, I move forward and consider literacy. Rather than asking myself what bits and pieces students will learn about *Beowulf,* I consider how I will facilitate students' transactions with *Beowulf* through reading and writing workshop structures and strategies connected to a larger unit focus, such as heroes.

Serafini (2001, p. 40) defined a *focus unit* as a "series of literary experiences that revolves around a central theme or focus." Thus, a unit focus encourages us to think more broadly and intertextually. When we workshop the canon, we interweave the study of a core canonical text with a variety of contemporary genres, helping students make connections more easily between a core text and their lives. We want to create a classroom workshop environment that immerses students in a focused unit of study that includes YA novels, picture books, nonfiction text (e.g., essays, articles, memoir, biographies, websites, reviews), graphic novels, short stories, movies and documentary films, poetry, plays, lyrics, and art. While our unit will include a core canonical text, the development of a unit focus encourages and guides us to include more diverse texts.

Consider *Julius Caesar,* Shakespeare's historical tragedy: What could be the focus for this unit of study? What idea will bind together a series of literary experiences and literacy engagements? I don't want to choose a genre as a focus, as this will limit the exploration of different kinds of texts. I want to be able to choose from a wide assortment of contemporary works to read alongside this play. My mind wanders to those larger topics always discussed when reading *Julius Caesar,* and I consider the relationship between power and corruption.

Such issues should appeal to students, and certainly a wide array of fiction and nonfiction texts will relate to this focus and enrich students' understanding and broaden their perspectives through hearing multiple voices.

When teaching *Romeo and Juliet*, the unit focus could be ill-fated love—rather a predictable choice, but adolescents relate well to this central idea. Who hasn't been unlucky in love? Who hasn't experienced a doomed or disastrous relationship? So I begin a new unit with students, reflecting and writing about unfortunate relationships. We consider iconic movies with not-so-tragic endings (e.g., *High School Musical, Twilight*) as well as those with tragic endings (i.e., *Titanic, The Fault in Our Stars, Star Wars: Episode II* and *Episode III*). We discuss star-crossed lovers on television: I show now-classic clips introducing Buffy and Angel in *Buffy the Vampire Slayer*. We listen to songs such as We the Kings' "Check Yes Juliet," Taylor Swift's "Love Story," and Gavin DeGraw's "We Belong Together." Then we consider those factors that might contribute to love being "ill-fated."

Commonly tied to a unit focus are *essential questions*, which are questions that relate to a unit focus and can be used to connect a core classical text to other genres as well. Effective essential questions accommodate many possible answers (Wilhelm, Smith, & Fredricksen, 2012). "What is ill-fated love?" isn't a strong essential question because there is likely agreement on the answer. "Are some relationships more ill-fated than others?" or "What is the relationship between love and fate?" work better because of the range of possible answers. In a unit focused around power, "Does all power lead to corruption?" is a better essential question than "What is power?" The best essential questions develop and deepen a unit focus, prompting higher levels of critical thinking across texts.

There can be many unit foci or essential questions for any given core canonical text. A teacher could create a unit around conspiracy or betrayal when teaching *Julius Caesar*; fate or young love when teaching *Romeo and Juliet*. Teachers should choose a unit focus to generate student interest, interweave diverse texts and genres, and prompt critical thinking. When Kayla teaches *Animal Farm*, for example, she focuses her unit around power and the corruption of government. Her essential questions include "How does power change a person's personality?," "What type of government is an ideal government?," "How much power should the government have?," "What rules should govern society?," and "What would happen to a country without rules?" When Lamar taught *A Raisin in the Sun*, he planned his unit around the untold stories of America and focused on counter-narratives that offered different points of view on the American dream. His essential questions included "How do race, class, and/or gender influence an individual's goals or aspirations?" and "What is the American dream?" To prompt your own thinking around essential questions, a listing of canonical texts with sample unit foci and essential questions is provided in Appendix A.

Collect Diverse Texts

After discovering a unit focus and essential questions, teachers collect *diverse texts*. Before we can workshop the canon, we require a wide variety of texts to include in the workshop structures. We need to select genres that will complement the core canonical text, expand the unit focus, and help us answer essential questions. Multiple texts provide more opportunities to immerse students in authentic literacy experiences, to increase student comprehension and motivation, and to foster diverse perspectives. I gather suggestions for pairing canonical texts with other literature from Herz and Gallo (2005), Richison, Hernandez, and Carter (2006), Kaywell (2000), and Short, Tomlinson, Lynch-Brown, and Johnson (2014). I ask media specialists and scour the Web for ideas and resources.

When teaching *Romeo and Juliet*, for example, I draw from a wide variety of YA novels related to ill-fated love, such as John Green's *The Fault in Our Stars*, Simon Elkeles's *Perfect Chemistry*, Rainbow Rowell's *Eleanor & Park*, Sabaa Tahir's *An Ember in the Ashes*, Gayle Forman's *Just One Day*, Stephenie Meyer's *Twilight*, Walter Dean Myers's *Street Love*, Mary E. Pearson's *Scribbler of Dreams*, Gordon Korman's *Son of the Mob*, Jasqueline Woodson's *If You Come Softly*, Sharon Draper's *Romiette and Julio*, Jamie Ford's *Hotel on the Corner of Bitter and Sweet*, and Jerry Spinelli's *Stargirl*. I gather a short, informational text about star-crossed lovers from the BBC and an article from *Science News* that informs readers about a pair of star-crossed love bugs. I remember Edgar Allan Poe's "Annabel Lee" and Ella Wilcox's "The Winds of Fate." A list of suggested YA novels, short stories, informational texts, picture books, music, art, and movies that supports the teaching of this unit focus can be found in Appendix B. Appendix B provides an extensive listing of canonical texts paired with sample unit foci, essential questions, and diverse texts to prod your own thinking about resources necessary to workshop the canon.

When Angela teaches Elie Wiesel's *Night* or Anne Frank's *The Diary of a Young Girl*, she focuses her unit around resilience. Essential questions include "What hope, if any, can be found in times of hopelessness?" and "How is resilience a ray of hope in dark spaces?" Though centered around texts immediately associated with the Jewish experience during the Holocaust, this unit is supplemented with additional works from other cultures to reinforce the idea of resilience in difficult times. For example, music selections, movies, and documentary films are incorporated from the African American and the Chicano/Chicana Civil Rights Movements, in order to build on and broaden the context for stories of resistance and remembrance that the core texts represent. A complete listing of Angela's supplementary texts for the unit she planned is included in Appendix B.

Once teachers discover a focus and find diverse texts for a unit, they can begin to workshop the canon through a variety of reading and writing workshop structures and strategies, as detailed in the following chapters.

Chapter Summary

Workshopping the canon interweaves authentic reading and writing processes into classrooms, increases student comprehension and motivation, reaches diverse learners, and fosters diverse perspectives. Workshop teachers utilize reading and writing workshop structures to prompt students' personal responses, foster the interpretive community, engage in formal analysis, and embark on critical synthesis. Our reading workshop includes time and opportunity for read-alouds, independent reading, shared reading, close reading, readers theater, response engagements, book clubs, Socratic circles, and a variety of mini-lessons (e.g., how-to, reading, literary, craft, vocabulary, and critical). Writing workshops evolve from reading workshops as students write in response to a unit focus, mentor/model texts, or other texts introduced throughout the unit. The writing process is supported through workshop structures such as writing plans, mini-lessons (e.g., how-to and craft), independent writing, conferences and/or writing circles, and publishing opportunities.

This chapter concluded with guidance for getting started with workshopping by finding a unit focus and collecting diverse text. Once teachers discover a focus and find diverse texts for a unit, they can begin to workshop the canon through a variety of reading and writing workshop structures and strategies, which are detailed in the following chapters.

2

Reading Matters

LORD POLONIUS: What do you read, my lord?
HAMLET: Words, words, words.
LORD POLONIUS: What is the matter, my lord?
HAMLET: Between who?
LORD POLONIUS: I mean the matter that you read, my lord.

—WILLIAM SHAKESPEARE, *Hamlet*

Reading matters and is the center of the workshopping classroom. As English teachers, it makes sense for us to value literacy, yet we allot so little time in class for the practice of reading. Students spend an average of 7.1 minutes a day reading in public schools (Paul, 1996). Why don't middle and high school teachers allocate more time for reading? We like to presume students read before they come to class, but, unfortunately, this doesn't always happen. We know readers develop by reading, and there is a definite correlation between the amount a child reads and reading achievement (Anderson, Wilson, & Fielding, 1988; Guthrie, 2004; Taylor, Frye, & Maruyama, 1990). It makes sense that, if we want students to become more proficient readers, we have to provide class time during which they can read.

Through reading, we extend our understanding of the world; we come to know ourselves and one another better. Students need to read more than they do now, and widely around different genres as well as deeply into a particular text. *Read-alouds* and *independent reading* are two foundational structures necessary for workshopping the canon, and this chapter introduces why and how to do both.

Why Read Aloud?

The value of read-alouds can be found in many childhood memories. A lot of us remember the feeling of sitting crisscross-applesauce on an alphabet rug after lunch while a teacher read aloud about the exploits of Curious George, Ramona, or Charlotte from the worn pages of a book. Others might recall curling up on a family member's lap, eagerly turning the pages to meet Brown Bear, Fancy Nancy, Bad Kitty, Amelia Bedelia, Flat Stanley, or even Walter the Farting Dog.

Equally, researchers have well identified the benefits of read-aloud experiences. For example, they boost vocabulary (Beck, McKeown, & Kucan, 2002; De Temple & Snow, 2003) because through them, students are exposed to language. Read-alouds increase word recognition (Stahl, 2003) and listening comprehension (Morrow & Gambrell, 2002; Stanovich, Cunningham, & West, 1998). Words surround and engulf everyone who hears them—reading is a natural medium for language learning.

Read-alouds increase fluency, too (Rasinski, 2003). As a teacher—presumably a proficient and practiced reader—reads aloud to students, he models appropriate phrasing, expression, stress, inflection, and intonation. The reading is smooth and the pacing consistent. The teacher thereby provides a powerful demonstration of fluent, phrased reading.

Furthermore, read-alouds build motivation (Palmer, Codling, & Gambrell, 1994; Trelease, 2013). As students are exposed to a greater variety of texts, desire and interest in reading is heightened. Read-alouds provide a means of introducing students to authors, genres, and topics they can later pursue. I can't tell you exactly how many books have disappeared from my classroom library shelves after snippets were read aloud, but it is a lot.

In response to my asking why teachers read aloud, Nicole mentions how reading aloud helps her build background knowledge in students: "There are so many gaps that I can help fill through short pieces that touch on themes, events, people, places, and ideas I want students to know about." Allen (2000, pp. 47–48) included the following in her justifications for read-alouds:

- exposes students to a wide variety of literature in an enjoyable way
- facilitates students' abilities to compare and contrast by providing opportunities to look at commonalities among themes, texts, authors, characters, and conflicts
- models effective reading behaviors
- provides opportunities to share a love of books with readers

I mention these specifically because each is relevant to why we read aloud in the workshopping classroom.

In the workshopping classroom, read-alouds are used to support the unit focus and essential questions as well as to expose students to a wider array of genres beyond a sole, classical text. A teacher reads aloud to introduce other fiction and nonfiction works to deepen and extend student understanding. For example, a teacher who reads aloud Kurt Vonnegut's "Harrison Bergeron" in a unit also including *1984* introduces students to two texts in lieu of one, and, as the two texts complement each other, knowledge of one text deepens understanding of the other.

A teacher utilizes read-alouds to facilitate either informal or formal comparison between texts. In this way, she can easily meet the College and Career Readiness (CCR) anchor standard for reading calling for the "integration of knowledge and ideas" (National Governors Association, 2010). She can encourage students to weigh their responses to the different texts, or to identify similarities and differences among more formal elements such as theme, plot, character, setting, point of view, tone, style, or symbols. Students may compare themes of survival or man's inhumanity to man in Richard Connell's "The Most Dangerous Game" and *Lord of the Flies*, or dystopian/utopian settings in John Lennon's "Imagine" and *Brave New World*. Such bases for comparison create atmospheres and opportunities for class discussion, generated from the read-aloud experience.

When a teacher reads aloud, he also provides students with opportunities to transact with texts, eliciting unencumbered and unfettered responses. Through his attitude, he relays a love of literature to students. While I admit that I was initially hesitant to read aloud to high school seniors, I quickly realized that no one is too old for this timeless practice. My students were mesmerized by the sound of picture books, short stories, newspaper articles, poetry, and—definitely—lyrics.

What to Read Aloud

Read-alouds are used to introduce as well as deepen and broaden student understanding of a unit focus, essential questions, and a core text. Although there are many textual possibilities for read-alouds, shorter texts are preferred when workshopping the canon. Certainly, YA novels can be read aloud, but this genre is better utilized with independent reading (discussed later in this chapter). A great way to introduce a unit focus or essential questions is through picture books.

Picture Books

Reading aloud a picture book can introduce a unit focus tied to a canonical work. When teaching around judgment and studying *The Scarlet Letter*, for example, a teacher might share Karen Gedig Burnett's *If the World Were Blind: A Book about Judgment and Prejudice*. Jenn reads aloud *Hurricane* by Jonathan London to introduce a unit focused around survival and *Lord of the Flies*. *The Children's Book of Heroes* by William J. Bennett encourages students to think about the role of heroes in *Beowulf*. If pondering the pursuit of science and knowledge when reading *Frankenstein*, then read aloud Toshi Maruki's *Hiroshima No Pika*. A desire for more is reflected in *Yertle the Turtle and Other Stories* by Dr. Seuss and *The Fisherman and His Wife* by Rosemary Wells, which can apply to both *Macbeth* and *Julius Caesar*. When teaching about social and equity issues and studying *To Kill a Mockingbird*, Lamar uses Margot Theis Raven's *Let Them Play*, as this book depicts the deep entrenchment of racism in the South during the Jim Crow era. Jenn suggests reading Amnesty International's *We Are All Born Free: The Universal Declaration of Human Rights in Pictures* alongside *Night* when introducing a unit focused around discrimination and human rights.

Reading aloud picture book adaptations can prepare students for the more challenging literature to come. Picture book versions such as Michael Rosen's *Romeo and Juliet*; Bruce Coville's *William Shakespeare's Romeo and Juliet, Macbeth,* and *Hamlet*; Marcia Williams's *Tales from Shakespeare, Chaucer's Canterbury Tales,* and *The Iliad and the Odyssey*; James Rumford's *Beowulf: A Hero's Tale Retold*; and Margaret Hodges's *The Kitchen Knight: A Tale of King Arthur* and *Merlin and the Making of the King* provide students with visual summaries of complex plays, tales, and epics.

Reading picture books aloud can also build the background knowledge required for a better understanding and appreciation of a classical work of literature. For example, Sally Pomme Clayton's *Tales Told in Tents: Stories from Central Asia* introduces storytelling and the frame structure, necessary concepts to be aware of before reading *The Canterbury Tales*. If teaching *Romeo and Juliet*, Dr. Seuss's *The Butter Battle Book* introduces feuds.

Picture books can complement canonical texts, one text setting off the other. Deborah Wiles's *Freedom Summer* or Jacqueline Woodson's *The Other Side* are counterparts for *To Kill a Mockingbird*. *Erika's Story* by Ruth Vander Zee supplements *Night* or *The Diary of a Young Girl*. William Miller's *Tituba* and Jane Yolen's *The Salem Witch Trials: An Unsolved Mystery from History* match with *The Crucible*. Jane Yolen's *Merlin and the Dragons* balances *Le Morte d'Arthur*. And Leonard Everett Fisher's *Cyclops* sets off *The Odyssey*. Lamar suggests Gary Soto's *Too*

Many Tamales as a complement to *Animal Farm* and Margot Theis Raven's *Circle Unbroken* for *A Raisin in the Sun*.

Short Stories

A teacher can also choose to read short stories aloud to students. In lieu of studying short stories as a genre, we interweave them into each unit in the workshopping classroom. Short stories make for thoughtful, brief read-alouds, and, just like picture books, they can build background knowledge, complement a canonical text, and deepen understanding of a unit focus or essential questions. When teaching *The Canterbury Tales*, read "The Tale of the Three Brothers" from J. K. Rowling's *The Tales of Beedle the Bard*. When teaching *Night*, read selections from *When Night Fell: An Anthology of Holocaust Short Stories* (edited by Linda Schermer Raphael and Marc Lee Raphael); when teaching *To Kill a Mockingbird*, read selections from *Short Stories of the Civil Rights Movement* (edited by Margaret Whitt). Nathaniel Hawthorne's "Young Goodman Brown" supplements *The Crucible*. Kurt Vonnegut's "Harrison Bergeron" and Ray Bradbury's "The Pedestrian" are provoking counterparts for *1984* or *Brave New World*. And Sylvia Plath's "Initiation" complements *Lord of the Flies*.

Informational/Explanatory Texts

Short, informational/explanatory texts make for great read-aloud material. When teaching *1984* or *Brave New World*, I like to read aloud a variety of short articles published in *Time* and *USA Today* that address such issues as animal organ transplants, tiny video cameras, house pet clones, eggs on ice, high-tech life forms, and social network data storage. Jenn suggests reading "A Prom Divided," a 2009 article from the *New York Times* that presents an example of modern-day segregation, when reading *To Kill a Mockingbird*. I also read essays culled from *The Bedford Reader*, *The Riverside Reader*, *The Prentice Hall Reader*, and *The Norton Reader* around issues of language, euthanasia, privacy, cloning, and drugs—all serving to broaden student understanding of issues addressed by the canonical core text.

Poetry

Sprinkle poetry across units as read-alouds. Poems are short yet powerful. They dance on the tongue. Read Emily Dickinson's "I Took Power in My Hand" or

Percy Bysshe Shelley's "Ozymandias" when teaching units featuring *Julius Caesar* or *Macbeth*. The ill-fated love of Edgar Allan Poe's "Annabel Lee" complements *Romeo and Juliet*. Robert Frost's "The Road Not Taken" or Walt Whitman's "Song of the Open Road" partner well with *The Odyssey*. Read aloud Margaret Atwood's "Half-Hanged Mary" when teaching *The Crucible*; Stephen Crane's "Think as I Think" when teaching *1984* or *Brave New World*; Abel Meeropol's "Strange Fruit" for *To Kill a Mockingbird*; Langston Hughes's *Montage of a Dream Deferred* for *A Raisin in the Sun*; Ricardo Sanchez's "I Yearn" for *The Great Gatsby*; Emily Dickinson's "Departed to the Judgment" for *The Scarlet Letter*; and William Blake's "A Poison Tree" for *Hamlet*.

Lyrics

Similar to poetry, lyrics can be utilized for read-alouds too. Students hum along or mock my musical tastes as they listen to Taylor Swift's "Love Story" when reading *Romeo and Juliet*; Evergrey's "Trust and Betrayal" when reading *Julius Caesar*; Twisted Sister's "We're Not Gonna Take It" when reading *Animal Farm*; The Clash's "Should I Stay or Should I Go" for *Hamlet*; Tina Turner's "We Don't Need Another Hero" for *Beowulf*; Rush's "Witch Hunt" for *The Crucible*; Pearl Jam's "Jeremy" for *Lord of the Flies*; Pink Floyd's "Another Brick in the Wall" or John Lennon's "Imagine" for *Brave New World* and *1984*; the Black Eyed Peas's "Where Is the Love?" for *To Kill a Mockingbird*; Sam Cooke's "A Change Is Gonna Come" for *A Raisin in the Sun*; Miley Cyrus's "The Climb" for *The Great Gatsby*; or Bob Marley's "Judge Not" for *The Scarlet Letter*.

If something is good for us, why stop doing it? Almost any text can be used for read-alouds. A wide variety to choose from is available in Appendix B. But a better idea is to become your own text collector. As you listen to music on your drive to and from work, does a song make you think of something you read in class? As you look through a magazine or newspaper during a rare break in the day, does an article remind you of a novel's character or a unit's focus? Nicole keeps an ongoing read-aloud file:

> Every time I see something interesting in the paper or hear a song I know will fit with something I'm doing, I print it and put it in a notebook I have set aside for read-alouds. If I know I'm going to use a particular piece, I generally pull it out the day before and read over it to see which words I'm going to emphasize, which words or ideas I might need to frontload, and what questions I want to develop for discussion.

How to Read Aloud

I think many of us who work in middle and high schools do not embrace workshop structures like read-alouds because we cannot envision what they might look like in our own classroom. It's one thing to picture a group of seven-year-olds, ribboned and wide-eyed, gathered around a carpet for story time with a big book; it's quite another to imagine how this same practice might look with our own pierced and tattooed, sometimes derisive but always beloved, students.

While I admit that I was initially hesitant to read aloud, student response was positive. Tempie, too, had a powerful experience when she read Natalie Babbit's *Tuck Everlasting* aloud:

> On the last day of the novel, when I got to the part in the epilogue when Tuck goes into the graveyard to read Winnie's tombstone, I choked up and couldn't read another word. For whatever reason, I started crying and just couldn't read anymore. I guess the book had been so special to me as a child, I became overwhelmed with sharing this transformative text with a group of children that I genuinely loved. A young lady named Sarah jumped up, grabbed the book from me, and finished the read-aloud. By the time she finished, I was composed again and could talk. I told the students that books had the power to change lives. I told them that books could take you to places you could only dream about and stir the very essence of your soul. I ended with "...and that is the power of a really great book!" At that very second, the bell rang; ...it was one of the best teaching moments of my life!

For this transformative read-aloud experience to happen, we have to prepare ourselves and our students—the magic doesn't occur without practice. Teachers need to plan for a read-aloud as much as they plan for a mini-lesson on onomatopoeia. We begin by introducing what we are going to read aloud to students, providing any necessary background information and generating interest in the text. For example, I might introduce Ray Bradbury's "The Pedestrian" as follows:

> Today, I am going to read a short story by one of my favorite authors, Ray Bradbury. This story introduces us to a futuristic society in which walking has become obsolete. As you listen, what do you notice about this futuristic setting? I picked this story to read aloud because I think it helps us think about our future, and who we are becoming as a society. I think it partners well with *1984*, which we are also going to read.

When reading aloud, make sure you preview the content. "I read it beforehand, practice it, and time myself so I know how long I can go on a given day in a given class," Tempie suggests. Middle and high school teachers especially need to practice reading picture books. It's not so easy to read aloud and show pictures at the same time. I had to find my rhythm and style, so I practiced at home, sometimes making the dog listen. I realized I prefer to read the words first and then show the pictures around the room to everyone, rather than trying to do this at the same time, which never seemed to work with twenty-seven students. When texts are available in digital format, they can be shared more easily.

Instead of hearing a classmate stumble his way through, teachers need to model fluent reading, increase comprehension, and generate interest in texts for students through read-alouds. Many ebooks now read to students as well. Your level of enthusiasm for read-alouds is contagious, so make it good. Act out parts, use hand gestures, move around while you are reading, and show the pictures—everyone wants to see the pictures!

Along with preparing yourself for the read-aloud, establish expectations before you begin, and review these often. Tempie's rules for read-alouds are as follows: "Actually listen to the read-aloud and do not interrupt. Call and response, if warranted, is fine, but don't ask questions out loud or engage in sidebar conversations." When Nicole reads aloud, she asks students to write or draw:

> They are instructed to use their hand to move any thought in their head while I am reading. I ask the students to write down any questions they may have to discuss at the end. I do ask them not to ask questions until I am done because I want everyone to hear the words. We always have at least a short discussion afterward. I sometimes read for beauty's sake, but I also like to see the metacognition going on because my students absorb so much and think about things that would never enter my mind.

Tempie has students complete a listening log (see Figure 2.1) to encourage response to her read-aloud of Sherman Alexie's *The Absolutely True Diary of a Part-Time Indian*.

Whatever you choose to read aloud and however you choose to engage students in the process, be sure to try it more than once. While teenagers can be overly expressive in the halls, they may provide little initial classroom response, or they might resist the practice early on, claiming read-alouds are for elementary school. As with any community-building workshop engagement, read-alouds take time and practice.

DATE:	Response/comment/question
Focus: Write down specific parts of the read aloud that catch your attention, including passages or phrases, individual words, or facts. You may paraphrase ☺	
DATE:	Response/comment/question
Focus: Draw something you could visualize in the read-aloud today.	
DATE:	Response/comment/question
Focus: What did you hear today that challenged a stereotype you might have had about Native Americans?	
DATE:	Response/comment/question
Focus: How do you connect to Junior's life?	
DATE:	Response/comment/question
Focus: How do you see the theme of Who Am I or One of Many in this book?	

FIGURE 2.1. Listening log for *The Absolutely True Diary of a Part-Time Indian*.

Why Independent Reading?

Along with read-alouds, we provide opportunity and space for independent reading in the workshopping classroom. Known by many acronyms (e.g., DEAR [drop everything and read], SSR [sustained silent reading], FVR [free voluntary reading], and SURF [silent uninterrupted reading fun]), this is time set aside for students to read in class, uninterrupted. The time allotted may vary, as will the teacher's role and students' accountability, but the occasion for continuous reading enjoyment remains.

We know we become better readers with practice, so it makes sense to carve out class time to read independently. But some middle and secondary teachers may struggle with relinquishing class time to just read. Similar to a math or a social studies teacher, we English language arts teachers have content we want to cover with students. Time spent reading is time not spent analyzing plot, characters, setting, symbols, or themes. We may have end-of-course and standardized tests based on content. The pressure is on. But research verifies the amount of time a student spends reading correlates with achievement (Wu & Samuels, 2004). A while back, Anderson and colleagues (1988) observed that children who scored at the 90th percentile on a reading test spent five times as many minutes per day reading books as children at the 50th percentile. A more recent study conducted by the National Endowment for the Arts (2007) found that students who read the most for fun scored the highest on standardized reading and writing tests. Apparently, increased experiences with independent reading improves writing style, vocabulary, spelling, and grammar (Krashen, 1993), and also increases motivation (Livaudais, 1985).

How to Read Independently

If we understand the value of independent reading, why don't we put it into practice in classrooms? While it's not uncommon to see students reading in elementary schools, it is still rare to see reading in a middle and, especially, a high school. Perhaps we are reluctant to encourage independent reading because it seems superfluous to our regular curriculum and teaching. On the contrary, though, carefully facilitated independent reading can help us meet a variety of standards as well as deepen and broaden understanding of a unit focus and essential questions. Independent reading involves much more than just the provision of time and space to read.

For the purposes of this book and with the middle and secondary language arts classroom in mind, *independent reading* refers to a classroom structure during which students read a teacher-guided noncanonical text and are provided a minimum of fifteen minutes in which to read it. Students keep a record of what is read, and the teacher monitors comprehension through conferences and other student-centered means. The students and teacher collaborate and set reading goals. For this to happen, teachers need to play an active role in facilitating and overseeing the process. Inspired by Routman (2003), I recommend *introducing, establishing, guiding, demonstrating, teaching, monitoring,* and *goal setting* as necessary components of independent reading in the workshopping classroom.

Introducing

First and foremost, teachers need to introduce independent reading as an important and valued workshop structure. Share your purpose, goals, and vision. Adolescents can see through us—if we don't deem reading as an important classroom activity, neither will they. It is vital we explain the reason and rationale for independent reading to students, parents, and guardians, as well as administrators and other educational stakeholders. In my justification, I often share research that supports the practice (see above) and am prepared to refute the report from the National Reading Panel (2000) and its lack of support for independent reading, based on the limited scope of their review—fourteen studies—and the requirements for their interpretation of sustained silent reading, which differs from ours in that students were not held accountable for what they read.

Establishing

Once you have introduced independent reading as a classroom structure, establish a reading schedule and classroom procedure to be used during the current unit of study. When will students read? On what days and for how long? Students need to have a predictable time to read freely, not counting the last five minutes of class when everyone is packing up. During a recent unit focused around *Romeo and Juliet* as the core text, we read YA novels on Monday, Wednesday, and Friday, and the core canonical text on Tuesday and Thursday; the following week, we alternated days. So we can all plan ahead for reading, I provide students a unit calendar (see Chapter 8) that includes time for independent reading.

Next question: Where will they read? Can students leave their desks and sit on the floor? What will they read? Will you provide an array of texts for them to choose from related to the unit focus and essential questions? How will they check out books? What will happen if they don't return them? It is important to clarify classroom procedures and establish behavior guidelines during reading time. For example:

> Find a comfortable place to read. You may sit or lie on the floor, but I must be able to see your eyes and hands. Once you have selected your place, stay there and read quietly. If you do this, you will receive two points toward your classwork grade.

Guiding

I guide student choices of texts for independent reading. While this may seem a bit unorthodox, often students forget to bring in a text, don't have access to one, or bring in something too easy or hard or of little interest to them—sometimes a book borrowed from a friend in between classes in order to get credit. It is both our responsibility and privilege to match students with books, and a work-shopping teacher builds text sets—related collections of different genres and media—for each unit. I want students to have reading choices, but steer them to select from an array of YA novels, across a variety of levels and genres, related to the unit focus and essential questions. We want to simultaneously empower student choices while monitoring their decision making. I introduce the assortment through book talks, book trailers, book passes, or online summaries at the beginning of a unit. Last year's iMovie book talks students made as projects are available on the class website. Amazon.com is rich with book summaries and reviews to browse. Once informed, students can make thoughtful selections.

Demonstrating

After students have something in hand to read, be sure to demonstrate your literacy commitment by reading with them on some days and conferencing with them on other days. We have to show students that we value reading. If we allot the time and space as well as follow up with students about what they are reading, then we are modeling a commitment to literacy. Talking with students about their reading takes five minutes or less: "What are you reading?," "What do you like about it?," "What do you not like about it?," "What does this text make you think about?," "How would you describe the author's style?," or "How is this text helping you grow as a reader and why?"

Teaching

On days we are not reading or conferencing, we teach a mini-lesson (see Chapter 6), to deepen comprehension. Before students read, I often review a comprehension strategy and ask students to practice as they read. Directed independent reading (Routman, 2003, p. 89) occurs when students read and are directed to do something as a follow-up, such as:

- Practice the reading strategy we have been working on.
- Notice how a character is behaving and what makes him behave that way.
- Visualize the setting the author describes.
- Make a connection to your life or something happening in the world.
- Be on the lookout for a strong chapter lead—an enticing beginning.
- Reread when you lose meaning.
- Use what you already know to figure out what words mean.

We want to be careful, however, not to encumber students' reading time with sticky notes or handouts, and instead balance intentional teaching with authentic reading experiences.

Monitoring

Monitor student comprehension during independent reading in a variety of student-centered ways. In lieu of sticky notes or worksheets, hold a pair-share or large-group discussion following independent reading. Each student is responsible for talking about his or her connections, predictions, inferences, visualizations, questions, or summaries with a partner or the class. This time for sharing provides the added bonus of introducing everyone to what everyone else is reading.

Another way to check student comprehension is through the use of reading logs and response blogs or vlogs. A *reading log* documents the extent of reading (i.e., date, title, pages read) and is easily completed following independent reading. But students also need to be held accountable for making meaning of what is read. This is best revealed through a response blog or vlog. A *response blog* (see Figure 2.2) prompts students to respond affectively to what they have read.

A *vlog* is a video form of a blog. Independent practice includes response (Routman, 2003), and teacher feedback is necessary to ensure readers are making meaning. When students blog or vlog, I post replies, and we engage in online reading conversations. Students also respond to one another. Just giving students time to read is not enough. If a student is not comprehending the text, we need to know, and a response blog or vlog allows some insight into student meaning-making. This, coupled with a reading conference, can provide a more accurate glimpse into a reader's interaction and transaction with a text. Reading

---

READER RESPONSE: *BRAVE NEW WORLD*

Kayla
Date: 10/2/16
Pages read: Chapters 3-4
Prompt: How does this book make you feel and why?

This book makes me worry about the current state of our nation. This setting may seem unlikely to come true, but, if we compare it to our own country, there are already many comparisons to be made. The part that concerned me the most was the segregation of the various groups. Lenina constantly mentions how she is glad she's not a gamma. In our society, this happens all the time. The prettier you are, or the more money you have deems your popularity and success in many instances. Gammas have no room to grow, and in many ways neither do children of poverty. It is very difficult to transcend one's social economic status, seen in society and the novel. This goes both ways though; children from affluent families have a future planned out for them as well. Free will only exists in our heads; we do not have the power to create our own future. Even though Bernard realizes the issues within society, there is nothing he feels he can do to change the system. I feel as though realizing one does not have free will and not being able to anything about it is worse than living in a dream world where one believes they have free will.

2 Comments
Amber 10/5/2016 08:47:45 pm
Hey Kayla, I completely agree with how unsettling this book feels when you compare it to our own world. Though their world uses hypnopaedia to help establish these castes, I suppose you could say that we are often influenced by what the media says (in addition to socioeconomic status etc.). I thought that your comparison of Gammas to children of poverty was an interesting point as well, and a very true one. The futility of Huxley's world certainly does reflect the struggles found in our own world—the only difference is Gammas, Deltas, and Epsilons seem perfectly content to be where they are in life.

Styslinger 10/10/2016 12:26:18 pm
I worry when I read this book as well; the obsession with pleasure and drugs is certainly reminiscent of our own society, as is the societal division—but I think your point about free will is very pertinent here. How much free will do any of us have in life? How many factors beyond our control determine our status and influence our decisions?

FIGURE 2.2. Response blog to *Brave New World*, with student and teacher comments.

logs and response blogs or vlogs allow teachers to monitor student comprehension, even though each student may be reading a different text. Rather than taking a computer-generated test, these offer student-centered means of promoting reading and response.

Goal Setting

Last—based on what we learn from reading logs and conferences, response blogs and vlogs—set goals with students. During a conference, ask a student how he or she wants to grow as a reader. Does he want to read a different genre? Does she want to read more? Does he want to improve his comprehension? Does she want to read books with male protagonists? In what way does a student want to become a more proficient reader? How does he or she plan to reach this goal? Check in with students at the next conference, and, once a goal is met, continue to set new goals.

What to Read Independently

Students need access to a wide variety of high-interest reading materials across an array of reading levels. From these, they can make selections for independent reading. We want to match students with a book they can both understand and enjoy. While the CCSS have foregrounded the issue of text complexity, independent reading is not the time to hand over a copy of Thomas Paine's *Common Sense* or John Steinbeck's *The Grapes of Wrath*. Our students need to start reading where they are and gradually tackle harder material. Save the more complex texts for shared and close reading (to be discussed in the following chapter).

When we workshop the canon, we read YA novels related to the unit focus during independent reading. This genre is high interest and more easily managed by students on their own. At the same time, students share and close read a canonical text (see Chapter 3) while a wide variety of other genres, including picture books, articles, essays, and lyrics, are read aloud. In this way, we are workshopping the canon and providing a range of novels, stories, drama, poetry, and nonfiction texts, helping us meet the scope of reading required by national, state, and district standards.

During independent reading, workshopping teachers provide approximately seven novel options (for an estimated class of twenty-eight) related to the unit focus and varied in level; then students make guided choices. For example, during a unit centered around utopia/dystopia, we share and close read *Brave New*

World, and students choose from the following for independent reading: Nancy Farmer's *The House of the Scorpion*, Gemma Malley's *The Declaration*, Veronica Roth's *Divergent*, Suzanne Weyn's *The Bar Code Tattoo*, Cory Doctorow's *Little Brother*, Anna Todd's *After*, Lauren Oliver's *Delirium*, or Neal Shusterman's *Unwind*. And while share and close reading *Romeo and Juliet*, students choose between Ally Condie's *Matched*, Simon Elkeles's *Perfect Chemistry*, John Green's *The Fault in Our Stars*, Rainbow Rowell's *Eleanor & Park*, Sabaa Tahir's *An Ember in the Ashes*, Gayle Forman's *Just One Day*, Sharon Draper's *Romiette and Julio*, Gordon Korman's *Son of the Mob*, and Jamie Ford's *Hotel on the Corner of Bitter and Sweet*. Sample lists of YA novels tied to unit foci and essential questions are provided in Appendix B. Be sure to include options that allow English language learners to make selections in their first languages.

This same YA novel read during independent reading will be utilized later in the workshop, during book clubs introduced and described in Chapter 5, so only four or five copies of each YA novel are provided per class. After each novel is introduced, students write down their top three choices in order, and the teacher makes final decisions overnight. If students don't get their first or second choice this time, they get priority in the next unit.

Choice is vital for independent reading. However, with choice comes responsibility. Provide students and parent/guardians a summary of YA novel selections for each unit on your class website. If a student or parent objects to reading a particular text, there is always another option available.

The text we eventually select needs to be appropriate for the individual reader, which means we have to know student readers as individuals—seems like common sense, but not always easy to manage when we average twenty-eight students per six class periods. Inspired by Atwell (1998) and Burke (1987), a reading survey (see Appendix C) can teach us a lot. I administer these at the beginning of the year or semester and encourage students to answer truthfully, as I use this information to guide reading selections. Conferences, logs, blogs, and vlogs can supplement what we learn about reading strengths and challenges from school-administered assessments. Guiding readers to texts is a challenging task, but the more we know, the easier it becomes. Get to know students' interests, proficiencies, and challenges and lead them to appropriate books.

When we workshop the canon, we interweave authentic reading processes, including independent reading and read-alouds. These two initial workshop structures expose students to a wider variety of texts and perspectives, extending their understandings of a unit focus and essential questions, not to mention the world and one another. Reading matters.

Chapter Summary

Workshopping the canon engages students in authentic reading experiences through a variety of structures, including read-alouds and independent reading, to support the unit focus and essential questions as well as expose students to a wider array of genres beyond the sole classical text. Read-alouds boost vocabulary, increase fluency, and build motivation and background knowledge among students. A teacher can utilize read-alouds to facilitate either informal or formal comparison between texts, or to provide opportunities to transact with texts, eliciting unencumbered and unfettered student response. Workshop teachers read aloud picture books, short stories, informational/explanatory texts, poetry, and lyrics. They plan for a read-aloud by previewing the text; practicing, to model fluency; introducing what is to be read aloud; and providing any necessary background information to generate interest in the text. Workshop teachers prepare students for read-alouds by establishing expectations and setting guidelines.

During independent reading, students read YA novels related to the unit focus for fifteen minutes or more during class. They keep a record of what is read, and teachers monitor comprehension through conferences and other student-centered means. Workshopping teachers are responsible for introducing the importance of independent reading; establishing a reading schedule and classroom procedure; guiding student choices for independent reading; demonstrating a literacy commitment, by reading and talking with students; teaching mini-lessons facilitating comprehension of texts; monitoring comprehension through student-centered means; and setting reading goals with students. Together, read-alouds and independent reading are the center of the workshopping classroom.

3

The Power of Language

It is only a novel …only some work in which the greatest powers of the mind are displayed, in which the most thorough knowledge of human nature, the happiest delineation of its varieties, the liveliest effusions of wit and humour, are conveyed to the world in the best chosen language.

—JANE AUSTEN, *Northanger Abbey*

Shared reading, close reading, and readers theater shed light and focus attention on the language of what is read. Similar to read-alouds, *shared reading* involves teachers reading a text out loud. However, during a shared reading, students have a copy of the text either projected or placed in front of them. Students follow along silently, seeing and hearing the text as the teacher reads. While a read-aloud models fluency, seeing the page as it is read encourages students to note the textual cues influencing phrasing and pacing. They become aware of text structures, sentence constructions, and word choices. They begin to perceive an author's syntactical and stylistic choices.

Shared reading is directly related to *close reading*. While definitions for close reading vary on particulars, the general process directs students to notice elements of style and structure utilized by an author to relay meaning. Beers and Probst (2013) described the close reading process as encompassing: working with a short passage; exploring the significance of words, sequence, characters, connections, etc.; extending from that passage to other parts of the text; encouraging exploratory discussion; and rereading with purpose. This detailed course of action fosters close reading.

Readers theater—minimal theater in support of reading—is another workshop structure that concentrates student attention on language. No memorization, movement, sets, costumes, or props are required. This way, the focus remains on the text, always visible to an audience. While similar to shared and close reading with its focus on wording and content, it differs in that students—not teachers—read aloud. During readers theater, students practice and perform reading in order to interpret and present a literary work in such a way as to draw attention to the author's craft. In order to communicate meaning to an audience, students focus attention on words, structure, organization, and meaning, deepening comprehension through their transaction and bringing life to the text with their voices.

Through the structures of shared reading, close reading, and readers theater, workshop teachers guide students to notice "the best-chosen language" as they simultaneously see and hear the pages before them.

Why Shared and Close Reading?

Seeing and hearing the pages alters a reading experience for students. Whereas a read-aloud can be, depending on the purpose of the lesson, primarily an aesthetic experience, a shared or close reading is more efferent, as students work to gain understanding of superficial and inherent elements and/or reading processes. During a shared reading experience, students can consider how and why they read a text, while, during a close reading experience, they can analyze how and why a text is written.

During shared and close reading, the teacher works with a more complex text, one typically beyond the reading level for most students in the class. Stahl (2012) referred to these as "stretch" or "heavy" texts, and Afferbach, Pearson, and Paris (2008) called them "Waterloo" texts, after the downfall of Napoleon. For us, the stretch, heavy, and Waterloo text is the core canonical work of literature around which we build a unit and workshop. While we may read aloud a wide variety of genres related to the unit focus, we always share and close read the core canonical text.

Shared reading provides students access to more difficult literary works as teachers simulate and facilitate reading experiences (Holdaway, 1979; Stahl, 2012). Comprehension, vocabulary, text structures, and text features are commonly addressed during a shared reading experience in intermediate grades (Fisher, Frey, & Lapp, 2008). Allington (2001) determined shared reading especially important for struggling readers, and Drucker (2003) recommended it for use with English language learners. While close reading is more commonly used at the secondary and college levels, it also has been proven to be an effective intervention resulting in significant increases in participants' self-perception and achievement as readers (Fisher & Frey, 2012).

Both shared and close reading allow for literature-based and holistic approaches to the teaching of reading strategies, literary devices, grammar, and vocabulary. In the workshopping classroom, we utilize the structure of shared reading to model comprehension-oriented strategies (e.g., connecting, questioning, predicting, visualizing, inferring, summarizing) as well as close reading to teach literary elements (e.g., allusion, conflict, irony, foreshadowing) and demonstrate language (e.g., conventions, usage, and vocabulary). Through shared and close reading, we can meet all of the CCR anchor standards for reading of "key ideas and details" and "craft and structure," as well as the CCR anchor standards for language of "knowledge of language" and "vocabulary acquisition and use," as further detailed in the sections below.

How to Share Read

In the workshopping classroom, we conduct shared reading with the core canonical text for each unit. We know the works of literature most commonly taught in middle and high school classrooms are difficult to comprehend, due to their complex content, structures, and themes, and that we can better support student meaning-making through a shared reading. How? We utilize shared reading to reveal a reader's means of making meaning of these complex texts. Too often, the processes of comprehending are invisible. Readers who struggle don't know how to go about understanding a text because no one ever shows them how to make meaning. During a *shared strategic reading*, we reveal the mysteries of our own meaning-making processes and model comprehension-oriented cognitive reading strategies for students.

Cognitive strategies foster meaning-making through constructive interactions with texts (Conley, 2008); comprehension-oriented cognitive strategies include activating relevant prior knowledge and using prediction, generating questions during reading, constructing mental images representing the meanings in texts, summarizing and clarifying the meanings in texts, and analyzing the structural components of narrative and informational texts (Pressley, 2006). Tovani has demonstrated cognitive strategy reading instruction in the classroom with her books *I Read It, but I Don't Get It* (2000) and *Do I Really Have to Teach Reading?* (2004).

Many of us are likely already familiar with strategy instruction, having seen posters in hallways calling for students to "connect," "predict," "infer," "visualize," "question," and "summarize." But, like many others (Conley, 2008; Fisher et al., 2008; Keene, 2010; Marcell, DeCleene, & Juettner, 2010), I am concerned with the "curricularization" of these strategies. We don't want to teach strategies in isolation. Shared reading as a workshop structure allows us to interweave strategy instruction effortlessly and holistically with the teaching of literature.

For example, during a shared strategic reading of a challenging classical work such as *Beowulf*, I demonstrate my meaning-making processes through a shared reading, modeling my use of strategies that help make the text more understandable. I project a page of text and mark as I read, displaying any connections, predictions, inferences, mental pictures, and questions for all to see (see Figure 3.1). When I finish reading a page, I might also summarize what I have read. Careful not to over-prepare, I want this shared strategy reading to be as metacognitively authentic as possible. My students often referred to this as a "reading brain spew."

As students read online in Nicole's classroom, they demonstrate their shared strategic reading with the help of Google Docs (https://docs.google.com/), a Web-based word-processing tool that encourages students to investigate their own reading strategies. Nicole describes how she facilitates online shared strategic reading as follows:

> We begin by discussing how students make sense of what they read. In an effort to foster metacomprehension, we question students initially about their meaning-making processes. Do they underline? Do they look up words they are unfamiliar with? Do they make notes in the margins? We then extend this discussion online, utilizing Google Docs for students to create what we call a "digital conversation" with the text. Students copy and paste text from their selected scene into a Document. Next, they chronicle their internal conversation with the text. If they are unsure of the meaning of a word, they can not only look up the definition, they can also see an image. Students are challenged to ask two questions, make five comments, and research two aspects of their scene. Last, students post and publish this conversation to a Google website [see Figure 3.2].

While the CCR anchor standards for reading fail to mention strategies to foster meaning-making other than inference and summary, shared strategic reading is necessary for students to comprehend literature at the expected grade-level text-complexity band proficiently; to understand these complex texts, students need the scaffolding provided by comprehension-oriented cognitive reading strategies. Shared strategic reading can provide the literacy support necessary to help students connect, question, predict, infer, visualize, summarize, and, ultimately, make meaning of more challenging works of literature. (See also Chapter 6, which discusses the use of mini-lessons to facilitate comprehension.)

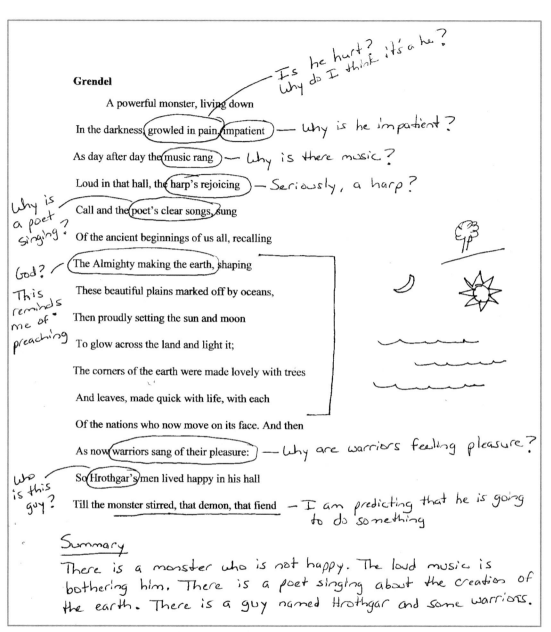

Grendel

Is he hurt? Why do I think it's a he?

A powerful monster, living down

In the darkness, (growled in pain) (impatient) — Why is he impatient?

As day after day the (music rang) — Why is there music?

Loud in that hall, the (harp's rejoicing) — Seriously, a harp?

Why is a poet singing? Call and the (poet's clear songs) sung

Of the ancient beginnings of us all, recalling

God? (The Almighty making the earth) shaping

This reminds me of preaching These beautiful plains marked off by oceans,

Then proudly setting the sun and moon

To glow across the land and light it;

The corners of the earth were made lovely with trees

And leaves, made quick with life, with each

Of the nations who now move on its face. And then

As now (warriors sang of their pleasure:) — Why are warriors feeling pleasure?

Who is this guy? So (Hrothgar's) men lived happy in his hall

Till the monster stirred, that demon, that fiend — I am predicting that he is going to do something

Summary

There is a monster who is not happy. The loud music is bothering him. There is a poet singing about the creation of the earth. There is a guy named Hrothgar and some warriors.

FIGURE 3.1. Shared strategic reading for *Beowulf*, with summary.

SCENE III. A churchyard; in it a tomb belonging to the Capulets.

Stay not, be gone; live, and hereafter say,
A madman's mercy bade thee run away.

PARIS

I do defy thy conjurations,
And apprehend thee for a felon here.

ROMEO

Wilt thou provoke me? then have at thee, boy!

They fight

PAGE

O Lord, they fight! I will go call the watch.

Exit

PARIS

O, I am slain!

Falls

If thou be merciful,
Open the tomb, lay me with Juliet.

Dies

ROMEO

In faith, I will. Let me peruse this face.
Mercutio's kinsman, noble County Paris!
What said my man, when my betossed soul
Did not attend him as we rode? I think
He told me Paris should have married Juliet:
Said he not so? or did I dream it so?
Or am I mad, hearing him talk of Juliet,
To think it was so? O, give me thy hand,
One writ with me in sour misfortune's book!
I'll bury thee in a triumphant grave;
A grave? O no! a lantern, slaughter'd youth,
For here lies Juliet, and her beauty makes
This vault a feasting presence full of light.
Death, lie thou there, by a dead man interr'd.

Laying PARIS in the tomb

How oft when men are at the point of death
Have they been merry! which their keepers call
A lightning before death: O, how may I
Call this a lightning? O my love! my wife!
Death, that hath suck'd the honey of thy breath,
Hath had no power yet upon thy beauty:
Thou art not conquer'd; beauty's ensign yet
Is crimson in thy lips and in thy cheeks,
And death's pale flag is not advanced there.

> **Comment [1]:** 00870555:
> QUESTION Why has Romeo been so sympathetic with his enemies throughout the novel?

FIGURE 3.2. Shared strategic reading for *Romeo and Juliet,* using Google Docs.

What to Share Read

Any of the genres utilized for read-alouds can be used for a shared reading experience (e.g., YA novels, picture books, short stories, informational/explanatory texts, poetry, lyrics). However, I select texts specifically for shared strategic reading that are more challenging for students to comprehend. Suzanne Collins's *The Hunger Games*, for example, is not the best choice for a shared reading, as most students will not struggle to understand YA novels. I always engage in shared reading with classical literature. Literary works such as *The Crucible, To Kill a Mockingbird*, and *The Great Gatsby* tend to humble any proficient and most adolescent readers. Note that English language learners should have access to stretch, heavy, and Waterloo texts in their first languages.

There can be no doubt the CCSS encourage us to read more complex literary and informational texts, and Gallagher (2009) reminded us that it is okay to challenge students with difficult text as long as we help navigate them through more demanding works of literature. I conduct shared reading with all of Shakespeare's plays, reading aloud or listening to dramatic audio recordings as students follow along. I project a page of text and demonstrate my metacomprehension, showing how I read stage directions, how I ask questions, how I infer to make meaning. Short stories with more sophisticated vocabulary and sentence structure, such as those written by Poe or Hawthorne, also work well for shared strategic reading, as do poems with more complicated structure and syntax, such as those written by E. E. Cummings or Walt Whitman. Shared strategic reading enables students to better meet the syntactic, lexical, and plot/theme difficulties these texts present.

How to Close Read

When I want students to observe something intriguing about the way a text is written, I stretch a shared reading into a close reading, and follow the process suggested by Beers and Probst (2013). Ideally, a passage for close reading is selected by students; challenge them to find an interesting paragraph or two from the assigned reading and to ponder the author's word choice, characterization, or imagery. Otherwise, the teacher directs attention to a specific passage of text, which is projected or provided, guiding students to contemplate how and why certain words are chosen, how and why a particular character is portrayed, or how and why a specific literary device is used. This *literary close reading* encourages students to: study the literary technique of the text individually, with partners, or in small groups, and consider the author's purpose; discuss and compare observations as a class; expand the discussion from the passage to other parts of the text; and, finally, reread with new insight.

For example, when reading *The Scarlet Letter*, I guide students through a close reading of passages in Chapter 16, "A Forest Walk," because I want them to ponder the symbolic nature of the natural world. Students are asked to reread particular passages and to draw the forest they see, labeling their description using quotations from the text. They then turn to a partner and share what they have drawn and written. I then ask them to flip their paper over and compare this natural world with what they have already learned about the Puritan community from their reading. They share with their partner again, then with the larger group. "What are the differences between the natural and the Puritan worlds?" "How do the laws in each setting differ?" "What purpose might the brook or sunlight serve?" "In which world would you prefer to live and why?" Following discussion, we reread the passage again, this time with renewed understanding. A literary close reading allows us to meet all of the CCR anchor standards for reading as regards "key ideas and details" and "craft and structure."

In their book *Notice & Note*, Beers and Probst (2013) provide a series of lessons designed to encourage close reading. The lessons are focused around six "signposts," or recurring textual elements, they identified after rereading the most frequently taught books in grades 4 to 10. Noting these textual elements can prompt students to ponder, for example, characters, plot, setting, themes, imagery, dialogue, and word choices. The signposts, described below, can be used to springboard a literary close reading:

- The *aha moment* is that time in the text when a character gains new understanding of himself, others, or the world around him. For example, what Chillingworth sees on Dimmesdale's chest as he sleeps causes him to rejoice. Aha!

- *Contrasts and contradictions* denote sharp contrasts between what readers expect and what we observe characters doing. Many of Chaucer's pilgrims, including the Miller, Friar, Prioress, Physician, Pardoner, Monk, and Manciple, are rich with contrasts and contradictions that students can notice and note.

- *Tough questions* express serious doubt or confusion, as when Hamlet ponders, "To be or not to be," or Juliet, "What's in a name?"

- *Words of the wiser* allude to advice or insight a wiser character offers about life to the main character, as when Merlin offers guidance to King Arthur.

- *Again and again* convey events, images, or particular words that recur again and again in a portion of a novel, such as the green light in *The Great Gatsby* or the flies in *Lord of the Flies*.
- And the *memory moment* is a recollection by a character that interrupts the forward progress of the story. In *Beowulf,* the narrator uses flashbacks to explain the history between characters, including Hrothgar and Unferth.

Along with naming and defining these signposts, Beers and Probst (2013) provide textual clues that students can notice to indicate a signpost, as well as a series of questions students should ask after noting a signpost.

In her unit focused around resilience, Brittany prompted students to conduct a literary close reading of Art Spiegelman's graphic novel *Maus,* using the memory moment:

> I place students in groups of three to four and ask them to describe the relationship between Art and his father. Then, I introduce the signpost memory moment. After a very brief mini-lesson, I direct them to review the novel and locate specific text that includes memories. Groups are asked to find textual evidence to support why they think Art has this kind of relationship with his father. After groups share, we then ponder the following questions in a class discussion: How do you think Art's father feels, reliving and retelling these painful memories? Based on what you know so far, how do his father's memories impact his actions toward his son? How does the role of memory work in both *Maus* and *Night*?

Along with concentrating attention on the literary, we can use close reading to guide a reader's attention to the language convention, style, or use evident in a particular text. Simply put, we can use close reading to teach grammar. Focusing on the positive, we make the author's "best-chosen language" visible in order to demonstrate how they have crafted a text in order to relay meaning. So much of our teacher energy in the past has centered on the negatives, as students circled or underlined improper pronoun case, dangling modifiers, or incorrect punctuation. Ironically, we directed students' attention to what is incorrect, rather than showing them what is correct.

Close reading integrates the study of language with the reading of literature. Rather than teaching grammatical conventions or language usage out of context, we interweave our study of language into the workshop structure of close reading. In this way, we can meet the CCR anchor standards for language including "knowledge of language" and "vocabulary acquisition and use." Our close reading of writing derives from the work of Noden (1999), Ray (1999), and Anderson (2005). These authors offered practical ways and means to promote the positive development of students' grammar knowledge and writing style through the use of powerful model sentences and passages found, scrutinized, and imitated in texts read.

We want students to have lots and lots of writing teachers. The way to achieve this goal is by offering mentor texts, texts written by professional and student writers demonstrating craft, technique, and conventions. Close reading and analyzing a mentor text invites students to read with a "writer's eye," studying and imitating structures and strategies used by skillful authors. Anderson (2005) encouraged teachers to find powerful model sentences in the stories and books read, and to present these sentences to our students as models for discussion (what he calls "noticing") and imitation.

When conducting a *language close reading*, a teacher draws on a sentence or passage from a text currently read as part of a unit of study. As with any shared reading, the teacher reads aloud while students follow along, seeing and hearing the text simultaneously. A teacher can guide student attention to Hemingway's use of nouns and verbs, Martin Luther King Jr.'s use of parallelism and repetition, or Faulkner's complex sentence structure. While the teacher can preselect and direct students' attention to particular words, sentences, or passages in order to meet a certain standard or lesson objective, I encourage students to collect their own words, sentences, and passages for language close reading. We want students to identify unknown vocabulary, discern sentence structure, notice artful parallelism, and observe correct punctuation independently. If students gather words during an initial shared reading, we can then explore and discuss the significance of these words, extending from the word to the sentence, to the paragraph, and to other parts of the text, rereading with renewed understanding during a language close reading. This language loot becomes the foundation for close reading and leads to such discussions as the relation of clauses to meaning or the effects of syntax on style. In Jessica's classroom, this is how language close reading is facilitated:

> As bell work, when students enter the classroom, I ask them to review the chapters they read for their book club for homework and find three things. They need to find (1) an unusual or unknown word, (2) a sentence they like, and (3) an interesting use of punctuation. Then, I ask them to get with their book club and discuss what they found. I project the following questions on the interactive whiteboard: What do you notice about the words you collected? Can you figure out what they mean? Can you group them in any way? Why do you think the author chose those

words? How do these words relate to the rest of the novel? Then: What do you notice about the sentences you chose? Why did you choose these sentences? What do you like or dislike about the way they are written? Have you ever seen sentences written like this before? In your own writing? In someone else's writing? Why do you think the author wrote her/his sentences in this way? Would you like to write sentences like this? Why or why not? And, last: What do you notice about the punctuation? Why do you think the author used punctuation in this way? Do think it would change the meaning of the novel if the author changed his/her word choice, sentence structure, or punctuation? Why or why not?

After noticing and noting, students discuss their findings.

What to Close Read

When facilitating a close reading around language use or literary devices, we want students examining a text rich with noteworthy grammar, style, and meaning. We need to teach texts students can read like writers. A mentor text—a text we can reread for many different purposes and later imitate—can be any piece of writing: a YA or classic novel, play, picture book, poem, short story, informational/explanatory text, lyrics, or even a comic book or graphic novel. The type of mentor text chosen depends on the goals of the overall unit as well as the purpose and objectives for the daily lesson.

Classical works are especially well suited for literary and language close reading. When teaching a unit focused around power and corruption, Kayla close reads Old Major's speech from *Animal Farm* because it parodies Karl Marx's theories of class struggle and exploitation of the working class. Students are asked to identify the craft of the passage, noting how Old Major manipulates and persuades his listeners. Not to be discounted, many YA novels are rich with examples of literary and writerly craft. As Jessica shows above, students can search their YA novels for sentences with particular parts of speech (e.g., adjectives, adverbs, conjunctions, nouns, prepositions, pronouns, verbs), sentences with particular phrases (e.g., absolute, appositive, gerund, infinitive, participial, prepositional), and sentences with particular clauses (e.g., dependent and independent), noting how structure affects meaning. They can investigate elements of style affecting voice and tone. And they can explore the ways punctuation is used by the author, such as her use of commas, colons, semicolons, dashes, apostrophes, or quotation marks. During a literary close reading, students can note the use of figurative language and literary devices and consider how these affect the novel's meaning and style.

Picture books are effective mentor texts to use with a close reading, as they often exhibit sophisticated craft, ideas, and structures and are short and easy to read. In a unit focused around journey, I read Allen Say's *Grandfather's Journey* and facilitate a literary close reading around irony and symbolism. In a unit centered around war, I read Eve Bunting's *The Wall*, and we contemplate point of view, while, with Patricia Polacco's *Pink and Say*, we consider symbolism. In a unit focused around gender, we explore satire in Munro Leaf's *The Story of Ferdinand* and voice in Robert Munsch's *Paperbag Princess*.

To facilitate a language close reading, have students analyze the author's language or convention and deliberate how these choices affect the book's meaning and style. When teaching a unit focused around justice, guide student attention to Jacqueline Woodson's sentence structure or dialogue in *The Other Side* or elements of persuasion in Eve Bunting's allegorical *Riding the Tiger* within a unit focused around power and corruption.

Essays and articles provide a springboard for close analysis of informational, explanatory, and argumentative text structures. For example, when teaching *To Kill a Mockingbird* within a unit focused around justice, close read Martin Luther King Jr.'s "I Have a Dream," Mary Mebane's "The Back of the Bus," or Judy Brady's "I Want a Wife." Close read articles about Trayvon Martin and Matthew Shepard published in the *New York Times*. And a wealth of short stories contain complexities of language to be explored, such as James Hurst's "The Scarlet Ibis" and Alice Walker's "The Flowers." Please see Appendix B for suggested supplementary texts.

Why Readers Theater?

Teachers want opportunities for students to practice reading, seeing, and interpreting the text before them. However, unprepared students should not be called on to read aloud. The practice of round-robin reading, when students are selected to read in a predetermined order, usually by desk arrangement, has been widely disputed by researchers for quite some time (Allington, 1980; Opitz, Rasinski, & Bird, 1998; Stanovich, 1980). Variants of this method include popcorn, Popsicle, and combat reading (Ash & Kuhn, 2006). No matter what cute name is given, these practices often lead to disconnected and dysfluent literacy experiences, because students are not allowed or encouraged to prepare for reading. If we are so busy taking turns, how often are students having a continued literacy experience? And, if we don't provide time to preview text, how well are students modeling a proficient reading? During popcorn reading, students read aloud in random order; students call on one another to read without prior knowledge of the text during combat reading; and a teacher draws indiscriminate names written on sticks during Popsicle reading. While stressful for more challenged readers, these practices are boring for those who are more skilled (Ivey, 1999).

An alternative—readers theater—provides the opportunity for students to practice reading in multiple and meaningful ways. It is unlike robin, popcorn, Popsicle, or combat in that it promotes an interpretive and prepared presentation of text in a nonthreatening setting. This workshop structure develops fluency and promotes thoughtful, enjoyable engagement with texts. We know practice makes for better readers. As students become more familiar with a text, they notice the rich vocabulary, interesting language, deeper meanings, and writerly craft. Research shows readers theater, because of the repeated readings it demands, yields improvement in word recognition, fluency, comprehension, oral communication skills, and reading motivation (Bidwell, 1990; Goodson & Goodson, 2005; Martinez, Roser, & Strecker, 1999; Rasinski, 2003; Uthman, 2002).

What to Read during Readers Theater

As the purpose for readers theater is to showcase the power of language, we begin with the selection of text. Any story, poem, essay, song, newspaper article, picture book, scene from a play, or chapter from a novel can act as a springboard for a readers theater performance. I once saw an amazing performance of readers theater based on letters compiled from the Civil War era. Julianne utilizes readers theater in her unit focused around fear and persecution with *The Crucible*. A shared class reading evolves into readers theater as students are grouped into scenes by number of characters and introduced to the value of performing a text.

While any text can be adapted for performance, it is best to select a work that deepens student understanding of a unit focus or essential questions, as well as challenges them to interpret characters and meaning. Bordering on close reading, students analyze textual style and structure to decipher meaning to be relayed through performance. Instead of merely talking about elements such as characters, plot, point of view, mood, and tone, students experience these first-hand as they are challenged to orally interpret text. Students become reader–performers and the teacher, a director.

How to Direct Readers Theater

Inspired by Black and Stave (2007) as well as Shepard (2014) and Rasinski (2003), teachers engage students in the readers theater process through repeated readings, script writing, vocal practice, performance preparation, and readers celebration, as follows.

Repeated Readings and Script Writing

The process begins as students are placed in small groups and provided a text to read and reread in order to identify main ideas and characters. Once students have initially comprehended the text, they write a script to be used for performance. The script should take around ten minutes to read, and students may make cuts and changes to the original text to make it easier to understand or perform. When Julianne directs readers theater, she asks students to adapt their assigned scenes from *The Crucible* into more modern language while maintaining the integrity of the play.

Obviously, some original texts are more easily adapted for performance. A scene from *The Crucible*, for example, already has characters delineated and dialogue assigned. However, even scenes from plays will need to be modified for a readers theater performance, as not all characters or dialogue need to be included to convey meaning. As above, students might also wish to change or update language. Once drafted, scripts need to clearly communicate the main information, ideas, and mood of the original text. It is okay to cut, combine, or split characters, but the script needs to include a narrator, as narration serves as the framework for the dramatic presentation.

It is often helpful to provide a mentor text—a sample readers theater script—as a visible guide for students. A wide variety of scripts appropriate for elementary students are freely available online, but it is a bit more difficult to find those appropriate for middle and secondary students. The author Aaron Shepard (www.aaronshep.com) has adapted a variety of folktales and fables from around the world, and I have located free script adaptations of *Beowulf*, Louis Sachar's *Holes*, and *To Kill a Mockingbird* with just a few clicks. Once students gain more experience with readers theater, they may write original texts or present self-selected materials related to a unit focus or essential questions. When reading *Lord of the Flies* as a core text, my students authored powerful readers theater scripts for a unit focused around bullying.

Vocal Practice, Performance Preparation, and Readers Celebration

Once students have a script written, they need to assign roles and practice vocal performances through repeated readings. Class time has to be allotted for rehearsals. Students can read for more than one character, or a character can be divided in half if necessary. Every student should have their own copy of the script, with their lines highlighted. Students practice reading to increase fluency and comprehension. They are encouraged to use lots of vocal expression and to consider their rate, tone, volume, inflection, and dialect.

Students prepare for performance by staging the script reading. No lines are memorized. The actual physical presence of the text reinforces its importance. But will students read sitting down or standing up? Where will chairs or stools be placed? No movement should detract from the spoken word, so actions are few and far between. But when are physical movements and facial expressions needed? Good eye contact and correct posture are always necessary. As we want to maintain focus on the text, I limit production elements such as costumes or props, but some may be necessary to identify characters, develop plot, or communicate meaning.

As students arrive at this rehearsal stage, we watch readers theater performances uploaded to YouTube or TeacherTube (www.teachertube.com), as well as clips from the Chamber Readers available on Aaron Shepard's website (www.aaronshep.com/rt/ChamberReaders). Recorded performances of last year's students provide encouraging and motivating models too. Finally, students are advised to plan how they will introduce their script at the readers celebration. And, during the readers celebration, groups perform their script readings for one another.

Because readers theater integrates reading, writing, speaking, listening, and viewing, a wide variety of CCR anchor standards for speaking and listening, reading, writing, and language can be met through this workshop structure. In addition, Julianne holds students accountable to the following criteria when they perform: scene encapsulation, participation, script, volume/clarity/inflection, and creativity.

Chapter Summary

Shared reading, close reading, and readers theater are workshop structures that interweave diverse text and deepen student comprehension of a unit focus and essential questions by directing their attention to the language and composition of what is read. When a text is visible, shared, or performed, students can perceive an author's syntactical and stylistic choices and ponder the effects on meaning derived from their transaction. Through shared strategic reading, teachers model how they make meaning of text with comprehension-oriented cognitive reading strategies. During a literary close reading, students consider the effects of literary devices on the meaning of text, while, with a language close reading, students deliberate grammatical, mechanical, and usage choices and their outcome for the reader. An alternative to the practice of round-robin reading, readers theater provides the opportunity for students to practice reading in multiple and meaningful ways. We utilize shared reading, close reading, and readers theater to support comprehension of complex literature. The power of language is revealed as students contemplate "best-chosen language."

4

Engaging Reader Response

But feelings can't be ignored

—ANNE FRANK, *The Diary of a Young Girl*

While the first few chapters of this book demonstrate why and how to workshop the canon using read-alouds, independent reading, shared reading, close reading, and readers theater, the present chapter offers reasons and resources for engaging students in reader response through these workshop structures and strategies. But, before we discuss why and how to engage students in reader response, it is important to broaden our understanding of the theory that influences this workshop practice.

A few general principles distinguish reader response as a theoretical framework. First, reading is believed to be a dynamic, active, and situated process. Text is unstable, so meaning is variable and changes with each reader. Meaning happens through an exchange between the reader and a text, through a sort of "dialogue" (Rosenblatt, 1994). Readers arrive at meaning through associative and personal responses. These responses are shaped by the cultural and social contexts in which the reading takes place as well as by the individual readers. As Rosenblatt (1995) summarized, a reader:

> brings to the work personality traits, memories of past events, present needs and preoccupations, a particular mood of the moment, and a particular physical condition. These and many other elements in a never-to-be-duplicated combination determine his response to the particular contribution of the text. (pp. 30–31)

Workshopping teachers structure classrooms that foster individual transaction with what is read, and then build on personal response toward formal analysis and critical synthesis, growing the interpretive community as a result.

We encourage students to transact with a picture book during read-alouds or a YA novel during independent reading. We foster personal response through shared and before close reading of a canonical work. Students need opportunities for unmediated, unencumbered responses to a wide variety of texts, and workshopping classrooms always nurture responses to what is read. After all, feelings can't be ignored.

Why Foster Reader Response?

The first reason for fostering reader response is simple. We want adolescents to enjoy reading. Students will not read, or subsequently improve as readers, if it is not a pleasurable experience. To improve as readers, students must read more often. To read more often, students must enjoy it. It is the transitive property of literacy. Our students are entitled to aesthetic experiences with texts. We want them to connect personally—thinking, feeling, and remembering as they read. We want them to relate personal to textual experiences. Sometimes, middle and high school teachers are tempted to move too quickly to the more formal analysis of text, but literature is not an artifact to be studied; it is an experience to be entered into (Probst, 2004). We enter into text through response.

Reader response encourages students to enjoy reading because, theoretically and pedagogically, it connects texts to selves. What middle or high school student is not interested in himself or herself? What adult, for that matter? When we facilitate reader response, we foster self-reflection and self-indulgence (Probst, 2004), guiding students to think about experiences, attitudes, and beliefs, and then considering how each of these shapes our meaning-making processes. Through reading response, we can come to know both our personal selves and reader selves better.

The implementation of reader response has been shown to have positive classroom effects. For example, when instruction is shifted from a formalist frame to a more response-oriented frame, students have been seen to become closely engaged by responding to novels more actively, sometimes passionately, as indicated by detailed oral and written responses (Patterson & Crumpler, 2009). Boyle (2000) found her students enjoyed reading more as a result of reader response being put into practice in the literature classroom. And Tucker (2000) found reader-response engagements combated the lack of interest in her introductory literature course. Providing students with opportunities to respond evidently increases appreciation for reading.

A second reason for implementing reader response is that it provides a starting point for formal analysis and critical synthesis. Response to texts does not equal interpretation of texts. While we want students to enjoy what they read, we also want them to leave classrooms thinking about what has been read. Reader response is a theory and pedagogy of reading upon which we build and extend. The aesthetic experience is not the end of a literary transaction; it is the first step. Both feeling and thought are legitimate components of literary interpretation (Rosenblatt, 1995), and any text, whether canonical or not, demands intellectual as well as affective responses from readers. Personal response is the initial means to a more formal and critical end. In the workshopping classroom, we interpret texts beyond personal connections.

While, in the 1980s, Rosenblatt's work influenced how we taught literature, from the early 1940s to 1970s, New Criticism was the prevalent theory guiding English instruction, and reader response can theoretically coexist with it. With New Criticism, meaning resides within the text. Readers are encouraged to identify specific literary qualities through close reading and to pay careful attention to the form and language of the text itself, seeking meaning within the author's techniques or intentions. Although New Criticism is certainly not new today, it has found renewed support in the CCSS. Any teacher who has read through these standards cannot help but notice the number of times the word *analysis* appears. New Criticism is the prevailing literary theory underlying the CCSS, which exclude other theories—including reader response and critical literacy.

While the more text-centered theory/pedagogy of New Criticism may seem at odds with reader response, it does not have to be. As Rosenblatt (2003) clarified, "Emphasis on the reader need not exclude teaching criteria of valid interpretation or application of various approaches, literary and social, to the process of critical interpretation and evaluation" (p. 7). In the workshopping classroom, we begin with reader response, allowing and encouraging students to bring prior knowledge—their personality traits, past events, present needs, physical conditions, moods, and preoccupations—to the text. These initial associations form the foundation on which we build, establishing an interpretive classroom community through sharing of personal responses, then engaging in more formal analysis and critical study. During formal analysis, we guide students in understanding how a text achieves its effects and, often, its meaning. When we embark on critical study, we view a text through one or more literary theories (e.g., historical/biographical, moral/philosophical, Freudian, feminist, archetypal, Marxist, formalist, rhetorical, deconstructionist, new historical, etc.).

There is constant interplay between the personal and the interpretive fostered through reader response, formal analysis, and critical synthesis. One informs the other. Reader response helps students develop an appreciation for multiple interpretations of literature as students begin their literary journeys with appreciating a variety of responses offered by classmates. Having gained an understanding of diverse perspectives, students are more ready to consider the many elements of formal analysis and view texts through a variety of theoretical lenses. Workshopping teachers address the personal, formal, and critical in recursive ways. Response enriches analysis as a reader's perspective shapes the literary work, while the work itself also has power to guide the reader's responses. The relationship between reader and text is reciprocal, each influencing the other. Teachers begin by fostering unmediated personal responses, on which are layered formal analyses, viewing the text through varied aforementioned theoretical lenses if desired, and finally the initial responses are revisited with a newfound understanding of the literary, social, cultural, and perhaps political contexts that shaped these responses. And this leads to a final reason why we should interweave reader response as we workshop the canon.

Reader response can guide students to critical reading and literacy. For some time, English and literacy educators have advocated for more critically and culturally responsive versions of reader-response pedagogies (Bean & Moni, 2003; Morrell, 2005; Sumara, 2000), arguing that teachers need to move beyond simply valuing students' personal responses to literature. After all, no reader's response is innocent. I was continually amazed by the array of student reactions to a character such as Shakespeare's Lady Macbeth. Whereas Calvin contended that she was personally motivated in her desire for power and suggested she manipulated Macbeth for her own ends, LaMyra argued Lady Macbeth wanted power only for the sake of her husband and influenced Macbeth for his own best interests. Most of us are well aware of the wide variety of student responses to any text, or elements within, such as character.

One facet of reader-response theory, cultural reader response, focuses on how such differences in roles, attitudes, and values, as well as larger societal and historical backgrounds, shape the responses of readers. Every reader brings a social, cultural, economic, political, and personal context. What forces led Calvin to blame Lady Macbeth and LaMyra to defend her? In my high school classroom, I often noticed how the context of gender, a factor of culture, influences literacy transactions (Styslinger, 1999, 2004). So many other factors of background and culture (e.g., race, religion, socioeconomic status, language, sexual orientation) shape transactions, and student responses to text reveal beliefs, values, assumptions, and attitudes that derive from certain ideologies. Critical literacy focuses on the social, cultural, and political forces that influence the creation and interpretation of texts and readers.

Just as reader response can coexist with New Criticism, so it can with critical literacy. Theories are permeable, and reader response acknowledges the influence of social, cultural, and political factors on the individual reader (Cai, 2008).

An analysis of response can "foster the development of critical and self-critical judgment" (Rosenblatt, 1995, p. xviii). When we layer critical literacy over reader response, readers can critically scrutinize initial responses to literary works for their social and cultural influences, reflect on their stance adopted toward a text, and examine their values and roles in society, thereby moving toward more critical readings.

Critical literacy tangles with formal analysis and literary criticism. In order to adopt a critical stance, students need to search for the author's underlying messages and assumptions. Readers reach to understand the text's purpose in order to avoid being manipulated by it. They question who is writing the text and contemplate who is deciding what is included and excluded within its pages. Critical literacy demands we consider whose voices are represented, whose are missing, and who gains and who loses by any reading.

When we workshop the canon, we juxtapose multiple genres and perspectives to foster critical literacy. Critical literacy depends on students having access to culturally diverse literature. Workshopping teachers make conscious and deliberate choices, choosing texts that introduce students to a variety of settings, characters, and situations. Reading allows the means to transport ourselves into the lives of others like and unlike us. If we read only a canonical text, our perspective would be sorely limited. Introducing other genres through workshop structures such as read-alouds, independent reading, shared reading, close reading, and readers theater, we provide the opportunity to enter the experiences and gain the perspectives of others. As a student once so aptly told Wilhelm (1997), "Reading is a way to get inside other people. . . . It's a way to learn stuff that's impossible to learn any other way because you learn from the inside" (p. 35). With the help of literature, we can provide access to possible ways of being in our classrooms.

When a text introduces characters, lives, and cultures less familiar to the reader, it can heighten self-consciousness and text consciousness. This is why independent reading selections are so important. We want students reading texts beyond the canon—works not just reflective of mainstream European Americans. At the same time, readers can be guided to a more critical stance when reading canonical works, reflecting on insights literature provides about their world and their relationships to one another, considering how their "situatedness" affects the meanings they construct—those contextual, textual, authorial, personal, and cultural factors influencing their responses (Knickerbocker & Rycik, 2006). Brooks and Browne (2012) examined ways in which literary interpretations are influenced by readers' ethnic backgrounds as well as the cultural milieu embedded in the stories they read. Teachers who workshop the canon encourage students to question where their responses come from and prod students to consider what these responses say about themselves as readers and human beings.

A final reason why we should encourage reader response is to better meet the needs of English language learners. There is much research supporting the practical application of this theory. Liaw (2001), for example, utilized a reader-response approach to teaching English as a foreign language, and her study revealed students went beyond comprehension of text and actively constructed meaning through a more complex transaction with texts. Amer (2003) discussed reader response as a pedagogically effective approach to teaching first-language narrative texts. And Carlisle (2000) utilized student-written reading logs in English as a foreign language literature teaching. Students made notes as they read, jotting down thoughts and feelings, interacting and responding to the text. Carlisle found this engagement particularly appropriate for second language use as it stimulates foreign language readers to move beyond the first barrier of semantic understanding toward a more critical appreciation.

When we engage students in reader response, we encourage an enjoyment of reading, provide a starting point for formal analysis and critical synthesis, offer opportunities for fostering critical literacy, and better meet the needs of English language learners. Now that we have an increased understanding of why we should translate theory into practice, let's consider the variety of texts that encourage response.

Which Texts Should Readers Respond To?

Workshopping teachers encourage response to every text read, beginning with the cornerstone canonical text. Rather than immediately providing background on the time period or information about the author, we begin by connecting some component of our students' lives with a component of the literary work. Of course, we may later interweave historical/biographical information into teaching; it is just not where we begin. We try to foster initial connections with upcoming characters, dialogue, ideas, setting, or plot. Rather than lecturing on the life and times of Shakespeare, we try to stir emotions and nurture associations, asking students if they believe in love at first sight; or making comparisons between hip-hop and iambic pentameter; or relating characters, events, and settings to past and present experiences.

Fostering personal response to canonical texts can be more challenging than expected, as many students already come to class carrying textual baggage. They have heard from classmates and adults about the challenges of reading

Shakespeare, Hawthorne, Golding, Fitzgerald, or Chaucer. They have already heard of balcony scenes, scarlet letters, pig heads, green lights, and gap teeth. Somehow, we must find a way to help students let go of scholarly, historical, and critical baggage associated with classical texts, in the hope of liberating personal response.

Along with classical texts, students should have opportunities to respond to novels read during independent reading. As students are reading different books, they can easily document their reading through personal responses. Students can then respond to one another, and the teacher can respond as well.

All texts read aloud or read independently throughout a unit—whether fiction or nonfiction, and including picture books, short stories, articles, essays, poetry, and lyrics—deserve response from readers. Students even can respond personally during a shared or close reading. While shared and close reading shift a reader's attention to how or why a text is written, we can foster responses before drawing students' attention to the text structures, sentence constructions, or word choices we want them to notice.

How to Foster Initial Reader Response

When teaching responsively, we help students recall experiences, elicit associations, and prompt reactions to what is read. We consider a literary work first personally, then more formally and critically, guiding students from personal to literary meaning-making. As we share responses, we foster an interpretive classroom community. Creating an active workshop environment in which students respond personally (as well as analytically and critically after that) to what they are reading is an important workshop goal.

Workshopping teachers can nurture student reaction to text in a variety of ways before, during, or after read-alouds, independent reading, shared reading, close reading, or readers theater. While most response is written, we don't have to limit students through medium; response can take musical, theatrical, visual, and spoken forms. In fact, performative responses (see Figure 4.1) allow students to create and express meaning in ways that go well beyond written or oral language, engaging creativity and imagination.

We also do not want to discount the role technology plays in promoting and recording responses from readers. While one of the most common ways to elicit response from readers is through a response journal (see Figure 4.2), this format can easily be updated to develop twenty-first-century literacy skills.

FIGURE 4.1. Student tableau in response to Act 5 of *Romeo and Juliet.*

Students can create a response blog as discussed and demonstrated in Chapter 2, or post on WordPress (https://wordpress.org/), another blogging platform available for free. WordPress offers artistic, even professional renderings of the blog template and provides another good option for housing journals and responses for students. Teachers and students can facilitate response-based discussions on Edmodo (www.edmodo.com), Padlet (https://padlet.com/), or Schoology (www.schoology.com), and PowToon (www.powtoon.com) even allows readers to create animated responses to their reading.

No matter the platform or format, students are presented with an array of prompts such as those provided below (some of which have been adapted from Myers, 1988, p. 65) to generate personal response during or following read-alouds, independent reading, shared reading, close reading, or readers theater:

- How does what you have read make you feel, and why? Do you have any similar feelings to those experienced by the characters? Why or why not?

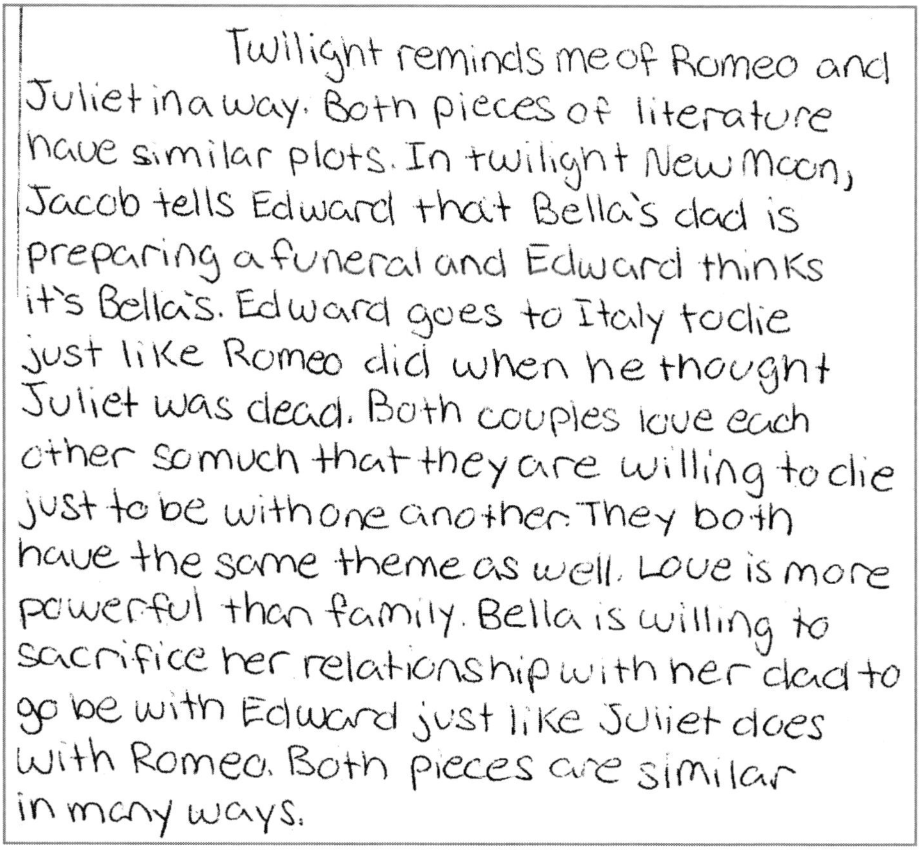

> Twilight reminds me of Romeo and Juliet in a way. Both pieces of literature have similar plots. In twilight New Moon, Jacob tells Edward that Bella's dad is preparing a funeral and Edward thinks it's Bella's. Edward goes to Italy to die just like Romeo did when he thought Juliet was dead. Both couples love each other so much that they are willing to die just to be with one another. They both have the same theme as well. Love is more powerful than family. Bella is willing to sacrifice her relationship with her dad to go be with Edward just like Juliet does with Romeo. Both pieces are similar in many ways.

FIGURE 4.2. Student response to *Romeo and Juliet*.

- What do you think is the most important word or sentence you have read so far? Why?

- Have you read anything that reminds you of someone or something else? What can you relate to? Explain.

- What confuses you about what you have read so far? Why do you think you are confused?

- What do you think is going to happen? Why?

- Describe what you are wondering about.

- Write a poem or lyrics in response to what you have read.

- Draw a picture or create a collage in response to what you have read, and write a paragraph explaining why you drew or created this.

- Describe what you like about what you have read so far. Why do you like this?
- Describe what you do *not* like about what you have read so far. Why don't you like this?
- Are there any characters you are very similar to or different from? How so?
- Does anyone remind you of anyone you know? Explain.
- Which characters do you like the best and least, and why?
- What qualities of which characters strike you as good characteristics to develop within yourself over the years? Why? Explain what the character says or does that you want to emulate.
- What would you do differently from the characters? Explain.
- How is this text like or unlike other texts you have read, movies you have seen, or experiences you have had? Explain.
- Do you feel there is an opinion expressed by the author through this work? What is it? How do you know this? Do you agree? Why or why not?
- What would you change about what you have read and why?

Following reading experiences, students are given time to talk through their responses.

When Emily was teaching a unit focused around utopia/dystopia, some students were independently reading Rodman Philbrick's *Last Book in the Universe*. In this futuristic novel, Spaz, who is not able to use the mind-numbing technology that others rely on, sets out on a quest to save his sister, and, in doing so, begins to see the real world. To foster personal connections, Emily asked students to imagine what songs the main character would download. Delaney responded with the following songs and rationales:

"Without You"—I think Spaz would relate to this song, because, without Bean, he feels lonely, depressed, and like nothing will ever get better.

"Wake Me Up When September Ends"—Spaz would like this Green Day song because the world he lives in, the Urb, seems really horrible to him. He is different than everyone else, and the Bully Bangers direct life. To me, it seems like Spaz would want to go to sleep, and not wake up for a while.

"Stronger (What Doesn't Kill You)"—I think Spaz would jam to this song, because he feels like he's been through a lot, and this song is good for that.

"I'm a Survivor"—This classic song would be one of Spaz's favorites, because he is on a journey to see Bean, and he isn't going to give up when he's so close.

"Safe & Sound"—This song would definitely be on Spaz's iPod because it talks about being safe, even though the world outside is on fire and in destruction. Spaz probably thinks Bean can make his world brighter.

As a result of this initial posted response, students engaged in a lively online discussion, arguing about the best song choices, revealing and increasing knowledge of characters' internal and external characteristics along the way.

Students in my classroom blogged responses to novels read during a unit also focused around utopia/dystopia, with *Brave New World* as the cornerstone text. Each week students were paired and would read and respond to each other's posts. Responses became layered (see Chapter 2) as students transacted not only individually with the text but collaboratively with each other and with me.

Similar to a response log or blog, a *double-entry diary* (Tovani, 2000) records connections, but students first select and copy quotations with page numbers from their reading on one side of the page, and then make personal, world, and textual connections to the selected quotations on the other side of the page (see Figure 4.3).

If students struggle to make connections to quotations, you can provide them with sentence starters such as the following to prompt their responses:

- I feel . . .
- I think . . .
- I see . . .
- I wonder . . .
- This reminds me of . . .
- I agree with this because . . .
- I disagree with this because . . .
- I can relate to this because . . .
- Based on my experiences . . .
- I don't understand this because . . .
- If I were . . .

Page Number	Quote	Connection
Page 1	*Mr. Utterson the lawyer was a man of a rugged countenance that was never lighted by a smile; cold, scanty and embarrassed in discourse; backward in sentiment; lean, long, dusty, dreary and yet somehow lovable. At friendly meetings, and when the wine was to his taste, something eminently human beaconed from his eye; something indeed which never found its way into his talk, but which spoke not only in these silent symbols of the after-dinner face, but more often and loudly in the acts of his life. He was austere with himself; drank gin when he was alone, to mortify a taste for vintages*	I can personally connect to this because I have many characteristics that are similar to Mr. Utterson's. I am usually the quiet one, the one who doesn't talk as much, nor contribute to conversations at hand. I like to be reserved but friendly as well, I am also very curious; just like Utterson, I always look for an answer.
Page 17	*"He must have lost his head, or he never would have left the stick or, above all, burned the cheque book. Why, money's life to the man."*	Nowadays people believe that the most important thing is money. Money has basically become the world's most important thing to possess. But I believe money can also lead to downfall, and this quote shows that money was and is still regarded by the world as being very important, and the statement "money is life to man" can also mean money is death as well. Because there isn't life without death.
Page 23	*"I sometimes think if we knew all, we should be more glad to get away."*	I really like this quote. This quote shows us that sometimes ignorance is bliss, and sometimes not knowing is better than being enlightened. Sometimes knowing less is better because the burden of knowing can be very difficult. Sometimes when we know more, we have more than we would ever wanted to know.
Page 24	*Within there was another enclosure, likewise sealed, and marked upon the cover as "not to be opened till the death or disappearance of Dr. Henry Jekyll." Utterson could not trust his eyes. Yes, it was disappearance; here again, as in the mad will which he had long ago restored to its author, here again were the idea of a disappearance and the name of Henry Jekyll bracketed. But in the will, that idea had sprung from the sinister suggestion of the man Hyde; it was set there with a purpose all too plain and horrible. Written by the hand of Lanyon, what should it mean? A great curiosity came on the trustee, to disregard the prohibition and dive at once to the bottom of these mysteries*	This was very interesting for me, because throughout the book I would wonder how I would be if I was Utterson. In this instant I'm not sure if I could be able to hold out and not upon the enclosure Lanyon gave Utterson. If I was Utterson, my curiosity would've gotten the best of me, and caused me to betray my friend's loyalty.

FIGURE 4.3. Student's double-entry diary entries for *Dr. Jekyll and Mr. Hyde.*

FIGURE 4.3. Continued.

Page Number	Quote	Connection
Page 25	*"You stay too much indoors," said the lawyer. "You should be out, whipping up the circulation like Mr. Enfield and me."*	This passage shows how friendship and companionship is really important for humans to have. In Frankenstein the whole story was based off how friendship and companionship was really important, it showed the true importance of having a friend to relate and talk to. Jekyll at this point tried to stay away from the company of others, but even Utterson could see the true importance of companionship.
Page 42	*And indeed the worst of my faults was a certain impatient gaiety of disposition, such as has made the happiness of many, but such as I found it hard to reconcile with my imperious desire to carry my head high, and wear a more than commonly grave countenance before the public.*	This quote can be related to the Lord of Flies. In the Lord of the Flies Jack always tried to wear a mask and portray what others expected of him. He wore a mask to gain respect and fear from the boys, the mask showed who he wanted to be seen as, but not he really was. Same thing with Jekyll his mask only showed who he wanted society to think of him. I think his mask was actually Jekyll and Hyde was who he was behind the mask, his true form.

In Nicole's English I classroom, students were reading *Dr. Jekyll and Mr. Hyde* as part of a unit focused around the essential nature of man and the complexity of duality. The class was considering whether or not duality exists or whether there is a single personality always in performance mode based on need. Nicole thought it crucial for students to collect evidence as well as interact with it. As students read, they were instructed to select two quotations per chapter that reflected duality (see Figure 4.3). Double-entry diaries thus served as an effective means of fostering student transaction with the core text and unit focus.

As teachers, we are always seeking ways to nudge responses from students. Probst, who so thoughtfully has translated Rosenblatt's theories into practice, devised a series of questions, including those featured below, that lead readers to dialogue with the text:

- What feeling or emotion did this text give you? Describe it briefly and explain why you think the text caused that reaction.

- What memory does this text call to mind—of people, places, events, sights, sounds, smells, or even something more ambiguous, such as feelings or attitudes?

- What did you see happening in the text? Paraphrase it, retelling the events briefly. When you discuss it, see if there are differences in the paraphrasing between discussion partners.

- Did the text give you any ideas or cause you to think about anything in particular? Explain briefly what thoughts it led you to.

- What is the most important word in the text? Explain briefly why you think it's so important.

- What image or picture did you see as you read the text? It might be something you remember and not something in the text. Describe it briefly.

- Does this text make you think of another text, song, TV show, or literary work? What is it, and what connection is there between the two pieces? (Probst, 2004, pp. 82–83)

When I was teaching the unit including *Brave New World*, my students and I conducted a shared reading of John Lennon's "Imagine." First, I read the lyrics aloud, and students followed along. Students then listened to a recording of Lennon singing the lyrics and, once again, followed along. Using Probst's questions as a springboard, students jotted down responses to questions, then engaged in conversation about the text with a partner and, later, the larger group. Latoya expressed how scary the words seemed—not being able to imagine a world without religion, which provided a strong guiding force in her own life. David said the words "join us" made him think of a cult. And Meagan questioned what people would have to give up to be "one." Students talked of movies they had seen (e.g., *Gattaca*, *The Island*, *Minority Report*) and books they had read (e.g., Lois Lowry's *The Giver*, Veronica Roth's *Divergent*, and James Dashner's *The Maze Runner*), making connections all along to *Brave New World*. (Appendix B includes a complete list of my supplementary texts for this unit.) Through dialogue, students remembered, explained, connected, considered, wondered, and reflected while laying the foundation necessary for formal analysis and critical synthesis.

There are so many creative ways to foster and relay response to a variety of texts utilized in a focus unit. In the guise of characters, students can blog, text, Snapchat, tweet, or post. They can write top-ten lists, articles, and diary entries; host talk shows, dinner parties, and self-help groups; design outfits, lockers, and bedrooms; make playlists, movie trailers, and pic collages. One of my favorite methods to elicit and share response is performative. Teachers place students in groups of five to eight and challenge them to create a tableau (see Figure 4.1) that demonstrates what they are thinking or feeling about a text. (A tableau is a freeze-frame or still picture. Think of the "mannequin challenge.") Students decide on the response they wish to convey, and then arrange themselves into a collaborative statue to relay meaning or ideas. No talking is allowed. Each group shares its tableau, and audience members guess its meaning.

Once students have engaged in this sort of initial response, we can move toward formal analysis and critical synthesis through mini-lessons (to be discussed in Chapter 6). As workshopping teachers, we also want to encourage critical literacy. While the above describes methods for engaging students in initial personal response, the following section will explain how to build on response in order to foster critical literacy.

How to Grow Critical Literacy

After students have responded to a text, it is important to encourage them to consider the contextual, textual, authorial, personal, and cultural factors that might be influencing their responses. In order to move students beyond an initial response, we can prod them to reflect on *why* they might have had certain responses to the reading. We can guide them to actively question the text and themselves.

I have found two frameworks especially helpful in provoking students to critically reflect on responses, those of Rycik and Irvin (2005) and McLaughlin and DeVoogd (2004). Both offer a series of questions to promote reading from a critical stance; drawing from them, I utilize the following prompts to guide critical discussion with my students:

- Reread your initial personal response to what you have read. Why do you think you responded in this way? What factors might have led you to respond in this way? Do you think your response was influenced by your family or friends? By your religion, race, gender, age, socioeconomic status, or sexual orientation? By your beliefs?

- What do you think the author wants us to think, and why?

- What do you already know about this author? What can you guess about this author? Do you think the author was influenced by his or her background when writing this text? Why? How?

- Are any voices missing from what you have read? Is there a different perspective that hasn't been shared or included in the text? Why do you think so, or why not?

- What do you think should be added to this text, and why?

Recently, in a classroom we were share reading *Romeo and Juliet* and independently reading novels including Simon Elkeles's *Perfect Chemistry*, Sharon Draper's *Romiette and Julio*, Mary E. Pearson's *Scribbler of Dreams*, John Green's *The Fault in Our Stars*, Ally Condie's *Matched*, and Gordon Korman's *Son of the Mob*. As a reading quiz, students were asked to write for ten minutes, selecting from a series of response-based prompts. They were then asked to reread their responses and consider why they responded in that way, and write about their reasons. In her thinking about her initial response to *Perfect Chemistry*, Alexis honestly wrote: "I think I am feeling this way toward this book because I have had a relationship with someone involved in a gang, so I can relate to this. I can also relate to Brittany because she tries to seem perfect and act happy, when, inside, that isn't the case." Lana, too, reflected on her response to *Scribbler of Dreams*: "I think I have a similar personality as Abby b/c we both have the same perspective toward life. We really care about what people think of us, and not letting people know what we really feel like inside, by blocking out all our feelings." We can encourage students to reflect critically on their responses using any format, including quizzes or tests, or the logs, blogs, journals, conversations, and performances previously discussed. We simply layer the critical atop the personal response.

While the previous questions can be used to prompt critical discussion about the forces influencing responses to texts, we also want to encourage student understanding of social, cultural, and political elements influencing the creation of a text. *Multivoiced journals* (Styslinger & Whisenant, 2004) offer a means for students to better understand a text's purpose, as they encourage responses to reading in varied, cultured voices of characters. Students write consistently as if they are characters representative of otherness in a text they are reading. For example, if a student was reading *To Kill a Mockingbird* as a cornerstone classical text during a unit focused around social justice, she might respond to the story as if she were Scout, Atticus, Calpurnia, Boo, Maudie, Tom, Mayella, Bob, or Reverend Sykes. Each of these characters would allow her the experience of "crossing" into the life of a cultured other: a tomboy struggling to understand herself and the events surrounding her, a single parent and Maycomb attorney assigned to represent Tom Robinson, a housekeeper and closest thing to a mother Scout has ever known, a mysterious neighbor who never comes outside, an avid gardener and one of Maycomb's most open-minded citizens, a black man accused of raping and beating Mayella, a nineteen-year-old white accuser, a patriarch who spends his welfare checks on alcohol and claims to have witnessed Tom attacking Mayella, the pastor at First Purchase African M.E. Church, or any number of lives caught in the crossfire of the growing Civil Rights Movement. With such an approach, students project and predict how literature speaks to/as others, as multivoiced journals direct personal response through cultural exploration. Journaling from varied perspectives can lead students to a better understanding of an author's purpose for characters, plot, setting, and point of view. Moreover, multivoiced journals have the potential to change student relationships with individuals, heightening sensitivity to issues of diversity such as race, religion, gender, or sexual orientation.

When utilizing multivoiced journals, what is most important is finding a text that includes a variety of characters representative of difference, perhaps through settings, characters, or situations. In Alison's middle grade classroom, students engaged in a unit focused around discrimination. As part of this unit, Alison read aloud *Crossing Jordan* to her predominantly white students. Adrian Fogelin's YA novel tells the story of friendship between two seventh-grade neighbors, Cass and Jemmie. They meet after Jemmie catches Cass spying through a peephole of a fence that Cass's father erected shortly after learning that a black family was moving in next door. The two girls soon learn they share a love of running and become fast friends. Unfortunately, they also share the challenge of parents who do not approve of their friendship. Cass's father disapproves of mixing with other races, and Jemmie's mother does not want her daughter playing with someone reared in a racist family. Luckily, the two have the wise advice and lessons from Nana Grace, Jemmie's grandmother, and the determination of a friendship that crosses the boundaries of race and authority.

At various points during the read-aloud, students were asked to journal in the voice of a particular character. For the purpose of the multivoiced journals, the places and characters whose voices in which they were to write were preselected. Alison purposefully chose points at which characters were dealing with racial tension. For example, students journaled from Jemmie's mother's perspective after coming home to find a fence built between their house and Cass's house.

Especially poignant was the writing from students that detailed the internal, racial conflicts of characters. As Cass and Jemmie grapple to understand their parents' perspectives in the novel, Carlos shared his frustration, writing from Cass's perspective: "I just met the girl next door, she is very nice, and says she can run. If I could, I would become friends with her. Momma probably wouldn't mind, but Daddy would get extremely upset." Student journals written from Jemmie's perspective also show the students' understanding of her internal conflicts. After Jemmie and Cass's first race in the novel, Meghan wrote in Jemmie's voice, "Hopefully Mama don't find out that we was out hangin-round today, or I'd get my butt cut so bad, I can't sit down for a week. Tomorrow I'm goin' to kick her butt so bad, I'll leave her in anotha time zone."

The student journals also indicated an understanding of the implications a school setting might have on Cass and Jemmie's friendship. Sarah's journal entry from Jemmie's point of view expressed Jemmie's fears of what might happen to her friendship with Cass when school started: "I can't help but wonder what is gonna happen with me and Cass. Will we still be friends when school starts. She doesn't have any other black friends so ppl [people] are gonna talk. I don't know, but I can't stand the thought of losing Cass as a friend. We are a team, Chocolate Milk! But will our team break up? Or will it stay together?"

It needs to be mentioned that, in order for multivoiced journals and consequent discussion to be successful, the classroom has to be a safe place for students to express their opinions. Initially, Alison's students were uncomfortable discussing the discrimination found in the book. "Wait time" was lengthy after questions, and it often had to be reiterated that everyone's opinions should be respected. Slowly, after a few journal entries and discussions of why Cass's father and Jemmie's mother acted certain ways, students started speaking more freely. Writing and then talking through ideas led to an increased understanding of the beliefs, actions, and underlying values of others.

Chapter Summary

When we engage students in reader response, we encourage an enjoyment of reading, provide a starting point for formal analysis and critical synthesis, offer opportunities for fostering critical literacy, and better meet the needs of English language learners. We help students recall experiences, elicit associations, and prompt reactions to texts read aloud or independently. There are many ways to foster and relay responses to a variety of texts utilized in a focus unit, including journals, diaries, dialogues, blogs, texts, Snapchats, tweets, or posts. Students can create top-ten lists, articles, and diary entries; host talk shows, dinner parties, and self-help groups; design outfits, lockers, and bedrooms; make playlists, movie trailers, and pic collages; or perform tableaux. After students have responded to a text, it is important to encourage them to consider the contextual, textual, authorial, personal, and cultural factors that might be influencing their responses. We also want to encourage student understanding of the social, cultural, and political elements influencing the creation of text through multivoiced journals. Creating an active workshop environment in which students respond personally—as well as, subsequently, analytically and critically—to what they are reading is an important workshop goal.

5

Ways to Talk

"I just want someone to hear what I have to say.
And maybe if I talk long enough, it'll make sense."

—RAY BRADBURY, *Fahrenheit 451*

When we finish reading something wonderful, we immediately want to tell someone about it. Whether reading *A Tale of Two Cities* or *Twilight*, each of us has probably nudged a partner awake in order to talk about Lucie or Bella. Not surprisingly, our students feel the same way. When they turn the final page of *Allegiant*, completing Veronica Roth's Divergent trilogy, they typically don't beg to showcase their knowledge on a five-paragraph essay. Instead, just like us, students want to share opinions, feelings, experiences, insights, and questions, as well as hear what their classmates have to say. Quite simply, they want to talk about what they have read.

We talk to make sense of ourselves, others, ideas, and the world that surrounds us. Wheatley (2002) compared talking with thinking, and we need to structure opportunities for doing both in large groups and small groups in classrooms. This chapter introduces why and how we talk while workshopping the canon.

Why Talk?

We cannot talk about talking without also thinking about responses and responding. It's like the chicken and the egg: which comes first? As discussed in Chapter 4, students need opportunities to respond to a text in order to have something to say, and talk is a means through which students can respond. Rosenblatt (1995) posited that a work of literature has no meaning until a reader has experienced a personal response. So, it is up to teachers to provide for those classroom experiences that facilitate responses through talking. After all, literature should evoke discussion. As Probst noted, we have a "rare opportunity" in the language arts classroom: "You have thirty kids and a book," he wrote. "You can talk" (2004, p. 72).

Unfortunately, we do not always allow for enough talk in the classroom. Historically speaking, teachers have always talked too much. More than a century ago, Stevens (1912) observed teachers talking 64 percent of the time during classroom discussions; Bellack, Kliebard, Hyman, and Smith (1993) found teachers talking three times more than students in the 1960s; Barnes (1992) identified teachers as doing the majority of the talking in the 1970s; and Goodlad (1984) found discussion accounted for only 5.1 percent of class time in the 1980s. Even in the 1990s, discussion took place for fewer than fifty seconds per class in grade 8 and fewer than fifteen seconds in grade 9 classrooms (Nystrand, Gamoran, Kachur, & Prendergast, 1997). The century may have changed, but Nystrand, Wu, Gamoran, Zeiser, and Long (2003) still found discussion in only 6.69 percent of 1,151 instructional episodes in grades 8 and 9. Beers and Probst (1998) described an all-too-familiar classroom scene in which a teacher dominated the conversation with her list of queries that moved logically from one topic to the next, frustrating students because they did not have an opportunity to ask their own pressing questions.

We want dialogue, not monologue, in the workshopping classroom. A discussion is not a lecture led by the teacher; it is instead a sharing of ideas within an interpretive community. Too many teacher-controlled discussions can alienate students from effectively responding to and talking about texts. But let's be honest. We have all led students through discussions with class handouts and study guides, heading toward a known destination. We have all tested students on answers to the questions and prompts appearing in those same class handouts and study guides. Yet there are equally if not more authentic means with which to engage students through talking, because talking is one thing tweens and teens can do.

We want to encourage talking, as it is a skill most students already possess. There is no mistaking a middle or high school corridor. Rich conversations reverberate through the halls as students chat about boyfriends, girlfriends, sports, phones, clothes, apps, music, parties, and movies. There are moments of rejoicing, spontaneous outbursts of song and laughter, and hugs, fist-pounds, chest-bumps, or squeals. In short, these wondrous creatures find a way to make noise.

There are many reasons why we want to promote talking in the workshopping classroom. Clearly, talking advances understanding. Applebee, Langer, Nystrand, and Gamoran (2003) found that dialogic approaches to literacy instruction have a strong effect on improving students' comprehension of literature. And Gilles (2010) made clear the connection between critical thinking and talk: "If we want students to do more critical thinking, to probe deeper into texts, and to build ideas with others, then we must rely on talk" (p. 11). Talking promotes ideas. Barnes (1992, 2008) defined rough-draft conversation as *exploratory talk*, during which students try to make meaning through talking with others, shaping their own thinking as well as that of others during the process.

The importance of talking in improving understanding has not gone unnoticed by students. In my analysis of responses to Socratic circles (Styslinger & Pollock, 2010), students clearly understood the reciprocal relationship between classroom talk and improved comprehension. As one student explained, "I like to talk about what we read in class because it helps me further understand the book by listening to other people's thoughts" and another admitted, "Sometimes I am confused about the book, and it is easier to understand once we talk about it" (p. 42). Student talk is a means to and measure of thinking, and, if a teacher dominates, then he or she is limiting opportunities for students to talk/think.

The importance of talking is recognized in the CCSS, too, with speaking and listening receiving their own anchor standards. Talking that occurs around a text can be invaluable to students' civic education as they hear and honor differing opinions and perspectives. As John Dewey (cited in Moyers, 1992, p. E15) affirmed, the habits of democracy include the ability to "grasp the point of view of another, expand the boundaries of understanding, [and] debate the alternate purposes that might be pursued." Talking enhances our understanding not only of texts but also of one another and the wider world, because it provides opportunities to hear varied viewpoints. As one student wrote, "I enjoy talking about what I read in class because it gives you everybody's perspective on many different things which helps you understand these people, understand the literature, and create your own perspective" (Styslinger & Pollock, 2010, p. 42).

We need to build intellectual communities through discourse in the workshopping classroom, guiding students to conduct themselves through an exchange of ideas; listen appreciatively to the ideas of others; frame their own thoughts with evidence and examples; speculate and hypothesize, evaluate and analyze; and show how they can extend their thinking and the thinking of others (Beers & Probst, 2013). We structure opportunities for active student talking, thinking, and listening around an assortment of texts and in a variety of ways, including book clubs and Socratic circles. This chapter will introduce each of these workshop structures and detail why and how to support talking within a focus unit, centered around a core classical text, incorporating a range of related genres.

Why Book Clubs?

Book clubs offer classroom space for students to participate in conversations around commonly read texts. The more commonly mentioned *literature circles* were popularized by Harvey Daniels (1994), and share some similarities with book clubs; however, the latter tend to be more flexible with regard to logistics, theory, and curriculum (O'Donnell-Allen, 2006). Book clubs are made up of a small group of readers who meet on a regular basis, engage in systematic discussion about texts of the members' choice, and use a variety of open-ended response methods to prompt discussion. Membership in book clubs varies and can involve the presence of a teacher or volunteer. They specifically differ from literature circles in that book clubs may stay together longer, draw on varied theoretical frameworks, and discuss topics that may be guided by teachers (O'Donnell-Allen, 2006). Both literature circles and book clubs have been credited with honoring student choice and moving beyond traditional instructional practices (Daniels, 2002; McMahon & Raphael, 1997; Short & Pierce, 1990); increasing student motivation to read (Lapp & Fisher, 2009); fostering critical discussion (Johnson, 2000; Latendresse, 2004; Long & Gove, 2003; Sandmann & Gruhler, 2007); improving student comprehension (Sweigart, 1991); as well as increasing critical thinking and bolstering problem-solving and practical decision-making skills (Blum, Lipsett, & Yocom, 2002).

In addition, book clubs have the potential to challenge traditional curricula, pedagogical practices, and culturally irrelevant texts. As groups self-select a book, students have the opportunity to read texts more culturally congruent with their own understandings of the world. More culturally responsive texts may allow students to learn life lessons as they see themselves and their circumstances reflected in the reading. Such texts may encourage students to explore ways of dealing with day-to-day issues and problems, examine political and social questions, and gain cultural insight and knowledge (Fredricks, 2012). Critical literature circles and book clubs specifically relate texts to members' historical, cultural, and social issues and provide a means to discuss social and cultural identities, offering insight into readers' theories on race, gender, and behavior (Park, 2012), making them a perfect vehicle for reclaiming voice, altering power dynamics, and creating spaces for students to learn routes for advocacy on issues important to them. As such, book clubs can be utilized to better prepare students to live in an increasingly diverse society.

What to Talk about in Book Clubs

As a reminder, in the workshopping classroom, we unite a variety of genres, including a classical text, around a unit focus and/or essential questions. We engage in read-alouds, shared reading, close reading, or readers theater with the cornerstone classical text while students independently read a variety of YA novels tied to the unit focus or questions. To provide students with more accessible texts, increase comprehension and motivation, reach diverse learners, and foster different perspectives, we also read aloud, share read, close read, perform, or have students read independently a range of picture books, short stories, informational/explanatory texts, poetry, and/or lyrics. Each of these workshop texts and structures offer matter and means for talking within a book club.

Book clubs bring smaller numbers of students—preferably no fewer than three and no more than five—together for a defined period of time around a common text for reading conversations. Topics for discussion come from students, but may be prompted by a response (see Chapter 4) or mini-lesson (see Chapter 6). Students bring notes to the conversation, but aim for open and natural conversations around what they have read. Book clubs provide an ideal setting for students to talk about YA novels, picture books, short stories, informational/explanatory texts, poetry, and/or lyrics. Reading is a social process, and students want to talk about their literacy experiences with one another. All we have to do is provide material, direction, and opportunity.

While students can conduct book clubs with any text used to expand the unit focus and support/extend the essential questions, it is best to practice book clubs initially with shorter texts, until students become more familiar with the procedures and expectations detailed fully in the following section. Before facilitating book clubs with YA novels related to a unit focus, I recommend practicing collaborative talking with shorter texts, including articles, stories, lyrics, poetry, or picture books experienced via read-alouds, shared reading, close reading, or independent reading. Appendix B offers an array of different genres workshop teachers can draw from.

For book clubs to be successful, students must have both a text and something to talk about. A teacher first nurtures student independent reaction to a text, and then creates an opportunity for student interaction. Chapters 4 and 6 provide a wide range of possibilities for facilitating responses and mini-lessons.

For example, students can begin discussions with their book clubs by sharing responses already recorded in listening logs, reading journals, blogs, or vlogs from read-alouds or independent reading; comprehension-oriented reading strategies from a shared strategic reading or independent reading; or vocabulary, structures, or punctuation from a language close reading. Opportunities for book club discussion abound during readers theater, as students read repeatedly, negotiate script writing, practice vocals, prepare performances, and plan celebrations. Mini-lessons, introduced in the following chapter, also provide matter for conversation. Book clubs are an organized forum for students to talk/think with one another.

How to Talk in Book Clubs

Talking is one of four language arts, in addition to reading, writing, and listening. Although we spend class time on reading and writing, how much do we allocate for talking and listening? When and how do we learn to thoughtfully exchange ideas with one another? Book clubs necessitate a great deal of preparation and practice in the arts of talking and listening.

When I first tried to facilitate book clubs, I failed miserably. I presumed too much. Because students were so talkative in and outside the classroom, I imagined they would thrive in a small-group, conversational setting. I was wrong. While students easily talked about parties, phones, and one another, they struggled for words when asked to converse about their reading. They needed scaffolds for both talk and topic, which I initially fell short in providing. Experience may not be the kindest teacher, but it left me with some powerful lessons to share.

Before beginning book clubs, students need to first observe then model appropriate, small-group dialogue. Watch a book club in action, making note of what you see and hear (see Figure 5.1). There are plenty of book club clips available on YouTube, but I like to show a snippet of the high school book club included in Daniels's (2001) *Looking into Literature Circles* DVD.

After students have recorded their observations, discuss what they saw, focusing on body language, and what they heard, concentrating on appropriate language. As a class, use these notes to develop a framework for small-group discussion, creating a positive list of expectations (see Figure 5.2) that can evolve into a rubric later used for self-evaluation as well as teacher observation.

What Do I See?	What Do I Hear?

FIGURE 5.1. Student handout for recording notes when observing a book club.

Guidelines for Participating in Book Clubs

- Come prepared
  - read
  - bring the text to class
  - bring notes to class

- Talk appropriately
  - be respectful and positive
  - stay on task
  - ask questions
  - make connections to your life and the world
  - contribute
  - use appropriate language

- Listen carefully
  - hear different views
  - look at one another
  - face each other
  - take turns

- Facilitate discussion
  - lead others to talk
  - ask others to contribute
  - validate what others say
  - ask questions of others

FIGURE 5.2. Student-generated guidelines for participating in a book club.

While we want to establish talk within a clear set of parameters, be careful not to corral student language use by defining too strictly when to talk, how to talk, and what to talk about. Too many rules can silence students. As teachers, we also need to be sensitive to the many different ways of talking, which may be affected by home culture or experience with ways of talking in school, as well as by access to opportunities to practice ways of talking (Gallas, Anton-Oldenburg, Ballenger, Beseler, Pappenheimer, & Swaim, 1996). Discourse is complex and is situated socially, culturally, and historically. We want to create classrooms that acknowledge and embrace the many forms of verbal expression.

After students have observed a book club, it is time to enact one. Rehearse the book club experience. As a scaffold for student talk, Nachowitz and Brumer's (2014) list of sentence starters provides language to practice the more complex literary thinking involved with textual conversations and expanding, justifying, and challenging ideas:

- I want to talk about . . .

- I noticed . . .

- I don't understand . . .

- I wonder why . . .

- I have a different idea . . .

- What in the text makes you believe that?

- I agree with you because . . .

- This reminds me of . . .

- At first, I thought . . . ; now, I think . . .

- Maybe this book is about . . .

Once sentence starters are in hand and talk guidelines reviewed, set up a fishbowl seating arrangement in which four to six volunteer students model a discussion while the rest of the class takes notes, or, even better, create a Twitter feed on what they notice, including positive examples of oral language, body language, eye contact, and active listening. As a class, share evidence and observations. In this way, we are helping students learn how to talk effectively with one another in small groups.

After watching and rehearsing, it is time for everyone to practice a book club meeting. As suggested above, select a short text linked to the unit focus or essential questions. I often begin with a shared reading of lyrics or a poem, followed by a response engagement. It is vital that we scaffold dialogue either through personal response (e.g., journals/blogs/vlogs, double-entry diaries, sentence starters, reader response questions, dialogue with a text) or by using mini-lessons (see Chapter 6). Students then have individual notes to discuss during the book club meeting. Once students have a common reading and something to share, set the purpose for this talk, post guidelines, provide sentence starters, establish a time frame, and then urge students to begin talking. Stop groups every once in a while to encourage reflection, asking questions such as "Is your conversation focused?," "Is everyone talking?," or "How are you demonstrating listening?" (Gilles, 2010).

Once students have practiced twice or more on different days with various genres, it is time to establish book clubs centered around YA novels (see Appendix B). These book clubs will remain together across the unit, and are formed around student choice. Each group may read a different or the same book as another group. An assortment of YA novels is first introduced through book passes, read-alouds, book trailers, book talks, or student reviews. Students then write down their top three choices on an index card. That night, the teacher establishes book clubs carefully, balancing student choice with other factors such as group dynamics, reading ability, and text availability. Book clubs are announced the next day, with the assurance that, if a student does not get their first or second novel choice this time, they will certainly get it in the next unit, which helps to ease disappointment.

Throughout the unit, book clubs meet according to a regular, predictable schedule, preferably twice a week for twenty-five minutes, to discuss their reading. At the first meeting, groups establish their reading calendar for the unit. During subsequent meetings, they use written notes to guide discussions. The aim of the groups is to have open, natural conversations about members' reading, so personal connections and some digressions are to be expected. A teacher serves as a facilitator but not a group member. Evaluation is by teacher observation as well as student self-evaluation, but, if warranted, teachers can still assess reading through more traditional means such as quizzes.

Less traditional and more virtual, book clubs are also capable of being rendered online, with technologies available such as Google Hangouts on Air (now YouTube Live), which provides the added benefit of being recordable with adjustable privacy settings, so that the videos can be viewed by group members and teachers at a later time. Angela recently took her book clubs online:

> Each book club was responsible for arranging an online meeting time to discuss salient points, ask clarifying questions, share connections, and critique ideas within the text. Students established the page ranges for each online discussion and brought their notes to the online meeting. The weekly facilitator was responsible for moderating the group discussion, and students were provided with helpful tips ahead of their first meeting, as well as the opportunity during the preceding class to test their Google Hangouts on Air accounts to make sure all things were operational ahead of the first meeting. Students anchored their discussions largely around issues the text brought up that reminded them of controversial issues within society or other texts they had read. The ability to ask clarifying questions also enabled students to help one another comprehend and analyze the text more deeply and adeptly. Though these students were used to discussing texts in person, they did not feel a disconnect in that interaction in an online setting, except for the few instances during which a group member temporarily lost an Internet connection.

Whether in twenty-first-century or bricks-and-mortar classrooms, book clubs are an effective way to promote student talk while workshopping the canon.

Why Socratic Circles?

Another way we encourage talking while workshopping the canon is with Socratic circles. Similar to book clubs, a Socratic circle provides students with an opportunity to talk about a text without the strict control of teacher-generated questions and "right" answers. Socrates was convinced the surest way to attain reliable knowledge was through the practice of disciplined conversation, which he called a *dialectic*. A dialectic is the art or practice of examining opinions or ideas logically, often through question-and-answer exchanges, so as to determine their validity, and a Socratic circle is a method with which to try to understand information by creating a dialectic, with participants seeking deeper understanding of complex ideas through methodical dialogue.

Socratic circles begin with a question. An opening question has no right answer; instead, it reflects a genuine curiosity on the part of the questioner. A good opening question leads participants to speculate, evaluate, define, and clarify the issues involved. Responses to the opening question generate new questions, leading to new responses. In this way, the line of inquiry in a Socratic circle evolves spontaneously, rather than being predetermined by a teacher.

Through Socratic circles, students have a conversation about a text or idea while gaining various perspectives. They are able to go back and forth through talking and finagle with various opinions, perspectives, and viewpoints. As Copeland (2005) wrote, "Socratic circles turn partial classroom control, classroom direction, and classroom governance over to students by creating a truly equitable learning community where the weight and value of student voices and teacher voices are indistinguishable from each other" (p. 3). My own research with students demonstrated a growing awareness of diverse viewpoints through participation in Socratic circles that positively affected students' written composition of counterarguments and rebuttals (Styslinger & Overstreet, 2014). Socratic circles are a way for student voices to not only be heard, but also developed, responded to, and valued.

What to Talk about in Socratic Circles

When workshopping the canon, we want to advance student thinking around the core classical text as well as the unit focus, essential questions, and supplemental texts. Since a Socratic circle is centered on collaborative inquiry, it makes sense to draw initial questions from the cornerstone classical text. For example, Jessica incorporated Socratic circles when share reading Shakespeare's *Romeo and Juliet.* Students were first asked to consider two questions: "To what extent are Romeo and Juliet victims of fate, or of their own poor decisions?" and "Who is responsible for the deaths of Romeo and Juliet?" These initial opening questions required students to take a stance and to find textual evidence to support their claims. Students participated in two Socratic circles.

The first circle occurred after Act 3. The class was divided into pairs, and they composed three open-ended discussion questions. Students in the inner circle were asked to participate a minimum of three times and make specific references to the text. Students in the outer circle were given netbooks (laptops), instructed to listen carefully, and asked to make a minimum of two comments or ask a minimum of two follow-up questions on the discussion occurring in the inner circle. The second Socratic circle occurred after students had completed reading the play. Students were asked to consider who was ultimately responsible for the deaths of Romeo and Juliet.

While a Socratic circle can focus on a specific text, it can also support inquiry into a more general unit focus or essential questions, encouraging students to draw examples and cite evidence from a variety of genres read throughout a unit, including YA novels read in book clubs, or picture books, short stories, informational/explanatory texts, poetry, and/or lyrics encountered during read-alouds, shared reading, close reading, or readers theater. In the section following, Tim and I explain how we facilitated Socratic circles around a unit focused on ill-fated love with *Romeo and Juliet* as the core text once again.

How to Facilitate Socratic Circles

In a Socratic circle, students read and take notes on a predetermined section or selection of text. They are then divided into an inner and outer circle, much like a fishbowl seating arrangement. The inner circle engages in a discussion while students in the outer circle silently observe, providing feedback to the inner circle once their discussion of the text is complete. The circles then exchange roles and positions (Copeland, 2005).

Just as students need guidelines for talking during book clubs, they want expectations for talking during Socratic circles. Similar to our preparation for book clubs, we first watch a Socratic circle, taking note of what is seen and heard. Following a class discussion, guidelines for participation in a Socratic circle are established (see Figure 5.3). Then it is time to read closely and generate questions.

Tim prepared his students for Socratic circles by first introducing the unit focus—ill-fated love—hoping to generate personal responses, leading to more

Guidelines for Participating in a Socratic Circle

Guidelines for Participation in the Inner Circle
- Bring your notes and text to the circle.
- Refer to your notes and the text to provide evidence and examples.
- Ask open-ended questions.
- Ask for clarification when confused.
- Take turns speaking (but you don't have to raise your hand).
- Listen carefully.
- Speak up. Make eye contact. Lean forward.
- Stick to the topic.
- Talk to each other, not the teacher.
- Open your mind to different ideas and perspectives.

Guidelines for Participation in the Outer Circle
- Be an active listener.
- Take notes about what you want to remember.
- Write down comments you want to add and new questions you want to ask.
- Synthesize ideas.
- Open your mind to different ideas and perspectives.

FIGURE 5.3. Student-generated guidelines for participating in a Socratic circle.

talking in the classroom. After exploring lyrics by Taylor Swift (2008) and James Blunt (2004), he made a connection with Stephenie Meyer's (2005) *Twilight*. Some boys rolled their eyes when the trailer for the movie played on the interactive whiteboard, but Tim pressed on.

He began a shared reading of the play, and students were instructed to write down a question and a comment each night that would stimulate good discussion. By encouraging students to prepare questions in advance, he provided them the opportunity to make sense of ideas before sharing them with a group—or what Probst (2004) called "verbaliz[ing] in solitude" (p. 75).

On the big day, everyone was ready. Desks were arranged in a large circle, and a round table was pushed in the middle and surrounded with ten chairs borrowed temporarily from the computer lab. Half of the class moved to the chairs in the middle to begin the discussion. The students in the outer circle were there to observe, all the while jotting down notes about nonverbal communication and positively framed suggestions about how the group could improve the discussion. To this extent, the role of the outer circle cannot be underestimated, as their feedback is crucial to fostering positive discussions.

Tim first attempted a "walk through" circle; nothing but the idea of "love at first sight" was predetermined. Students were asked to generate questions and comments on their own. The conversation floated around the surface level, but interest had clearly been sparked. Two days later, a more formal circle gathered. Scared to lose them on the first real attempt, he elected to stay safe with literary-based prompts, offering the following predetermined topics:

1. Mercutio's death: "A plague o' both your houses!"
2. Romeo's revenge—Tybalt's death:
    o "Either thou or I, or both, must go with him."
    o "I am fortune's fool!" (fate/destiny).
    o A honeymoon kicked off with murder of a family member.
    o Romeo's banishment/exile.
3. Juliet's reaction:
    o "Back, foolish tears, back to your native spring."

The inside circle spoke for about ten minutes. The outer group offered feedback for approximately three to four minutes, and then Tim followed up with positive reinforcement and a few specific suggestions for each group. Then he reformed the circles, and the process repeated.

Reading continued over the next few days, but students still resisted the obvious connection to the two teenagers on the pages of the play before them. Would a return to a more personal Socratic circle encourage the desired responses and talking? Tim provided students with the following topics to consider:

- Have you ever felt like Romeo—so upset that you act in a way you normally wouldn't? What situation made you feel like that?
- Have you ever felt like Juliet—unable to tell a secret to those close to you? What does that feel like, and does it make you sympathize with Juliet? What else?
- Who in your life has given you advice that you didn't want to hear, or advice that is good for you but too hard to accept?
- Do you ever feel that your parents', teachers', or coaches' way of seeing things is not the way you see things? How does this relate back to R and J?
- What other general thoughts, opinions, or connections did you make while reading the play—or now, as you think back to your reading?

Two more circles followed, both of which attempted to merge the literature with life experiences. Students had plenty to say about Romeo, who became a quick target for criticism when discussing the relationship between the two star-crossed lovers. The majority of those who spoke were not impressed with the fast-talking Romeo; in fact, several were put off by his advances, as this exchange shows:

FEMALE STUDENT: Romeo was all over Juliet.

FEMALE STUDENT: It was kinda weird on page 59 [when Romeo and Juliet share their first kiss] . . . [pause] . . . I was like . . . [pause] . . . kissing their faces already!

MALE STUDENT: And they were talking about pilgrims!

FEMALE STUDENT: He was all in love so fast.

MALE STUDENT: Romeo seems kinda like a player.

FEMALE STUDENT: And on page 57 . . . [long pause] . . . Juliet's like calling him a perv!

FEMALE STUDENT: Yeah, like he was going too fast.

Another class's exchange on the same topic went like this:

MALE STUDENT: Okay, here's the question: Is Juliet a good fit for Romeo?

FEMALE STUDENT: So far, I don't think it's gonna work out.

FEMALE STUDENT: If their parents loved each other, they might have a chance.

MALE STUDENT: Romeo goes from high to low really fast.

MALE STUDENT: He's a crybaby!

MALE STUDENT: He's going crazy.

FEMALE STUDENT: He kissed Juliet and they didn't even know their names.

FEMALE STUDENT: I'm surprised he didn't get slapped.

MALE STUDENT: I don't know why they didn't introduce themselves.

FEMALE STUDENT: It's like making out with a hobo!

A third class took the same topic but ventured into gender differences:

FEMALE STUDENT: Can a thirteen-year-old really fall in love?

MALE STUDENT: Puppy love, not actual love.

FEMALE STUDENT: 'Cause we haven't gone through that stuff.

MALE STUDENT: We're still adolescents; we are still confused.

FEMALE STUDENT: I think that it's possible.

MALE STUDENT: It wouldn't last long.

MALE STUDENT: Are you saying they could be—

FEMALE STUDENT: Maybe.

FEMALE STUDENT: I agree, what if [long story about two people meeting, going away, and then coming back together]?

MALE STUDENT: That's like a movie.

FEMALE STUDENT: They would have to put in a lot of time.

FEMALE STUDENT: Maybe it just hasn't happened to you yet, [boy's name].

FEMALE STUDENT: My parents knew each other when they were [ninth graders] in high school.

FEMALE STUDENT: Why do you think Romeo and Juliet can't be in love?

FEMALE STUDENT: People were different then.

MALE STUDENT: They died younger.

MALE STUDENT: [Seeking support from other males] Who thinks they cannot fall in love?

[Several boys say "me" or raise their hands.]

FEMALE STUDENT: Yeah, but y'all [boys] think of stuff differently. You don't want to be in love.

MALE STUDENT: I'm thirteen; I don't want to be in love. . . . I love my dog.

An especially poignant, personal connection that resulted from the above conversation was from a young man who shared about the death of his dog, who had been "like 117 in dog years." The student said that, after the dog's death, his "whole house died," and he compared that situation to Romeo's lost love of Rosaline. But, just as Juliet reignited Romeo's love, the presence of a new dog "relit the fire in the house."

We need to talk more about talking in classrooms, helping students realize the importance of its relationship to understanding. Talking is a practice through which we make meaning of all that surrounds us, including the concepts of love or loss. Sometimes, students believe that, in order to talk in class, you need to already understand the text. While they recognize talking increases comprehension, they also admit they would talk more "if I understood the book a little bit better" and "if I was very knowledgeable about the subject" (Styslinger & Pollock, 2010, p. 42). For Socratic circles and book clubs to be successful, we need to make clear that understanding does not have to be a precursor for talking. Understanding is a consequence of talking. If we talk long enough, it will all make sense.

Chapter Summary

Talking enhances our understanding not only of texts, but also of one another and the wider world because it provides opportunities to hear varied viewpoints. When workshopping the canon, we structure opportunities for active student talking, thinking, and listening around a range of texts with book clubs and Socratic circles. Book clubs offer classroom space for students to participate in conversations around commonly read texts. Students bring notes to the conversation but aim for open and natural conversations around what they have read. Before beginning book clubs, students need to first observe and then model appropriate, small-group dialogue. While we want to establish talking within a clear set of parameters, though, be careful not to corral student language use by defining too strictly when to talk, how to talk, and what to talk about. Once students have modeled and practiced book clubs with shorter texts, they are ready to embark on book clubs with YA novels related to a unit focus.

Another way we encourage talking while workshopping the canon is with Socratic circles. In a Socratic circle, students read and take notes on a predetermined section or selection of text. They are then divided into an inner and outer circle. The inner circle engages in a discussion while students in the outer circle silently observe, providing feedback to the inner circle once their discussion of the text is complete. The circles then exchange roles and positions. A Socratic circle can focus on the core canonical text, or it can support inquiry into a more general unit focus or essential questions, encouraging students to draw examples and cite evidence from a variety of genres read throughout a unit.

6

Mini-Lessons to Teach

....

"I have to catch everybody if they start to go over the cliff—I mean if they're running and they don't look where they're going I have to come out from somewhere and catch them. That's all I do all day. I'd just be the catcher in the rye and all."

—J. D. SALINGER, *The Catcher in the Rye*

Teachers can help students see where they are going with *mini-lessons*, which are interactive lessons that include teacher demonstrations in language arts procedures, strategies, craft, conventions, and perspectives. We teach mini-lessons before, during, and after workshop structures such as read-alouds, shared reading, close reading, readers theater, book clubs, Socratic circles, and independent reading and writing.

In our workshop, there are how-to, reading, literary, craft, vocabulary, and critical mini-lessons. A *how-to* mini-lesson explains classroom policies and procedures. *Reading* mini-lessons encourage comprehension through making connections, fostering predictions, generating questions, constructing mental images, summarizing meanings, analyzing structural components, and formulating inferences. *Literary* mini-lessons help students analyze story elements, figurative language, and literary devices as well as interpret texts through schools of literary criticism. *Craft* mini-lessons encourage students to unravel techniques and conventions utilized by an author worthy of imitation. *Vocabulary* mini-lessons provide for word study in the context of what students are reading. And *critical* mini-lessons lead students to question what they are reading, how they are reading, and what they are taking away from reading. This chapter introduces why and how we teach a variety of mini-lessons as we workshop the canon.

Why Teach Mini-Lessons?

Mini-lessons follow student-centered, constructivist theory that advocates learning as an active process. Students are supported in their individual meaning-making through mini-lessons that provide new information, connect it to prior understandings, and allow students to practice and apply new learning collaboratively and independently. Mini-lessons encourage learning as personal and dynamic, interactive and collaborative.

We know learning occurs in social contexts, and students need interaction with others. Mini-lessons offer a collaborative forum for teachers and students to think–talk–demonstrate–practice what they are coming to know together. Workshop teachers provide information, modeling, and guidance during a mini-lesson, but then take a step back and allow students the necessary talk space to think through new ideas and practice new learning, resulting in more individual responsibility for the learning experience. Workshop teachers are not sole providers of knowledge to silent students.

Along with supporting constructivist principles and encouraging collaborative and interactive learning, teaching mini-lessons can also improve students' writing (Danoff, Harris, & Graham, 1993; Feng & Powers, 2005) as well as their reading (Dionisio, 1989). And workshop teachers teach mini-lessons to increase literal, interpretive, and critical comprehension (McMahon, 2008) of text that is both read and written by students during a focus unit.

Literal comprehension involves understanding what is explicitly stated. Reading and vocabulary mini-lessons help students better understand what an author has written; students also make use of vocabulary mini-lessons as they author texts. With the help of mini-lessons, teachers can guide students to better understanding and producing written meaning.

Interpretive comprehension requires more than recall. When we interpret a text, we draw from prior personal and textual experiences to make meaning. We look between the lines and combine pieces of information to make inferences about the author's intent and message. Literary as well as certain reading and vocabulary mini-lessons direct students in their analysis. When we note the craft of a text we read or employ craft in a text we write as a result of mini-lessons, we are also developing our interpretive comprehension.

Critical comprehension draws on readers' dispositions or values, and may lead to any of the following: "1) an opinion after reading, 2) an evaluation of positions, either within the book or held by the reader, 3) an assessment of the relevance or reliability of information provided within a text, and/or 4) the formulation of inferences beyond the text to other contexts" (McMahon, 2008, p. 13). Critical mini-lessons encourage reflection on personal, societal, and political values, leading students to question what and how they read and write.

Which Texts to Use during Mini-Lessons

Some mini-lessons are more text-driven than others. For example, when teaching a *how-to mini-lesson*, we can draw from any text, as lessons do not originate with the text itself but with the needs of students. What is the desired process or procedure we want students to learn? The purpose and content of the lesson is related more to a course of action and less to a work of literature. For example, a teacher could provide a mini-lesson on how to ask questions during a Socratic circle and model questions gathered from *The Scarlet Letter* just as easily as from YA companion texts such as Laurie Halse Anderson's *Speak* or Hillary Jordan's *When She Woke*. The purpose and content of the mini-lesson is not derived distinctively from the canonical or supplemental text. As teachers plan for how-to mini-lessons, they reference texts to demonstrate a desired process or procedure.

Conversely, *reading mini-lessons* rely heavily on the text selection. We teach reading mini-lessons to improve both literal and interpretive comprehension. We know certain works of literature commonly taught in later middle and most secondary classrooms are difficult to comprehend due to their complex content, structures, and themes, and we want ways to better support student meaning-making. We specifically teach reading mini-lessons in an effort to increase student comprehension of the core texts for our units, such as *The Crucible*, *To Kill a Mockingbird*, and *The Great Gatsby*—all canonical texts that tend to humble any proficient and most adolescent readers.

While a majority of canonical texts necessitate the teaching of reading mini-lessons, we have to be careful not to teach such lessons in isolation. Students need opportunities to convey new kinds of thinking across reading. For example, we don't want students to associate specific reading strategies only with certain texts, failing to see their transferability. We don't only predict with *Lord of the Flies* or infer with *The Scarlet Letter*. The use of related texts, fiction and nonfiction, allows students to experience the process of deepening understanding across texts, which also advances knowledge and strategy building. As we workshop the canon, we want to provide opportunities for students to deepen their comprehension across the core and supplemental texts inclusive of a wide variety of genres, encouraging students to transfer different kinds of thinking to new texts and learning.

Literary mini-lessons derive from the text and increase students' interpretive comprehension. Workshop teachers engage in formal and critical analysis to enhance student meaning-making, with the work of literature determining what form, language, or theory is to be addressed in any mini-lesson. Scrutinizing the structure of an essay, analyzing the elements of a novel, or exploring the language of a poem increases formal literary meaning, and this is why we teach selective literary mini-lessons focused on story elements, language choices, and/or literary criticism.

Any work of literature can undergo formal or critical study, but some more easily than others. For example, a Marxist reading of *1984* is more straightforward than a Freudian reading of *The Great Gatsby*. A Freudian reading of *Hamlet* is more effortless than a deconstructionist reading of just about anything. A study of characterization rather than plot makes sense when reading the *General Prologue* to *The Canterbury Tales*, and symbols such as Piggy's glasses practically jump off the page in *Lord of the Flies*. Poetry is always analyzed as so much depends on a red wheelbarrow. But these genres are not the only ones worthy of formal and critical consideration.

Often overlooked by middle and high school teachers, many picture books are rich in form, language, and meaning. Recently, in a unit focused around social justice, I read aloud Eve Bunting's *Smoky Night*, and we analyzed onomatopoeia; a few days later, I read Patricia Polacco's *Pink and Say*, and we tackled the book's symbolism. In another unit focused around gender, we interpreted Anthony Browne's *Piggybook* and Munro Leaf's *The Story of Ferdinand* through a feminist lens. In Nicole's classroom, she read aloud Shaun Tan's *The Arrival*, and her class analyzed cultural differences and ideas of belonging in a unit focused around otherness. Another picture book, Doreen Cronin's *Click, Clack, Moo: Cows That Type*, provided her students with an amusing entry into a new unit focus on power structures in America. When interwoven into units, picture books, along with novels, plays, poetry, lyrics, essays, stories, articles, and memoirs, all have potential for formal and critical study.

We teach *craft mini-lessons* when any text demonstrates models of grammar and convention we want students to emulate. We select authors and texts from core and supplementary literature to show students how to write well, utilizing mentor texts as a focus during mini-lessons. Quality crafting can be found across all genres. I have crafted mini-lessons around Ray Bradbury's imagery, personification, and parallel structure in "There Will Come Soft Rains"; John Green's use of simile and metaphor in *The Fault in Our Stars*; Eric Carle's use of dialogue in *Mister Seahorse*; Melvin Berger's use of process description in *Why I Sneeze, Shiver, Hiccup, and Yawn*; and Rick Reilly's use of just about everything in a variety of sports articles. But I don't always direct students to worthy examples; I want them to make their own discoveries of model writing when reading.

During a *vocabulary mini-lesson*, students are encouraged to notice new words in the context of authentic reading experiences. When we read classical works by the likes of Shakespeare, Poe, Hawthorne, Chaucer, Conrad, Orwell, or Huxley, we engage in word study with students, playing with the language and discovering meanings for unfamiliar vocabulary. We teach vocabulary mini-lessons to increase literal and interpretive comprehension of text. But word study need not be limited to traditional texts—the more modern *Feed* by M. T. Anderson, with its futuristic vocabulary, is certainly not null for our units and unettes. Vocabulary mini-lessons emerge from all text.

Critical mini-lessons enhance critical comprehension and may be taught across all texts responded to in a unit. We teach critical mini-lessons to reflect on those factors that may influence our transaction with text, the construction of the text itself, or any word spoken or action made in relation to text. While we may reflect critically across all genres, it is particularly relevant to teach critical mini-lessons in relation to a core canonical text. Beers and Probst's (2013) survey of the twenty-five most commonly taught novels in grades 9 to 10 included only four female authors, four minority authors, and one female minority author. Students need to scrutinize the contents and meaning of classical literary works for their social, cultural, historical, and political influences through critical mini-lessons. If we only read canonical texts and fail to engage with these critically, our perspectives will be sorely limited.

Workshopping teachers teach a variety of mini-lessons across the core and supplemental texts in order to meet district, state, and national standards as well as textual demands and student needs. We are careful to teach procedures, strategies, craft, conventions, and perspective with an integrated approach, keeping the text at the center, and using mini-lessons as a means to unravel content and unlock meaning.

How to Teach Mini-Lessons

As we plan for mini-lessons in procedure, strategy, craft, convention, or perspective, we want to keep in mind the gradual release of responsibility model (Fisher & Frey, 2007; Pearson & Gallagher, 1983), which acknowledges the role of the teacher in guiding students to independent practice and application. Our ultimate goal as workshop teachers is to steer students toward independence, and mini-lessons are unlike lectures in that students are active and social participants. Teacher speaking time is limited. Each workshop mini-lesson begins with whole-class instruction, including teacher modeling, followed by opportunities for guided, collaborative, and independent learning.

Whole-class instruction occurs as the teacher introduces the topic, purpose, and content for the mini-lesson. For example, a teacher might plan a mini-lesson around any of the following: identifying positive verbal and nonverbal language for book club discussion (how-to); discovering ways to infer during reading, to improve comprehension (reading); analyzing imagery in a text, to deepen understanding of setting (literary); recognizing an author's use of parallelism, to enhance personal writing (craft); defining new vocabulary from reading, to increase understanding (vocabulary); or questioning whose voices are not heard within a text (critical). The topic, purpose, and content of mini-lessons can derive from standards, but, more important, they need to arise from what students are reading and writing.

Teacher modeling is an important component of a mini-lesson. Once the topic, purpose, and content for the mini-lesson have been clearly established, teachers explicitly demonstrate the desired procedure, process, strategy, craft, convention, or perspective. For example, during a how-to mini-lesson, teachers could model how they select a book during a book pass; or, during a strategy mini-lesson, teachers model how they question to make meaning; during a literary mini-lesson, teachers model how they determine similes and metaphors; during a craft mini-lesson, teachers model how they balance subject and verb agreement; during a vocabulary mini-lesson, teachers model word-solving strategies; or, during a critical mini-lesson, teachers model how they reflect on an author's perspective.

Next, teachers begin to transfer responsibility for learning to students through guided instruction. Teachers move from center stage to backstage. During guided instruction, the teacher directs students through tasks directly related to the mini-lesson's purpose and content. This is typically accomplished with small, purposefully selected groups of students. For example, once a teacher has modeled how she questions when reading during a mini-lesson, she might place students in small groups and have them write down their questions as she reads aloud a shorter passage of text. Next, collaborative learning occurs as students share and compare their questions with group members, then with the whole class. Once students have practiced questioning text and had the opportunity to talk through their thinking with one another, they move finally toward independent learning, which occurs as each student practices on his or her own. For example, independent learning is fostered as students read and question a text independently.

Thus, using the gradual release of responsibility model, we teach a variety of mini-lessons when workshopping the canon. The following sections explain and demonstrate how-to, reading, literary, craft, vocabulary, and critical mini-lessons in more detail.

How-to Mini-Lessons

This type of mini-lesson explains "how to" do something. For example, students need to learn how to listen during read-alouds, how to select books for independent reading, how to keep a response journal, how to conduct a Socratic circle, and how to organize a book club meeting. Not all students have experienced a read-aloud in middle or high school, have chosen a book for independent reading, journaled or blogged, or spoken up in a large or small group. We prepare students for engagement in workshop structures through mini-lessons that establish expectations, detail procedures, offer guidelines, provide examples, and specify assessments. We teach how-to mini-lessons through whole-class instruction, such as modeling, followed by opportunities for guided, collaborative, and independent learning. How-to mini-lessons ensure structured management in the reading and writing workshop.

These types of mini-lessons are explained first because their importance cannot be overemphasized. While seemingly simple, how-to mini-lessons are often overlooked by later middle and high school teachers. In our eagerness to implement book clubs, we forget to teach students how to make a thoughtful book selection, how to organize a reading calendar, how to respond to reading in a blog, how to talk about books with classmates, or how to go about a book club meeting. Then we wonder why students fail to meet expectations. Frustrated, some of us may abandon book clubs, declaring students are not ready for this literacy liberty. The success of workshop structures relies heavily on the successful teaching of how-to mini-lessons.

Before engaging students in a Socratic circle, for example, the teacher needs to implement a number of how-to mini-lessons. Questions ensure the quality of discussion, and students need to learn how to ask open-ended, thought-provoking, and clear questions to promote critical thinking among participants. Here, a how-to mini-lesson establishes the purpose for the lesson: to develop questioning strategies in order to facilitate deeper understanding of the ideas in the text through collaborative discussion. Next, the teacher provides whole-class instruction, introducing the characteristics and types of questions to be asked during a Socratic circle, focusing on interpretive and evaluative questions. Interpretive questions ask students to interpret text, whereas evaluative questions encourage students to share their own experiences, positions, and opinions. The teacher provides sample questions to foster interpretation and evaluation of the text, such as:

- What is the main idea in the text?
- What is the author's perspective?
- Do you agree or disagree with the author's perspective? Why or why not?
- What does [a particular quotation] mean?
- Which are the most important words, sentences, or paragraphs?
- Is there something in the text you don't understand?
- How do any of the ideas in the text relate to your life?
- What does this text mean to you?
- Why is this text important?

The teacher can also provide sample questions to ask other students, in response to their ideas:

- Can you clarify what you mean by that?
- Why do you think you think that?
- Has anyone changed their mind as a result of reading this text?
- How does this text relate to what [someone else] said?

Students are then guided in their construction of questions for a specific text, and, when finished, share their questions in small groups. Last, students draft questions independently. A follow-up how-to mini-lesson will introduce expectations for discussion during a Socratic circle.

Reading Mini-Lessons

The purpose of a reading mini-lesson is to provide direction in how to increase literal and interpretive comprehension of text. Teachers facilitate mini-lessons based on cognitive reading strategies, which include activating relevant prior knowledge and using prediction, generating questions during reading, constructing mental images representing the meanings in texts, summarizing and clarifying the meanings in texts, and analyzing the structural components of narrative and informational texts (Pressley, 2006). More simply put, to increase student understanding, workshopping teachers teach reading mini-lessons that help students connect, predict, question, visualize, summarize, infer, and analyze before, during, and after reading. Each of these components is discussed in the following subsections.

Making Connections

In order to make sense of texts, students need strategies that help them connect what they already know to that which they will come to know through reading. All of us best understand when we are able to relate new information to old knowledge or prior experience. For example, when I first read Suzanne Collins's *The Hunger Games*, I was reminded simultaneously of visiting the Roman Colosseum, watching *Survivor* on television, and reading *Lord of the Flies* in high school. All of these recollections helped deepen my literal understanding and increase my interpretive comprehension because I was able to draw from prior experiences to make new meaning.

Workshop teachers help students make connections before reading. This is especially important with canonical texts, as they often include settings, characters, plot, language, and themes that can seem far removed from students' current realm of experience. To foster connections before reading, introduce the unit focus and explain why it is important for students to relate new ideas with what they already know. Model a few connections to the unit focus, then have students work independently and collaboratively. When I introduced a unit focused around ill-fated love, I shared a song, movie, work of art, video game, television show, book, and YouTube clip that demonstrated ill-fated love. I asked students to list their own ill-fated love connections to various media independently. Then students partnered up and compiled a listing. A lively whole-class discussion followed, and the interactive whiteboard was filled not only with connections to our unit focus, but also oodles of supplemental resources.

One of the easiest ways to cultivate connections in students during or after reading is to have them respond to any of the following prompts in their response journal, blog, vlog, or double-entry diary:

- This reminds *me* of . . .
- This reminds me of another *text* (e.g., movie, book, article, story, song) because . . .
- This reminds me of something happening in the *world* . . .

In this way, students are making personal, textual, and social connections. Students can even record their responses on sticky notes as or after they read independently, later to be shared collaboratively, perhaps with book clubs.

In Charles's classroom, students practiced making connections to themselves, texts, and the wider world while reading *To Kill a Mockingbird*. First, Charles modeled his own connections as he read aloud a passage from the novel. He then read a new page, encouraging students to draw a small globe, a stick figure, or a book in the margins of their notebook paper. Then they attached at least one sentence to their picture that explained the connection they made. As students shared in small groups, they became more aware of how they were thinking. This metacognitive aspect shed light on the thought processes involved in the reading of text. Students then practiced making connections to their companion novel in their double-entry diaries as they read independently.

Fostering Predictions

Proficient readers make predictions before and during reading. Predictions help students anticipate reading and demonstrate active thinking while reading text. Teachers encourage students to make predictions through mini-lessons. Using the gradual release model, we establish the purpose for prediction (i.e., increased comprehension through anticipating the text) and demonstrate our own predictions as we read. We then guide students as they make predictions independently as well as collaboratively, using any of the following methods.

To foster prediction, Beers (2003) suggested an engagement she adapted from Sue Perona called Tea Party. Teachers distribute an index card or slip of paper to each student that has one phrase on it copied from the text students are about to read; some are repeated phrases. Students are then instructed to (1) share their card with as many classmates as possible and (2) listen as many others read their cards. If your class size is large, break into two or three groups to minimize walking around. Once students have exhausted reading, break into groups and have students discuss how these cards might be related and speculate on what the cards, collectively, might mean. Ask students to discuss what they presume will happen in this text and to record their predictions by writing a "We think . . ." statement.

There are many methods for nurturing prediction, and two of my favorites are Word Splash and Floorstorming. A Word Splash is a collection of key words or concepts chosen from a text students are about to read. Using Wordle (www .wordle.net) (see Figure 6.1) and the interactive whiteboard, splash some important words or phrases together and have students write a prediction statement about what the text might be about, based on these words.

Instead of words, Wilhelm's (2004) Floorstorming uses images to promote predictions. A teacher creates a visual display of images for a text about to be read, and the exhibit is placed where all students can see it easily (e.g., on the floor). Use more than one display if needed for different groups. Ask students to look carefully at the images, describe what they see, notice commonalities and relationships, and, based on their observations, make predictions about the new text.

FIGURE 6.1. Word splash to generate predictions for *Bar Code Tattoo*.

After explaining the importance of predicting and modeling how he made predictions while reading Jacqueline Woodson's companion picture book, *The Other Side*, Charles arranged students in small groups so they could make their own predictions for *To Kill a Mockingbird*. During this guided instruction, he moved around the room, listening to conversations and providing necessary support. With minimal prompting, students were soon wondering how Jem broke his arm, why a girl would want a nickname like Scout, and why everybody is afraid of Boo Radley. Naturally, these questions led to predictions among group members. Students were reminded that making predictions does not begin and end with a certain unit or text; in fact, readers make predictions all the time, regardless of the genre, class, or assignment. This notion was continued as Charles introduced another related text, Martin Luther King Jr.'s "Letter from a Birmingham Jail."

Generating Questions
Too often, it is the teacher's questions that are answered, or that go unanswered. Instead, students need to be the ones wondering about and inquiring into text.

Rather than passively answering, students need to be actively interrogating. Tovani (2000) observed that readers who ask questions assume responsibility for learning and improve comprehension by interacting with text, by motivating themselves to read, by clarifying information in the text, and by inferring beyond the literal meaning.

Workshop teachers encourage students to question with mini-lessons during and after reading. Teachers also plan for mini-lessons, drawing on a variety of methods. Tovani (2000) encouraged students simply to pose "I wonder" questions. This open-ended approach promotes discovery and curiosity. Raphael and Au (2005) challenged students to learn how to interpret and create questions that will help them comprehend text. "Right There" questions can be answered in the text, with the words used in the question and answer usually found within the same sentence. Such questions support students' literal comprehension. A second type of question also supporting literal comprehension is "Think and Search." These differ from "Right There" questions in that the answer is embedded in more than one place in the text. "Author and You" questions foster interpretive comprehension, as the answer is not in the text and students have to think about what they know, what the author says, and how they fit together. "On Your Own" questions also promote interpretive comprehension, as students must rely on what they already know in order to answer them.

Jesse read *The Great Gatsby* as a shared reading with students. After he introduced questioning as a strategy and modeled his inquiry process (a vital step in any mini-lesson), he guided students to collaborate in small groups and develop their own questions on a section of the novel. After reading further, students regrouped, returned to the questions they were able to answer, and cultivated new questions. Questioning became the prominent reading strategy they used to decipher the text.

At Nicole's school, the district has adopted Google Apps and each student has access to a Gmail account, which includes a suite of tools in their Google Drive. Nicole began her mini-lesson, detailing how we make meaning. In an effort to foster metacomprehension, she questioned students initially about their meaning-making processes. Do they underline? Do they look up words they are unfamiliar with? Do they make notes in the margins? She then extended this discussion online, utilizing Google Docs for students to create what we called a *digital conversation* with the text. Students copied and pasted text from selected scenes in *Romeo and Juliet* into a Document. Next, they chronicled their internal conversation with the text (see Figure 6.2). Students were challenged to ask two questions, make five comments, and research two aspects of their scene. Last, students posted and published this conversation to a Google website.

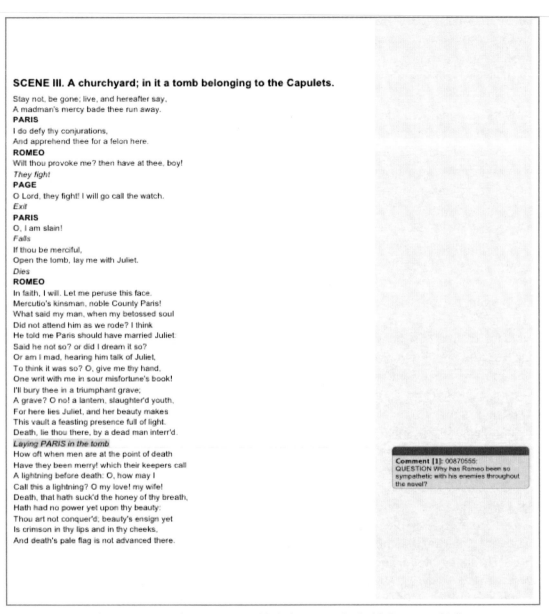

SCENE III. A churchyard; in it a tomb belonging to the Capulets.

Stay not, be gone; live, and hereafter say,
A madman's mercy bade thee run away.
PARIS
I do defy thy conjurations,
And apprehend thee for a felon here.
ROMEO
Wilt thou provoke me? then have at thee, boy!
They fight
PAGE
O Lord, they fight! I will go call the watch.
Exit
PARIS
O, I am slain!
Falls
If thou be merciful,
Open the tomb, lay me with Juliet.
Dies
ROMEO
In faith, I will. Let me peruse this face.
Mercutio's kinsman, noble County Paris!
What said my man, when my betossed soul
Did not attend him as we rode? I think
He told me Paris should have married Juliet:
Said he not so? or did I dream it so?
Or am I mad, hearing him talk of Juliet,
To think it was so? O, give me thy hand,
One writ with me in sour misfortune's book!
I'll bury thee in a triumphant grave;
A grave? O no! a lantern, slaughter'd youth,
For here lies Juliet, and her beauty makes
This vault a feasting presence full of light.
Death, lie thou there, by a dead man interr'd.
Laying PARIS in the tomb
How oft when men are at the point of death
Have they been merry! which their keepers call
A lightning before death: O, how may I
Call this a lightning? O my love! my wife!
Death, that hath suck'd the honey of thy breath,
Hath had no power yet upon thy beauty:
Thou art not conquer'd; beauty's ensign yet
Is crimson in thy lips and in thy cheeks,
And death's pale flag is not advanced there.

> **Comment [1]:** 00870555:
> QUESTION Why has Romeo been so
> sympathetic with his enemies throughout
> the novel?

FIGURE 6.2. A student annotation demonstrating a "digital conversation" with *Romeo and Juliet*.

Students reported that this digital conversation prompted a deeper understanding of the text. First, the act of engaging in online questioning required them to slow down and read for meaning. They also reported that it encouraged them to research aspects of the text they otherwise would have skipped over, possibly losing meaning in the process. For example, while working with Act

3, Scene 5, one student commented, "The Nurse prefers Paris for Juliet rather than Romeo, but I like how she helps Romeo anyway because she knows that he makes Juliet happy," showing she understood the nurse's motivation—to see Juliet content with her life (Styslinger, Walker, & Lenker, 2014, p. 19). This strategy allowed students to clear a roadblock in their minds for deeper thinking, and they self-reported that this was worth their time and was a strategy they would like to use in the future.

Applications such as Stixy (http://stickyapps.se/) or Lino (http://en.linoit .com/) can help more visual students question text. Both create boards for posting messages, images, documents, and lists. Teachers can paste in quotes from the text and ask students to post questions. An account is required, but it is free to use. Lino also has an iPad app available. Another resource for questioning is to ask students to create a question-and-answer conversation with the text using ifaketext (http://ifaketext.com/). Students can create a conversation between themselves and the text and then save the conversation as an image for sharing.

For the more visual student, ThingLink (www.thinglink.com) allows him or her to link to a website, upload an image, or import images from Flickr (www .flickr.com). Students can then bookmark exact points on the image and type notes at these hotspots. They can use this app by taking a screenshot of the text they are annotating. They can then upload the text as an image and click where they would like to add their ideas. They can link to other websites or add their own ideas as pop-up notes. ThingLink is free and Web based. Finished Thing-Links can be shared via a link or embedded directly into a blog.

As our classrooms become more digitized, it is essential that we teach students ways of both asking questions and seeking answers that are compatible with their lifestyles as digital natives.

Constructing Mental Images

Reading is seeing, Wilhelm (2004) reminded us. Ultimately, comprehending text relies on a student's ability to create images, story worlds, and mental models while reading. As teachers, we foster visualization with mini-lessons, guiding students as they tap into and create visual experiences.

To help students see the action of text, we draw on a wide variety of visual media as we plan for mini-lessons. Of course, students can draw or sketch as they read, creating images to represent understanding. Commonly referred to as Sketch to Stretch, this method asks students to visualize a passage or portion of text, interpreting it through drawing. These renderings can be factual, to encourage literal comprehension, or more symbolic, to prod interpretive comprehension. Sometimes I stop intermittently as I read aloud and ask students to sketch what they are seeing in response journals.

Or students can work collaboratively to create body biographies: visual representations of a character drawn from the reading. Use a cutout of a recognizable literary character (e.g., Edward, Bella, or Jacob from *Twilight*) to demonstrate the process. Strategically place quotations and symbols from the novel on the character cutout to create and represent meaning. Once you have modeled this, place students into groups to create their own portrait illustrating a character's traits. Students will need to review happenings in the text, select quotations, and draw symbols to place strategically on their portrait.

Below, Julianne explains how she taught visualization while share reading *The Crucible*:

Each day began with a mini-lesson that clarified the purpose of a cognitive reading strategy. One focus lesson introduced and encouraged visualizing while reading. Visualization is necessary for students reading this play in order to imagine dramatic elements, including the setting, stage directions, and characters. After I introduced the strategy of visualization, students listened and followed along as I read aloud a related text, Margaret Atwood's "Half-Hanged Mary," and drew what they saw [see Figure 6.3].

In response to the poem, one student sketched her interpretation of a village relishing in the triumph of persecution. Later that same day, students were instructed to close their eyes and listen to descriptions in *The Crucible*, mentally picturing characters, repeating and practicing what was learned by way of a different genre. These focus lessons included modeling, as students witnessed me engaged as well. I made my thinking visible on a different day during another lesson as I read aloud and projected a picture book, William Miller and Leonard Jenkins's *Tituba*, and demonstrated my questioning process: How is Tituba characterized in the picture book? How is she characterized in the play? Why are these different? How do these images suggest her characteristics are valuable to the progression of the play? Guided instruction occurred as students worked in small groups creating images with textual support, displaying the town of Salem portrayed in Act 1, visualizing the setting [see Figure 6.4].

Two students collaborated and pictured Salem Village, making apparent intertwining relationships among community members as well as with the outside world. While students worked together, they were still accountable for individual work. I introduced all of the lessons, guided instruction, and then phased out, as is necessary with the gradual release model.

FIGURE 6.3. Student visualization sketch of "Half-Hanged Mary."

Nicole added a twenty-first-century classroom twist to visualization as she read *The Strange Case of Dr. Jekyll and Mr. Hyde*. She wanted students to "see" characters, plot, and settings, and wanted to peek into their visual meaning-making processes. Using their imaginations, how would students picture people, places, and events? How could they share their mental pictures with others? She first asked students to create six-panel comic strips featuring quotes from the novel, coupled with images, to represent their understandings of the text. Using a class set of iPads and a comic book creation app called ComicBook!, students brought their artistic talent and ideas to life. They used the iPad camera and Skitch, a drawing and photo marking app, as well as a collage app called Pic

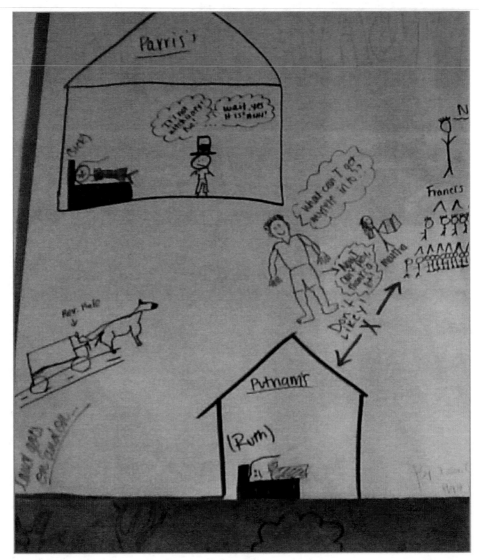

FIGURE 6.4. Student visualization of the setting in *The Crucible*.

Stitch to create the right images before uploading them to the comic panels. Both apps are free from iTunes. Once the images were uploaded, students could add filters to create the proper tone in accord with their vision. Students published finished comic strips on a Google site so that everyone could view their work (see Figure 6.5). Visualizing with comic book apps is particularly effective for teachers who wish to differentiate instruction, as they encourage us to honor the multiple modalities of learning that students bring to the classroom by interweaving technology, visual arts, and literacy.

FIGURE 6.5. Student visualization of *Dr. Jekyll and Mr. Hyde* using ComicBook!

Summarizing Meaning

While students are barraged with information in 140 characters or fewer outside of school, they often have difficulty distilling information from what is read. Berke and Woodland (1995) indicated that "no greater challenge to the intellect and no more accurate test of understanding exist than the ability to contemplate an idea and then restate it briefly in your own words" (p. 370). Summary challenges students to recap, limit, and organize ideas drawn from text. A summary reveals what students take away from a reading, offering us insights into their focus, their knowledge of details, and the relationships between the two. The importance of summary is reflected in the CCR anchor standards for reading, key ideas and details, which state that students need to be able to "summarize the key supporting details and ideas" (National Governors Association Center for Best Practices, 2010).

Nicole began her reading mini-lesson by explaining the importance of summary and then sharing a synopsis she had written of a scene students had read the day before. Next, she assigned students a different scene from *Romeo and Juliet* to summarize in approximately 200–250 words, including at least one direct quote. Students then created a headline and newspaper article from their summary (see Figure 6.6). Students used Google Chromebooks (www.google.com/chromebook) to access one of two websites that generate newspapers based on the text they input. Stephanie Locsei's newspaper generator (www.homemade-gifts-made-easy.com/newspaper-generator.html) is a free online tool students can use to upload writing and one image. Fodey.com's alternative (www.fodey.com/generators/newspaper/snippet.asp) is part of an entire suite of entertaining generators, including talking tomatoes and clapperboards. This application may be a better choice for more reluctant writers, as it allows for approximately 65 words. When finished, students publish and share their newspapers, labeled by scene, to a class website.

The newspaper summaries demonstrate how students were able to construct meaning from a text despite possible language barriers by using note-taking, questioning, and research skills. Their comprehension of the text allowed them to participate in an act of reciprocal teaching, as they posted the summaries, study aides written authentically in student-friendly language, to a central website.

Other digital resources to foster précis include two free iPad apps, Puppet Pals and Sock Puppets. If iPads are not available, VoiceThread (https://voicethread.com/) provides a means for students to summarize verbally. It is completely Web based and free; students simply need a microphone and Internet

The Verona Gazette

28 MAY 2013

Montague and Capulet Feuding Continues!

By TIANNA MYERS

Reuters

From ancient grudge break to new mutiny, where civil blood makes civil hands unclean. These words rang true yesterday evening as yet another feud broke out between the Montague and Capulet families. These two families, of similar social classes, have allegedly been ancient enemies ever since trading deals between the two went bad. The peaceful city of Verona has turned into a bloodbath for all of its citizens, even those not involved in the feud. The fight yesterday evening allegedly started after a servant from the Montague home bite his thumb at a servant from the Capulet home. The two men drew their swords and the vicious duel began. No one was killed but both men were badly injured. Officials even say that an innocent man was dragged into the commotion and badly injured as well. However, each family has a child that is of marrying age. The Capulets have a daughter named Juliet and the Montagues a son named Romeo. Hopefully this new generation of Montagues and Capulets can eliminate this vile fighting. There may even be a love interest between the Capulet and Montague children which could ultimately lead to not only tragic deaths in both families, but also the end of this ongoing feud and finally bring peace. This will inevitably leave Verona, Italy the safe place it once was.

International Moose Count Underway

By BOB O'BOBSTON

The UN-sponsored International Moose Census got off to a flying start today with hopes for an increase in the worldwide moose population compared to last year's disapointing figures. Among the traditional early reporters were Egypt, returning figures of six moose, a twenty percent increase on 2011's figures of five, and Uruguay whose moose population remains stable at eleven.

According to Robbie McRobson, head of the UN Moose Preservation Council, worldwide moose numbers are expected to grow markedly on last year due to the traditional moose strongholds of Canada and the United States, with the larger developing moose ecologies also poised to make gains. The largest percentagee increase in moose will likely come from China", says McRobson, The Chinese government has invested heavily in moose infrastructure over the past decade, and their committment to macrofauna is beginning to pay dividends". Since 2004 China has expanded moose pasture from 1.5 of arable land to nearly 3.648 and moose numbers are expected to rise to 60,000 making China a net moose exporter for the first time. This is good news for neighbouring Mongolia, a barren moose-wasteland whose inhabitents nonetheless have an insatiable desire for the creatures. The increase in Beijing-Ulanbataar trade is anticipated to relieve pressure on the relatively strained Russian suppliers, but increase Mongolia's imbalance of trade with its larger neighbour.

Historically the only competitor to China in the far eastern moose markets has been Singapore but the tiny island nation is set to report a net loss, expecting a decrease of more than five percent on last year's 50,000 moose counted. The head of Singapore's Agency for Agriculture, Jing-Feng Lau, explained to an incredulous Singaporean parliament yesterday that bad weather had contributed to this season's poor showing, most notably when a cargo of 150 moose were swept out into the Indian ocean in a monsoon.

Yet again the global demand for moose will be met largely by the US and Canada. The recession-hit States is taking comfort in its moose growth figures with gross production expected to break 700,000 and net exports to grow by 2. The worldwide dominance of Canada shows no signs of abating though with this year's moose population expected to match last year's record figures of one hundred million billion.

Europe's rise as an international moose power will slow slightly this year as a response to the European Union's move towards standardising the European moose. Stringent quality controls are holding back the development of the eastern european populations compared to last year when they contributed significantly to europe's strong growth figures. Norway, which is not an EU member but has observer status, strenghted in numbers relative to the Euro area with numbers of Norweigian moose, known locally as elk" expected to rise for the tenth consecutive year, particularly thanks to a strong showing in the last quarter.

As moose season reaches its close, researchers world wide are turning to

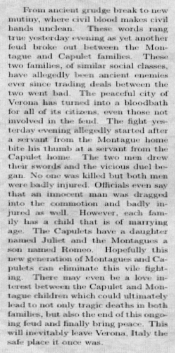

FIGURE 6.6. Student summary of the Prologue of *Romeo and Juliet*.

access. The use of digital tools as a summary strategy provides a more authentic experience for student learning. It utilizes a format they experience in everyday life while emphasizing a twenty-first-century workplace skill.

Analyzing Structural Components

When we workshop the canon, we include a variety of texts. Whereas our core text is typically a narrative, we want to utilize other texts, including informational/explanatory pieces, as well as arguments and topics related to the unit focus. Writers organize their information in purposeful ways, and it is helpful to provide mini-lessons to students on relevant structures and features to heighten awareness and increase comprehension. Students need a plan for reading, and workshopping teachers design mini-lessons that introduce organizational patterns and guide students to see the arrangement of and relationships between written ideas.

What are the structural components? Text structure refers to how information within a written piece is organized. Let's begin with *narrative*. Most familiar to language arts teachers, narratives are stories that generally reveal what happened, who did what to whom, and why. Narrative text has its own unique structure, organized into a story grammar. Story grammars are a set of rules that generate a structure for any story (Rayner & Pollatsek, 1989), and they identify the parts of a story and show how these parts relate to one another. There are different story grammars, but we are most familiar with setting, theme, character, plot, mood, and point of view. We teach mini-lessons about these organizational structures to heighten narrative text awareness and deepen literal and interpretive comprehension.

Informational/explanatory texts have structures different from narratives, and students utilize alternative strategies to comprehend these different texts. Informative/explanatory text structures include listing and naming, summary/précis, description, process description, definition, compare–contrast, classification, cause–effect, and problem–solution (Wilhelm et al., 2012), each of which is explained here. A list connects and arranges names to connote meaning. Summary/précis recaps, limits, and organizes main ideas. A description enables readers to see, experience, and understand what is described. Descriptions may be organized spatially, as parts of a whole, or chronologically. A definition explains the meaning and limits of a term or concept. There are two kinds of definitions: short and extended. Short definitions are those found in a dictionary, whereas extended ones are utilized when explaining concepts, making comparisons, or classifying examples. Compare–contrasts help us see similarities despite differences and differences despite similarities. Information is organized by either the block method, XXX–YYY, or the point-by-point method, XYXYXY. Classification groups elements or examples of a topic group into subgroups that share important defining characteristics so that various kinds of relationships, such as similarities and differences, can be perceived and explained. Cause–effect structures explain the relationship between a set of causes and consequences for events that have already occurred. A text can begin either with a cause or an effect. The effects may constitute some kind of problem, which is why cause–effect is usually a subset of problem–solution and often embedded in that pattern.

Different from both narrative and informational/explanatory text, an *argument* includes a claim that is both defensible and controversial. Often recognized as a thesis, a claim is supported with data. Following the data is a warrant that explains why the data matter. An argument also includes a rebuttal that addresses what someone who disagrees with any portion of the argument might say. The structure of argument differs from its counterpart, persuasion, in its reliance on logos and logical appeal rather than ethos and emotional appeal.

When I teach a mini-lesson to heighten awareness of a text structure, I begin by establishing the purpose: Writers use text structures to organize information, and, when we better understand the characteristics of these structures, it increases our comprehension when reading. Better understanding of the structure also enables us to emulate such organizational patterns when writing. Following an overview of the text features, I provide a think-aloud as I read a passage of text, highlighting the structural components as I read. I then guide students to continue reading on their own. In small groups, students share what they noticed individually. Finally, I ask them to collaboratively create a Say/Do table (see Figure 6.7), which is an adaptation of Wilhelm et al.'s (2012) "Author Says/Does Analysis."

In the left column, students list important ideas gathered from the text; in the right column, they list what the author does to relay this idea. During a unit focused around individual freedom with *Fahrenheit 451* as the core canonical text, students read Stanley Milgram's "The Perils of Obedience" and analyzed the essay's structure, paying particular attention to the author's use of evidence.

Formulating Inferences

Inferring involves drawing conclusions or making interpretations about that which is not explicitly stated. Human beings make inferences all the time; we interpret facial expressions, body language, and vocal tone as we pass colleagues in the hall, surmising when an administrator is in a bad mood based on the way she walks, talks, or scowls. We spend minutes each day trying to select or "read" emoji expressions in a text message sent or received. We read between textual lines as well, noticing a character's actions and drawing conclusions. Proficient readers infer when they combine background knowledge and

Say	Do
In this column, list the main ideas from the essay you have read. What does the author have to say?	*In this column, for each idea you listed on the left side, explain what the author did to relay this main idea. What did the author do as a writer to make his or her point?*
•	•
•	•
•	•
•	•

FIGURE 6.7. Say/Do table for use with text structure mini-lessons (adapted from Wilhelm et al., 2012).

merge this with clues in a text to formulate an educated guess. Readers assume, deduce, and suppose when they infer. They make reasonable predictions, testing and revising these predictions as they read further, resulting in dynamic interpretations of text that are adapted as they continue to read and even after they have completed reading. When our students read inferentially, they are actively involved with the text at a higher level—reflecting on information, considering background knowledge, and drawing logical conclusions. Perhaps this is why inference is noted in the CCR anchor standards for reading key ideas and details, which state that students should be able to "read closely to determine what the text says explicitly and to make logical inferences from it" (National Governors Association Center for Best Practices, 2010).

Authors leave clues behind for readers to find, and workshopping teachers provide mini-lessons to guide students along the processes of analyzing textual information and drawing reasonable conclusions. We help students first see the clues, then encourage them to combine their background knowledge with the textual evidence. We help them avoid what Tovani (2000) referred to as "outlandish responses" (p. 97) by clearly differentiating between an inference and an opinion and focusing on sound, text-driven conclusions.

One of my favorite methods for guiding inference is Beers's (2003, pp. 165–71) "It Says–I Say." With this visual scaffold, students organize their thoughts, connecting what is stated or seen explicitly in the text with what is not stated or seen in the text. In a unit focused around judgment and persecution with *The Scarlet Letter* as anchor text, my students and I slightly adapted this table and used it to make inferences (see Figure 6.8) as we read together.

Question	It Says	I Say	And So
Write down any question you have about what you have read.	*Find information from the text that will help you answer the question.*	*Write down what you already know about that information.*	*Combine what the text says with what you know to come up with the answer.*
Who is the father of Hester's baby?	"'People say,' said another, 'that the Reverend Master Dimmesdale, her godly pastor, takes it very grievously to his heart that such a scandal has come upon his congregation.'" (Chapter II)	Sometimes, it is the least likely person you expect who does something bad. This makes for a good story.	I think he is the father.
Who is Chillingworth?	"When he found the eyes of Hester Prynne fastened on his own, and saw that she appeared to recognize him, he slowly and calmly raised his finger, made a gesture with it in the air, and laid it on his lips." (Chapter III)	Hester knows and recognizes him. He doesn't want her to acknowledge him.	I don't know who he is, but I think he is someone close to Hester and important.

FIGURE 6.8. It Says–I Say–And So table for use with inference mini-lessons.

When planning for an inference mini-lesson, begin as always with an explanation of purpose. Adolescent students are more willing to adopt a strategy when they understand why and how it helps them as readers. Explain the importance of inference. Make connections to daily life. Project pictures, images of people going about their daily lives, and have students infer what is happening and explain why they think this. Ask questions about the pictures. What is he thinking? What is she feeling? What kind of person is he? Why do you think this? Have students cite evidence from the image to support their deduction. Then, transition to written text. Model your own educated guesses as you share read a short text, perhaps a picture book, poem, or lyrics, using Beers's (2003) visual scaffold to record your thinking process. Next, have students read a passage of text on their own and complete the chart, then share collaboratively with a small group.

Literary Mini-Lessons

Closely related to reading mini-lessons, literary mini-lessons guide students in their analysis of text, increasing interpretive comprehension. A text demands intellectual responses from readers, and we teach literary mini-lessons to maneuver students through the study of a range of literature encompassing works of fiction, drama, poetry, and nonfiction. Through literary mini-lessons, students discover story elements like plot, character, setting, point of view, tone, style, or theme. They explore figurative language such as the author's use of simile, metaphor, personification, alliteration, onomatopoeia, hyperbole, or idiom. Students consider literary devices, including allegory, allusion, irony, symbol, imagery, foreshadowing, or rhyme. Or students consider text from varied schools of literary criticism, contemplating historical and autobiographical context. Literary mini-lessons are used to foster interpretation, and teachers want to create an active workshop environment in which readers respond analytically and critically.

Workshop teachers layer textual interpretation on personal response and reading mini-lessons. After engaging students personally with text, we transition and scaffold, identifying specific literary qualities through close reading, noting form and language, and seeking meaning within the author's techniques or intentions. Teachers may also extend reading mini-lessons into literary mini-lessons. For example, there are obvious connections between the teaching of visualization and imagery. Or we can utilize questioning as a means to access plot or theme. We can utilize inference and prediction as we make guesses about characters and their relationships or actions. Workshop teachers thus unite literacy with the literary.

During literary mini-lessons, teachers guide readers in understanding how a text achieves its effects and meanings. We may embark on critical study, viewing a text through one or more literary theories (i.e., historical/biographical, moral/philosophical, Freudian, feminist, archetypal, Marxist, formalist, rhetorical, deconstructionist, new historical, etc.) and consider why a text is written. Literary mini-lessons center on an author's choice of form, language, or idea and attempt to explain its significance.

A literary mini-lesson may concentrate on the form of a text. Depending on the genre, such lessons may explore elements of plot, character, setting, point of view, tone, mood, style, or theme. A literary mini-lesson might explore the choices and effects of the author's language, helping students to unravel the figurative and connotative, dialect and diction, rhythm and rhyme, repetition and parallelism, and even imagery created through the use of simile, metaphor, onomatopoeia, or personification. A literary mini-lesson can also provide theoretical lenses through which to view a text, leading students to practice varied critical perspectives and develop literary tools for approaching any text.

The text itself determines the form, language, or theory to be addressed in any literary mini-lesson. Workshop teachers do not embark on formal analysis or critical synthesis with a list of predetermined terms in hand, imposing them on the page, but alternatively address these as the text demands. Gallagher (2009) has warned us about committing "read-i-cide," which is "the systematic killing of the love of reading" (p. 2), and we have to be careful not to overanalyze texts with literary mini-lessons. Instead, we want to find the "sweet spot" (Gallagher, 2009, p. 106) and teach mini-lessons within an authentic reading context, with topics for lessons arising naturally from the novel, play, poem, lyric, essay, story, article, or memoir under study within a focus unit.

English teachers likely have the most background for and experience with teaching literary mini-lessons. However, we want to be sure to teach in ways that are constructive, encouraging students to create their own understandings of text. Rather than lecturing about form, language, and idea, we guide students through their own textual discovery. With mini-lessons, we provide the purpose, introduce the literary tool(s) necessary for analysis, model our process of critical thinking, interpret texts using literary tools, share an analysis with others, hear alternative perspectives, and finally clarify and refine our initial interpretations.

Teachers most often engage students with formal and/or critical discussion questions during a literary mini-lesson. Such questions can be used to prod and extend student meaning-making. We just need to be careful not to ask questions that imply there is one best interpretation of the text. For example, when I was teaching Charlotte Perkins Gilman's "The Yellow Wallpaper," a short story included in a unit focused around gender, I divided students into groups

Historical/Biographical
- When and where was this short story written?
- What was happening in society at this time?
- Who wrote this story?
- What did you discover about the life of the author that might connect to the story in some way?

Feminist
- Who are the women in this short story, and how is each portrayed to the reader?
- Describe the relationship between the female and male characters in this story.
- Who has the power in this story, and how do you know this?

Marxist
- What do you think is the role of social class in this story?
- How does this story support or challenge power relationships?
- What issues of social justice and/or injustice do you believe this short story is addressing?

FIGURE 6.9. Critical questions to guide group discussion of "The Yellow Wallpaper" during a literary mini-lesson.

of three. After introducing the purpose of literary criticism and providing a very brief overview of the historical/biographical, feminist, and Marxist perspectives, each group was assigned a critical lens through which to view the story. Students conducted further research online, and were given a series of open-ended questions to guide their thinking (see Figure 6.9). Once students were confident in their collaborative critical analysis of the story, I jigsawed the groups, creating new groups consisting of members from other schools of criticism, allowing students to hear alternative perspectives of the same story and then refine initial interpretations.

Craft Mini-Lessons

Literary analysis leads naturally to the study of craft. As students examine characters, setting, point of view, tone, simile, metaphor, personification, alliteration, onomatopoeia, hyperbole, idiom, allegory, allusion, irony, symbol, imagery, foreshadowing, or rhyme, they notice not only what a text is saying but *how* it is being said. Craft mini-lessons encourage us to unravel such techniques and conventions utilized by an author that are worthy of imitation. Mini-lessons in the workshopping classroom do not end with a search for meaning; they continue to explore how meaning is achieved through the study of an author's craft.

Craft mini-lessons direct students to make observations about the ways in which a text is written. But, before engaging in craft study, students need to enjoy the aesthetic experiences of reading and transacting with a text; only then are they ready to move to a more intellectual response. Once students have engaged personally, workshop teachers can foster more analytical responses, guiding students to consider not only the effects of the author's language but also the cause of the effects; that is, the grammar and style utilized by an author to achieve meaning. During craft mini-lessons, we guide students to notice characteristics of convention and technique during and after reading experiences—while students are immersed in workshop structures such as close reading, independent reading, or book clubs—in order to increase both literal and interpretive comprehension.

When we workshop the canon, we teach grammar, usage, and mechanics just as we teach formal analysis and critical synthesis. And we do so from the inside out. We teach principles that guide the structure of sentences and paragraphs (grammar), rules that govern the practice of language (usage), and conventions that regulate the use of punctuation, capitalization, and paragraphing (mechanics) during authentic reading and writing experiences. Drawing from the core and supplementary literature in a unit, teachers select mentor texts as a focus during mini-lessons and inquire into the author's craft. As Smith (1988) and Ray (1999) have recommended, we teach students to read like writers.

Students can learn what they need to know about writing from reading. To do so, workshop teachers transition students from reading as readers to reading as writers, moving them from generating readerly to writerly responses. During craft mini-lessons, teachers guide students to notice particular elements of writerly craft and engage in collaborative inquiry to determine how these elements of text are achieved through writing. Anderson (2005, 2007), for example, encouraged teachers to find powerful model sentences in texts and to present these to students as models for discussion. Like artists, students study and learn from model sentences written by accomplished authors, becoming sort of craft apprentices.

Along with teachers, students can identify examples of writerly craft. After directing students to be intentional readers (through a how-to mini-lesson), we encourage them to read like writers. What do they notice about how a text is written? What are examples of craft worthy of replication? Students collect examples of imitable grammar, mechanics, and usage in their response logs during independent reading, later to be shared during a book club meeting. Or, they engage in collaborative inquiry during a close reading, rereading passages and uncovering how a text is artfully written to relay meaning. We want students to see writing craft in multiple ways, across multiple genres, and practice reading like writers through multiple workshop structures.

We also want students to utilize such techniques when writing. Workshop teachers provide craft mini-lessons to support both student writing and reading processes, but we select topics for mini-lessons based on rhetorical needs. When analyzing student writing, we look for patterns and choose what is most important as lesson topics. For example, Nicole noticed her students were struggling to use powerful descriptors when writing a memoir. So she designed a mini-lesson showing students how to use words economically but with powerful impact, drawing examples from Walter Dean Myers's *Harlem*. Each student was given a page of the book and directions to scour the text for a single word or short phrase that created a specific image, realizing through this process that often few words evoke the strongest emotional response from a reader.

If you are unsure of topics for craft mini-lessons, Robb (2012) has suggested a range of options to draw from, including thesis/focus statements, leads, endings, strong verbs, specific nouns, show-don't-tell, figurative language, dialogue, direct quotations, paragraphing, transition sentences, sentence openings, run-ons, faulty pronoun references, punctuating complex sentences, using prepositional phrases, and comma usage. Anderson (2005) proposed a series of lessons based on sentences, pronouns, verbs, adjectives and adverbs, and punctuation.

Once topics for craft mini-lessons have been decided, be sure to provide students with an explanation of purpose. Why is it important to read like writers? We teach craft mini-lessons to improve the application of grammar, usage, and mechanics. Having established the purpose, teachers next have the option of organizing the lesson deductively or inductively. If teaching the mini-lesson deductively, introduce the grammatical, usage, or mechanical rule and demonstrate the rule in a work of literature included in the unit of study. As we want active and social participants in the lesson, arrange students into small groups, guiding and instructing them to search for other examples of the crafting technique in a supplementary text. Conclude the mini-lesson with independent and authentic crafting practice.

If teaching the lesson inductively, think aloud with students during a shared reading of a passage of text. Model your craft inquiry process, rereading words, phrases, and sentences with students. What do we notice about the way this text is written—about the structure and the "way with words" (Ray, 1999, p. 45)? We might notice the author's use of parallelism, verbs, dialogue, or transitions. However, we might also notice craft for which we do not have a name. If so, label the technique together. Place students into small groups and have them engage in a similar collaborative inquiry process, utilizing close reading as a structure, and simply asking, "What do you notice about how this text is written?" Ray (1999, p. 120) suggested guiding students in their process of reading like a writer as follows:

1. *Notice* something about the craft of the text.

2. *Talk* about it and *make a theory* about why a writer might use this craft.

3. Give the craft a name.

4. Think of *other texts* you know. Have you seen this craft before?

5. Try and *envision* using this crafting in your own writing.

Once students have worked in small groups, have them practice crafting during independent writing.

Certain methods can be utilized to encourage identification and association with an author's writing style. Students can practice crafting through a variety of apprentice writing experiences, adopting and adapting found examples of craft. Aspiring writers can surround model words, phrases, or passages with visual images. They can translate artful phrases or passages into their own words, re-creating and rewriting craft in their own language. "Official plagiarism" (Milner et al., 2012, p. 386) encourages students to restate or reorder another writer's words, rearranging them to create new versions of text. Students can utilize another author's craft as a springboard—borrowing a simile, metaphor, or symbol—and then create their own written work. Imagine the power of rhetoric imitated from Martin Luther King Jr.'s "Letter from a Birmingham Jail" as students model the author's use of parallelism, diction, or allusion.

All writers can hone their craft through the study of written models. Following mini-lessons, encourage students to utilize new techniques when writing and have them edit for craft with writing circles (see Chapter 7). Always showcase positive student examples of writerly craft when celebrating and publishing student work.

Vocabulary Mini-Lessons

Similar to the study of craft, vocabulary mini-lessons focus on the author's word choice. They help students better understand *what* an author has written as well as *how* an author has written, increasing both literal and interpretive comprehension. A vocabulary mini-lesson provides an opportunity for word study in the context of what students are reading. Students also make use of vocabulary mini-lessons as they produce their own text. With the help of mini-lessons, teachers can guide students to better understanding and producing written meaning.

Teachers who workshop the canon have numerous opportunities to increase word knowledge across a variety of meaningful contexts. We grow our vocabulary by encountering new words. Read-alouds, shared reading, independent reading, close reading, and readers theater immerse students in language-rich environments. Students discover a wealth of new words through these work-shop structures. However, workshopping teachers balance this incidental learn-ing with the intentional teaching of vocabulary mini-lessons before and during reading experiences, across a wide variety of genres.

Before reading, workshopping teachers can activate background and word knowledge in relation to the unit focus. We want to develop students' initial understanding of concepts. For example, if we are about to read *Julius Caesar* and our unit focus is fate and free will, it is vital that students gain a general understanding of these abstract ideas in order to make connections across tex-tual experiences. So we frontload the unit focus by having students engage with a List–Group–Label task (Allen, 2007; Taba, 1967), in which they first list all the words they can think of related to the unit focus (in this case, fate and free will). Destiny. Choice. Chance. Doom. Then we have them work with a partner to group the words they listed and place them into categories. Finally, students decide on a label for each group. A lively class discussion follows, preparing and motivating students to read.

When a text, most often the core canonical literary work but sometimes a book club selection, includes challenging vocabulary, we teach mini-lessons during reading to increase comprehension. There is a direct correlation between reading comprehension and word knowledge, so we want to teach vocabulary mini-lessons in meaningful and memorable ways. Rather than handing out pre-fabricated lists of decontextualized words, stems, or roots, we teach vocabulary important and critical to understanding. As they read, students collect unfamil-iar words, and we unravel their meaning during vocabulary mini-lessons.

To make new words visible, we create word walls. An alternative to the dreaded bulletin board, these visual language displays surround students with new vocabulary. As students discover words related to the unit focus, core text, or supporting readings, we post them on the wall, placing words in view so stu-dents can see them and use them when speaking and writing throughout a unit.

Workshopping teachers provide direct vocabulary instruction to support reading. We teach, rather than assign, vocabulary. We want students to identify words they do not understand, and then we provide strategies for unraveling meaning during mini-lessons. Students can work out words in a variety of ways beyond looking them up or using context clues. Allen (1999) suggested that teachers support students' word knowledge with visuals, connections, repeti-tion, description, definitions, comparisons, contrasts, and rephrasing. Shared, independent, and close reading as well as read-alouds and readers theater offer optimal opportunities for teaching vocabulary mini-lessons. During any of these reading experiences, students can collect words they do not know, to be shared and worked out later with book clubs or during a large-group discussion.

There is a wide variety of strategies available to help students learn new vocabulary. Three of my favorites are *verbal and visual word association* (VVWA) (Eeds & Cockrum, 1985), *vocabulary tableau*, and *word theater*. VVWA combines a vocabulary word and its definition with both a visual of the term and a personal association or characteristic of it. With this strategy, students:

1. Select unfamiliar vocabulary from the text being read.
2. Draw a rectangle divided into four sections.
3. Write the vocabulary word in the upper-left box of the rectangle.
4. Write the definition of the term in the lower-left box.
5. Draw a visual representation of the vocabulary word in the upper-right box of the rectangle.
6. Write a personal association, an example, or characteristic in the fourth box at the lower right.

Figure 6.10 shows an example of VVWA for vocabulary drawn from *Beowulf*.

FIGURE 6.10. VVWA for the word *boast*, selected from *Beowulf* during a vocabulary mini-lesson.

A bit more out of the box is a vocabulary tableau, in which students practice and perform a living statue of an assigned word. They might also create a drawing, mime, photograph, video, or dance. Finally, requiring a bit more direction and rehearsal, word theater asks students to select a focus word and to dramatize it. They perform words for one another, and classmates are asked to guess the meaning through reference to a word bank. Workshopping teachers can interweave a variety of such strategies to foster language learning during mini-lessons.

As with any mini-lesson, begin by establishing the purpose: the purpose for a vocabulary mini-lesson during reading is to increase comprehension through knowledge of vocabulary. Next, select words from student listings, focusing on new vocabulary that will help students understand the text being read. We model how we make sense of unknown and unfamiliar words in the context of reading either a core or supplemental text in the unit, talking through our processes of using context, structure, prior knowledge, and resources to make meaning. Then we guide students in collaborative and/or independent practice of new vocabulary through a strategy such as any of those described above.

Critical Mini-Lessons

Critical mini-lessons lead students to question what and how they read, speak, or act. Such lessons derive from the theory and practice of critical literacy, which focuses on the social, cultural, and political forces influencing the creation and interpretation of texts and readers. No reader or reading is pure; there are personal, cultural, social, historical, and political factors shaping our reactions to text. Neither is any text untarnished, as the same factors can shape the creation of a text. Nor indeed is any word or action innocuous. We teach critical mini-lessons to reflect on those factors that may influence a reader's transaction with a text, the construction of the text itself, or any word spoken or action made in relation to text.

Just as we layer textual interpretation on personal response, we layer critical literacy over personal response and/or textual interpretation. Let's think about that. In order to adopt a critical stance, students need to reflect on their initial reaction to the text and may consider as well the author's underlying meaning. Before a reader can become critical, he or she must first have experienced a reaction to the text and considered the author's intent. During a critical mini-lesson, we encourage students to question the reader, author, and text, as follows: How did you respond to the text? What did you say or how did you act because of the text? Why do you think you responded in this way? What did the author include as well as exclude from the text? Why do you think the author did this? Whose perspectives are represented and missing from the page? Workshop teachers critically scrutinize opening responses to literary works and the contents and meaning of literary works for their social, cultural, historical, and political influences.

Critical mini-lessons are especially vital when teaching a core canonical text. As the vast majority of classical literature represents a Eurocentric perspective, readers need to be guided toward a more critical stance, considering how and why these texts were created and are read. We want to heighten self-consciousness and text consciousness among readers. Teachers who workshop the canon encourage students to question where their responses come from, prod them to consider what these responses say about themselves as readers and human beings, and lead them to ponder those factors influencing authorial intent.

An ideal time to teach a critical mini-lesson is after students have completed some sort of response engagement, such as a reading journal, blog, or double-entry diary as introduced in Chapter 4. However, students can also be encouraged to reflect on their oral responses after a book club meeting or Socratic circle. To promote reading from a critical stance, ask students to consider the following after a book club meeting:

- Reflect on your conversation today. Be honest, and write down what you remember saying during the meeting.

- What do you think influenced what you said (e.g., past experience, family, beliefs, race, gender, religion, sexual orientation, or status)?

- Consider what your language says about you as a reader and a human being. Does your response reveal you for who you are and/or who you want to be?

- Do you think other perspectives were missing from the conversation? If so, whose? Why do you think so?

- What do you think the author of the text would say about your response?

Students reflect individually. The teacher models his or her own critical reflection and encourages students to share their critical thinking in small groups, reminding students they do not have to share all of their responses if they do not want to.

Critical mini-lessons encourage students to scrutinize initial responses for their social and cultural influences, reflect on their stance adopted toward a text, examine their values and roles in society, and conduct more critical readings of text. These lessons can help students unravel assumptions, explore numerous perspectives, hear more than one narrative, and identify the voices that were present and absent within a text.

Chapter Summary

Mini-lessons are interactive lessons including teacher demonstrations in language arts procedures, strategies, craft, conventions, and perspective. Teaching mini-lessons supports constructivist principles, encourages collaborative and interactive learning, and improves students' reading and writing. Workshop teachers teach mini-lessons to increase literal, interpretive, and critical comprehension. Some mini-lessons are more text driven than others, but teachers need to be careful not to teach mini-lessons in isolation.

We teach mini-lessons before, during, and after workshop structures such as read-alouds, shared reading, close reading, readers theater, book clubs, Socratic circles, and independent reading and writing. As we plan to teach mini-lessons, we keep in mind the gradual release of responsibility model. Mini-lessons begin with whole-class instruction, including teacher modeling, followed by opportunities for guided, collaborative, and independent learning.

In our workshop, there are how-to, reading, literary, craft, vocabulary, and critical mini-lessons. A how-to mini-lesson explains "how to" do something. To increase student understanding, workshopping teachers teach reading mini-lessons that help students connect, predict, question, visualize, summarize, infer, and analyze before, during, and after reading. Literary mini-lessons help students analyze story elements, figurative language, and literary devices as well as interpret texts through schools of literary criticism. Craft mini-lessons encourage students to unravel techniques and conventions utilized by an author worthy of imitation. Vocabulary mini-lessons provide for word study in the context of what students are reading. And critical mini-lessons lead students to question what they are reading, how they are reading, and what they are taking away from reading.

7

Need to Write

A written word is the choicest of relics. It is something at once more intimate with us and more universal than any other work of art. It is the work of art nearest to life itself.

—HENRY DAVID THOREAU, *Walden*

Along with all of the structures that immerse students in reading, talking, and listening, workshopping teachers provide many and varied opportunities for writing and researching in the classroom. We use the written word both to clarify and confirm our thinking. When we workshop the canon, students engage in both writing as process and writing as product.

Students write throughout a focus unit, clarifying their meaning-making as they listen during a read-aloud; respond during independent reading; connect, question, predict, visualize, infer, and summarize during a shared reading; analyze literary, grammatical, and mechanical elements during a close reading; compose scripts for readers theater; prepare for book clubs and Socratic circles; and engage in mini-lessons. Students in the workshopping classroom also write in response to a unit focus or essential questions as a culminating experience at the conclusion of a unit. In this way, they are not only clarifying meaning for themselves, but also making their meaning-making known to others through a composing task. Students may create narrative, informative/explanatory, argumentative, literary, multigenre, or research-based papers or projects that meet the CCR anchor standards for writing and demonstrate their thinking.

Teachers support the writing process and products through a variety of workshop structures, including mentor texts, writing plans, independent writing, writing circles, craft mini-lessons, and publishing opportunities. This chapter discusses why and how to support workshop writing with the canon.

How do we teach formal writing when the world has become significantly less formal? What is the value.

Why Writing?

Too often, writing is the "neglected R" (College Entrance Examination Board, 2003), overlooked in secondary classrooms by teachers who favor reading and discussing literature. A National Council of Teachers of English (2007) policy research brief revealed that 40 percent of high school seniors never or rarely write a paper of three or more pages. If students don't practice writing, then it follows they aren't writing very well. The National Center for Education Statistics (2012) found about 27 percent of students perform at or above the *proficient* level and about 80 percent of students perform at or above the *basic* level for grades 8 and 12. Graham and Hebert (2010) determined roughly one-third of high school graduates are not ready to succeed in an introductory-level college writing course. If we want students to grow as writers, then they need more opportunities to write.

When we workshop the canon, we interweave the teaching of reading with the teaching of writing. Writing and researching emerge naturally from reading, thus avoiding the "schizophrenic" split (Langer, 1990, p. 812) between the teaching of writing and the teaching of literature. Students in workshopping classrooms create a culminating narrative or informative/explanatory, argumentative, literary, multigenre, or I-Search paper or project to demonstrate their thinking around a unit focus and essential questions.

For example, in a unit focused on decisions, a student could write the story (narrative) of an important choice; in a unit centered around identity, a student could conduct research (I-Search) on his or her family; in a unit concentrated on survival, a student could design a manual (process description) for incoming ninth graders; in a unit exploring the American dream, a student could contend whether this dream is equally accessible (argument). What is written provides a counterpart for what has been read throughout a unit.

How to Workshop Writing with the Canon

When workshopping the canon, we design units centered on a core text, thematic focus, and essential questions. We engage students in a variety of genres that provide varied perspectives and prompt exploration of the focus and questions. Throughout the unit, students think–talk–listen–write about what they are reading—clarifying, sharing, and reflecting on their meaning-making. As previous chapters in this book offer ways and means to engage students in writing as a meaning-making process, this chapter will focus on writing as a product.

The following section provides a review of text structures that can be utilized when workshopping the canon. These structures include the types of student writing cited in the CCSS and the National Assessment of Educational Progress framework. According to these national guidelines, high school students are expected to engage in three mutually reinforcing writing capacities: writing to persuade (40 percent), writing to explain (40 percent), and writing to convey experience (20 percent). The listing below is school and standards based, and there are certainly more genres to include within a unit. Just as we want to immerse students in many different literary genres, we want to encourage them to craft a variety of text structures when workshopping writing with the canon.

Narrative

The most familiar genre to English language arts teachers, a narrative tells a real or imagined story. While the CCSS and the National Assessment of Educational Progress framework grant narrative the least amount of attention in secondary school (20 percent), this mode of discourse is foundational to writing informational/explanatory texts and crafting arguments/analyses because it relays meaning. Through the telling of story, we guide others to perceive, know, feel, and experience. As a result of storytelling, we are better able to make sense of the world and others around us. Therefore, the importance of narrative should not be discounted in middle and high school classrooms.

To write narrative, students first select a topic worthy of writing about. What is the meaning or relevance they want to share with others? Students then develop the same conventions they so often analyze in other stories: setting, characters, plot (i.e., exposition, rising action, climax, falling action, and denouement), point of view, dialogue, and theme. In the workshopping classroom, students may develop narrative in response to a unit focus or essential questions. In the past, I have asked students to write narratives about a heroic moment when reading *Beowulf*, about important decisions when reading *Hamlet*, and about a life-changing journey when reading *The Odyssey*.

Informative/Explanatory

Regaining popularity because of their mention and attention in the CCSS, informative/explanatory text structures include listing and naming, summary/précis, description, process description, definition, compare–contrast, classification, cause–effect, and problem–solution (Wilhelm et al., 2012). While listing and naming and summary and précis may not receive the same attention in middle and secondary school classrooms, they are necessary components for creating the other text structures.

Listing and Naming

When we list, we denote importance. In order to list, we must name. When we name, we confer both meaning and power. We can arrange and categorize that which we have named into lists to connote more and different meaning. Let's say, for bell work, we ask students to make a list of the characters in a YA novel they are reading independently. We ask them to list descriptive characteristics and attributes beside each of the characters. Next, we ask students to share the names and lists with their book club. Finally, we ask the book club members to create categories of characters in their novel based on characteristics and attributes exhibited. As students name each category, they designate and relay more meaning.

Summary/Précis

Once we have listed and named, we are capable of creating a summary or précis that includes key details that are related and shaped to communicate meaning. As soon as students have listed, named, and categorized, they are ready to organize these categories into a coherent whole that synthesizes and conveys meaning. Workshopping teachers can ask students to summarize in a variety of ways. Have students create a bumper sticker that encapsulates meaning. Students can choose the most important word in a poem, story, or novel. 3–2–1 is an adaptable strategy that prompts students to summarize their thinking; students may write three things they learned, two questions they have, and one opinion they have about the topic. Students might also perform a tableau, as introduced in Chapter 4, which offers a snapshot of meaning, or create newspaper articles as described in Chapter 6.

Description

Description further develops details and enables readers to see, experience, and understand what is described. This is accomplished using sensory details. A student who writes a description fleshes out each detail, demonstrates relationships between details, and even includes some judgment about the details. A thorough and thoughtful description inspires a response from an audience.

A description may be organized spatially, whereby details are presented as if they are in space (i.e., top to bottom or left to right). Students can describe or draw elements of a setting. Likewise, a description could be organized as parts of a whole. Certain characters might be grouped in some way, such as feuding families. Or a description might be organized chronologically; students could describe how the plot unfolds. Or a description might be organized by order of importance; students could depict the most important people, places, things, or ideas.

Process Description

Process description describes in detail the steps or course of an action. It allows us to consider, practice, and reflect on a specific activity. Long gone are the days when we described how to make a peanut butter and jelly sandwich or bake chocolate chip cookies. Instead, students can create a recipe for how to fall in love, after reading Suzanne Collins's *The Hunger Games* or *Romeo and Juliet*; they can create a how-to manual for survival, after reading *Lord of the Flies* or Gary Paulsen's *Hatchet*; they can fashion a pamphlet for how to defend civil rights, after reading *To Kill a Mockingbird* or Alex Haley's *The Autobiography of Malcolm X*.

Definition

While definitions can be short, an extended definition relies on thorough description and deep understanding of a term, concept, or phenomenon. Students can craft extended definitions in relation to the unit focus or in response to essential questions. Once students have read around, talked through, and listened to ideas about a unit focus, such as a journey, they can begin to create an extended definition. List–group–label and VVWA techniques, as described in Chapter 6, can help them generate and organize initial meaning. Students can then place "journey" within a group of ideas to which it most closely belongs; gather, generate, and analyze examples, counterexamples, aspects, and forms of a "journey"; identify specific criteria that designate a "journey"; and differentiate it from other terms, such as "trip" or "vacation" (Wilhelm et al., 2012). Students can engage in an authentic research process as they survey and interview others in their efforts to clarify the term.

Compare–Contrast

When we compare and contrast, we analyze the similarities and differences of two or more subjects that we deem important. Meaning is relayed and an argument made through the analysis of the subjects. For example, in the work-shopping classroom, students can compare and contrast any of the wide variety of genres read throughout a unit—most easily, a core canonical text with a YA novel. Students might compare and contrast such features as the setting, plot, characters, and themes of the two works. A Venn diagram with its overlapping circles can help students visualize that which is similar and different. Also helpful, a semantic features analysis prompts students to create a chart, listing the

	Setting	Plot	Characters	Theme
Romeo and Juliet				
Perfect Chemistry				

FIGURE 7.1. Semantic feature analysis comparing and contrasting a canonical core text with a young adult novel.

subjects for comparison down the left-hand column while, across the top, they list the features or points of comparison (see Figure 7.1).

Once students have selected points to compare–contrast in respect to their subjects, they develop a thesis or claim (e.g., which is better and why) and decide on an organizational structure. Students can arrange their points in one of three ways: (1) subject by subject, in which all of the points about one text are combined and followed by all of the points about the second text; (2) point by point, in which the similarities and differences between each of the settings, plots, characters, and themes are combined; or (3) likenesses and differences, in which all of the similarities between the two texts are combined, followed by all of the differences.

Classification

Classification helps us see and explain patterns and relationships among ideas. When we classify, we sort things into groups or categories to say something meaningful about how a whole relates to a part or a part relates to a whole. We guide students through the process by determining a subject for classification, sorting the subject into useful categories, ensuring the categories fit the same organizing principle, determining a thesis or claim related to the classifications, and providing examples of each category that support the thesis or claim. While workshopping the canon, students might classify in relation to a unit focus (e.g., kinds of journeys, types of dreams), an essential question (e.g., How do we persecute others? What are different types of heroic action?), or texts read (e.g., types of characters, attributes of setting).

[handwritten marginal note:] What are we really teaching? Why do we insist on doing it the most boring way possible?

Cause–Effect

Cause and effect text structures are concerned with why something happens (cause), what happens as a result (effect), and the relationship between the reason and the consequence. This structure typically takes one of two forms, either explaining how a cause produces specific effects or how specific effects are produced by a cause. Rarely is there a single cause for an effect or a single effect for a cause, so consider the many possibilities. If your cause or effects are previously unknown (and you have discovered either), then you are writing an argument and need a claim, even though the CCSS refer to cause–effect as informational/explanatory text. If a cause or effect is known, then you are writing to inform and need a thesis. Following the claim or thesis, students will include a description of the cause, description of the effect, and explanation of (or argument for) the cause–effect relationship.

Certain essential questions can lead to an exploration of cause–effect relationships. For example, in a unit focused around individual freedom, we could ask, "What are the effects of censoring thoughts, speech, language, and expression?" In a unit centered on decisions, "What are the effects of our choices and actions on others?" Texts read within a unit may also warrant an exploration of cause–effect relationships: "What are the causes and effects of Macbeth's demise?" Or "What are the effects of the utopian/dystopian society on characters in *Brave New World*?"

Problem–Solution

Closely related to cause–effect, this explains the relationship of a problem to a solution, or, if the solution or problem is previously unknown, it makes an argument for the solution or the problem. Students identify a topic; research the problem and solutions; identify the causes of, or solutions to, a problem; write a thesis to inform/explain, or a claim to argue; and then present their ideas. Students become active problem seekers and solvers through engaging in this inquiry process. When workshopping the canon, a unit focus, essential questions, and certain texts lend themselves to the problem–solution format: How can we promote social justice in our school and community? How does our school violate individual freedoms? What could Romeo and Juliet have done other than commit suicide? What difficulties does Hester face in *The Scarlet Letter* and how could she surmount them?

Argument

Writing arguments fosters critical thinking. It is mainly about logical appeals and involves claims, evidence, warrants, and rebuttals. A *claim* can be the starting point for an argument. Similar to a thesis, a claim needs to be both debatable and defensible. There needs to be at least two positions on a topic, and the claim argues one of these positions. "Some freedoms need to be curtailed in the interests of national security" is an example of a claim written by a student in response to a workshop unit focused on freedom of expression.

To prove a claim, students gather and organize data. Data provide the *evidence* to substantiate a claim. Students can cite experts, provide facts, list statistics, and state reasons to support the claim. They can collect data from texts, interviews, surveys, observations, even experiments. When debating the need to curtail certain freedoms, as in the claim above, a student interviewed and surveyed others as well as gathered textual support. Engaging in such a detailed and authentic research process encourages students to understand different points of view. In this way, arguments may begin not just with a claim but also with the research process itself. After engaging with the data, students then can state their position and make a claim with more authority.

A *warrant* explains why the data matter. Data can be used to support a variety of positions, but a warrant clarifies the connection between the claim and the data. A warrant may be stated or assumed. For example, data can be used to support either the freedom of expression or the curtailing of certain freedoms, but a warrant presumes that certain freedoms can be dangerous and that people value national security.

A *rebuttal* addresses the opposing position. In an argument, we present and refute that which disputes the claim. We acknowledge and counter differing perspectives. For example, the rebuttal "There are those who believe that the rights listed in the First Amendment must be protected at all costs" introduces an alternative view to the claim presented above. Subsequently, the student presents reasoning or evidence intended to undermine or weaken the claim of an opponent.

Literary

Students in the language arts classroom are specifically challenged to construct literary arguments, making a defensible yet debatable claim about a work of literature. As Smith, Wilhelm, and Fredricksen (2012) explained, evidence comes from mining a work of literature in support of a claim. The warrant offers a reason about what an author might have intended something to mean, or posits how he or she might have made different choices if wanting to imply a different meaning. The rebuttal considers other perspectives.

Foundational to a literary argument is the need for alternative interpretation. If a claim is to be debatable and rebuttable, then a text (and the teacher) needs to encourage and support diversity of meaning-making. While workshopping teachers may include a classical core text, students read a wider variety of genres more open to interpretation and less venerated by the public. Let's face it: the literary arguments surrounding *Romeo and Juliet*, *Lord of the Flies*, *The Scarlet Letter*, and *The Great Gatsby* are simply too well known and too accessible for online purchase. Enough about the stars, glasses, woods, and green light. Students are much more likely to formulate a unique claim about John Green's *The Fault in Our Stars*, Suzanne Collins's *The Hunger Games*, Jay Asher's *13 Reasons Why*, or Sherman Alexie's *The Absolutely True Diary of a Part-Time Indian*.

When workshopping, students can create analytical arguments about YA novels, picture books, short stories, informational texts, graphic novels, and poetry interwoven within a unit. Since workshopping teachers include media and the arts, students may construct arguments about movies, television shows, songs, dances, and works of art. No matter the genre, literary arguments can make assertions about characters, themes, plot, literary devices, settings, or craft. Students can make judgments about characters and their actions: "Augustus commits a selfish act when he takes Hazel to Amsterdam in *The Fault in Our Stars*." Students can write arguments about the central ideas of a text and evaluate those ideas: "*The Hunger Games* offers a social commentary on society's preoccupation with reality TV." Or students can write evaluative arguments, offering evidence as to the quality of the text itself: "The characters, plot, and theme of *The Absolutely True Diary of a Part-Time Indian* reveal the real-world challenges faced by many teens today."

Multigenre

Once students have been introduced to a variety of text structures, they are ready to create multigenre papers or projects. When students write multigenre texts (Romano, 2000), they represent their thinking through a variety of different genres and subgenres, each independent yet connected by a common theme, topic, language, image, or content. In contrast to the more traditional and singular essay, a multigenre work interweaves multiple text structures and threads them together. As Romano (2000, pp. x–xi) summarized:

> A multigenre paper arises from research, experience, and imagination. It is not an uninterrupted, expository monolog, nor a seamless narrative, nor a collection of poems. A multigenre paper is composed of many genres and subgenres, each

piece self-contained, making a point of its own, yet connected by theme or topic and sometimes by language, images, and content. In addition to many genres, a multigenre paper may also contain many voices, not just the author's. The trick is to make such a paper hang together.

To help such a paper "hang together," students include an introduction, table of contents, and a reflection that makes clear the relationship between the multiple genres for the reader. Such papers and projects fit effortlessly into the workshopping classroom, as they may be centered around a unit focus or essential question yet allow students to respond through a variety of different forms beyond the school-based genre repertoire, including multimodal.

In a unit focused around gender, my students and I read works by A. R. Ammons, Maya Angelou, India Arie, Gwendolyn Brooks, Lucille Clifton, Rita Dove, Nikki Giovanni, Donald Justice, Doris Lessing, Alice Munro, Marge Piercy, Theodore Roethke, and Virginia Woolf. These authors guided our explorations of gender and its relationship to language, media, bodies, careers, family, and relationships. As a culminating assignment, students wrote a multigenre paper that represented their thinking through class readings and conversations about gender.

I asked students to answer one of our essential questions: "What role does gender play in daily life?" I wanted them to embrace research as a personal and organic experience—as a means of exploring their self(ves), their values, and their role(s) in society. Their ways of seeing and saying could appear in multiple forms, such as poetry, prose, lists, drama, art, and exposition. They could mix fact with imagery and memory with imagination in their efforts to convey thinking and knowing to others.

This multigenre approach encouraged students to play with a variety of voices, perspectives, and ideas. For example, Felicia, a self-identified female, wrote:

> I hate girls. They are always trying to play with us boys. Why can't they leave us guys alone? They wear stinky perfume. They have cooties. Girls are always combing and brushing their hair. They are stupid. They always cry about everything. I hate it when they run up and try to kiss you. Gross. They don't know how to play football, and they don't know how to play war. They just don't know how to die right.

When students are no longer limited by the singleness of voice, perspective, or form, they are no longer constrained by singularity of idea. Multiple forms can prompt multiple representations of knowing. Rather than a singular demonstration of a truth, students are encouraged to explore varied truths, a task much better suited for fostering critical thinking within democratic, diverse societies.

In another class, I challenged students in each book club to create a collaborative, digital, multigenre paper in response to their chosen YA novel. Students used Google Sites (https://sites.google.com/) and Wix (www.wix.com) to create nine genres that represented their group meaning-making through the use of narrative, informational/explanatory, and argumentative text structures. Kayla created a cause–effect flow chart (see Figure 7.2) for her group, showing why Allyson should go to Paris, for their multigenre paper titled "To Go or Not to Go" based on Gayle Forman's *Just One Day*.

And Erin created a bio poem (see Figure 7.3) and an argument (see Figure 7.4) for her group's paper based on Rainbow Rowell's *Eleanor & Park*. The multigenre approach offered students a forum to collaboratively make meaning and represent their thinking through practice with a variety of text structures.

I-Search

Another format that allows students to demonstrate their research around a unit focus or in response to essential questions is the I-Search. These papers are student focused and encourage writing around a researcher's journey. More process oriented than a traditional research paper, an I-Search shares the details of how a student has come to discover something new.

Macrorie (1988, pp. 62–64) defined the steps of the I-Search process as follows:

1. Allow your topic to choose you.
2. Find people; locate experts or authorities.
3. Read as much as you can about your topic before you actually meet people.
4. Interview people who know a lot about your topic.
5. Test the statements of experts against those of other experts.
6. Consult firsthand sources.
7. Tell your search as a story.

For example, a student researching journeys could interview others, asking them to define *journey* and to describe the kinds of journeys they have had in their lives. They could list, name, describe, define, classify, and compare–contrast these personal journeys with the journeys they have read about throughout

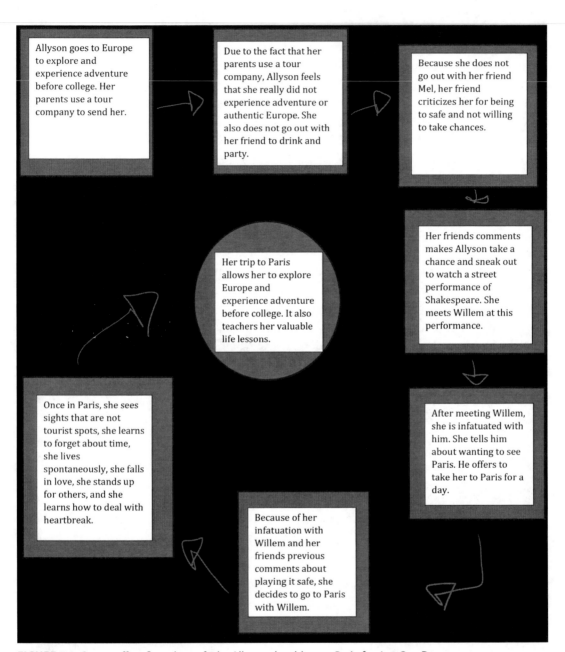

FIGURE 7.2. Cause–effect flow chart of why Allyson should go to Paris, for *Just One Day*.

> *Eleanor's Bio Poem*
> by Erin
>
> Eleanor
> Who is a kind of hero.
> Who needs a friend.
> Who feels attacked.
> Who fears her stepfather.
> Who gives everything for her mother and siblings.
> Who would like to see her family happy again.
> Who is definitely not like the other girls at school.
> Who typically wears crazy clothes that draw even more attention to her.
> Resident of a too small, worn down, 'home' that will never feel like home.
> Who is like a muggle Luna Lovegood.
> Who is made of frizzy red hair, a full figure, eccentric clothes, and unlimited sass.
> Who spent a year sleeping on couches before she could come back home.

FIGURE 7.3. Bio poem about Eleanor for *Eleanor & Park*.

> Eleanor the Hero
> by Erin
>
> Christopher Reeve once said that "a hero is an ordinary individual who finds the strength to persevere and endure in spite of overwhelming obstacles," and Eleanor perfectly embodies this definition of a hero. Throughout the novel, Eleanor shows extreme resiliency in the face of abuse from both her family and her classmates.
>
> After being kicked out of the house by her stepfather and spending a year living with her mother's friend, Eleanor returns home to her family. Despite clear signs of abuse from her stepfather, she decides that it is better to stay with her mother and siblings than to continue living away from them. One night after a fight between her parents, Eleanor wakes up and "A horrible thought came to her, and she got up, stumbling over the kids and the blankets. She opened the door and smelled bacon. Which meant that her mother was still alive….You couldn't not notice the bruise on the side of her face. Or the hickey under her chin" (49). This shows that Eleanor clearly believes Richie is capable of worse violence against her family because she feared for her mother's life. Still, she takes it upon herself to help take care of her younger siblings and shield them from abuse whenever possible. Additionally, she faces bullies at school for her weight and the way she dresses. Specifically, a group of girls on the bus call her "rag head" and put her clothes in the toilet during gym class. Despite this abuse, Eleanor keeps a 'cool tone' no matter how much they make fun of her.
>
> This shows Eleanor's resilience because resilient people encounter hardships, but do not lose who they are because of the obstacles they face. They stay true to themselves. Some may say that Eleanor should be stronger by standing up to the bullies in her family and at her school. She should force Richie to leave rather than living with this abuse and she should fight back against the students who mock her at school.
>
> However, I would argue that Eleanor chooses to stay not because it is easier, or because she is weak. She stays because she still values her family and wants to ensure that they are safe. This willingness to subject herself to the abuse she faces at home makes her a strong character. Additionally, her resilience does ultimately lead to her mother taking the children away from Richie. When Eleanor is finally forced to leave again, Park still goes by her family's house and says, "Sometimes the truck was there, sometimes, it wasn't, sometimes the Rottweiler was asleep on the porch. But the broken toys were gone, and there were never any strawberry blond kids playing in the yard. Josh said that Eleanor's little brother had stopped coming to school. Everybody says they're gone. The whole family.' 'That's great news,' their mother said, 'Maybe that pretty mom woke up to bad situation, you know?'" That final fight forced Eleanor's mother to face the situation she had been putting her family in and convinced her to take the rest of the children away from Richie. This probably would not have happened if Eleanor had stayed away. This shows that Eleanor's resilience actually saved the rest of her family.

FIGURE 7.4. Argument for *Eleanor & Park* multigenre paper.

the unit. Imagine the power and possibility of I-Searching other unit focuses such as social justice or civil liberty.

Once students have completed their search, they write up the process of their research. Rather than focus solely on the products of their inquiry or answers to their questions, they share the details of their process. Not so easily found on the Web, these first-person narratives detail why a topic is important and what a student initially knows about his topic, how she researched the topic, and what he learned about the topic. Macrorie (1988, p. 64) suggested the following format for the I-Search:

- What I Knew (and didn't know about my topic when I started out).
- Why I'm Writing This Paper (Here's where a real need should show up: the writer demonstrates that the search may make a difference in his life).
- The Search (story of the hunt).
- What I Learned (or didn't learn. A search that failed can be as exciting and valuable as one that succeeded).

Students document the story of their research process, from beginning to end, relating their search to the self.

How to Support the Workshop Writing Process

Teachers support the student writing process with a workshop environment. Described and encouraged by Atwell (1998), Calkins (1994), Fletcher and Porta-lupi (2001), Graves (1983/2003), Murray (2004), and Ray and Laminack (2001), writing workshops are student centered, social, and collaborative. Students are empowered with choices and encouraged to take responsibility for their own writing projects. Teachers allocate class time for reading, writing, and talking. Teachers design mini-lessons and share their sample writing to guide the individual writing process. Expectations are high, but the workshop environment is ensured through a variety of workshop structures, including mentor texts, writing plans, independent writing, writing circles, craft mini-lessons, and publishing opportunities. Each of these pieces fit together to form the whole of a writing workshop.

Mentor Texts

As we introduce diverse genres within a unit, workshopping teachers purpose-fully include *mentor texts*. We offer an array of models written by professional and student writers that provide examples of structure, craft, and technique. A mentor text can be any piece of writing: a novel, poem, short story, essay, comic book, play, newspaper/magazine article, or picture book. The type of text depends on the need. For example, if students are expected to construct an argument as a culminating unit assignment, then we need to provide a written model that demonstrates the structure and style of an argument. If students are expected to craft a narrative, then we need to include examples of story. If students are supposed to write a cause–effect paper, then we need to share sample essays. Mentor texts are related to the unit focus or essential questions whenever possible.

Students conduct a close reading of mentor texts, as described in Chapter 3, and teachers facilitate mini-lessons around structural components, as discussed in Chapter 6. For instance, when introducing students to a model classification essay, I asked students to discuss the following:

- What are the categories this author writes about?

- What do you notice about how this is written?

- What does the author do to make her categories clear? Describe? List? Itemize? Explain? Illustrate? Compare? Provide examples? Develop?

Mentor texts are studied and then imitated. In this way, we guide students to try new writing structures and strategies.

Writing Plans

A plan can take any form: a web, a list, a chart, notes, an outline, a graphic orga-nizer, or even a storyboard. The structure for a plan is influenced by the men-tor text. After analyzing the claim, evidence, warrant, and rebuttal of a model argument, students will want to include the same elements in their plan. For a classification essay, students might include categories as well as definitions and examples of each. A plan helps students organize their ideas.

Independent Writing

Opportunities for writing are the greatest gifts we can offer students in the workshopping classroom, as this will provide them a supportive community in which to grow with words. It is time uninterrupted and unencumbered for writing.

Writing Circles

Once students have begun drafting, they will want occasions to talk about what they are writing. *Writing circles* (Vopat, 2009) are small groups of students who gather together and respond to one another's writing throughout a unit. Writing circles evolve naturally from previously established book clubs. Students bring drafts and questions to the conversation, but groups aim for open and natural conversations around what they have written. Just as with book clubs, the teacher serves as a facilitator, not a member of the groups, and rotates among them. Writing circles gather more than once to support the writer through the process of drafting, revising, and editing.

Craft Mini-Lessons

As students are drafting, revising, and editing, a teacher provides support through mini-lessons. A *craft mini-lesson*, as discussed in Chapter 6, directs students to make observations about the ways in which a text is written. Noden (1999) and Anderson (2005) utilized authentic and accessible text to draw student attention to grammar and style. Robb (2012) has offered guidance for mini-lessons on strong verbs, specific nouns, show-don't-tell, figurative language, dialogue, direct quotations, paragraphing, transition sentences, sentence openings, run-ons, faulty pronoun references, punctuating complex sentences, using prepositional phrases, and comma usage. When we teach craft mini-lessons, our students learn to read like writers and write like readers.

Publishing Opportunities

Teachers also support the workshop writing process when they provide opportunities to *publish writing*. When students post a book review on Amazon.com, read ninth-grade survival manuals to eighth graders, present multimodal multigenre projects to the community, they perceive themselves as writers. They recognize a purpose for writing and see an audience for their written material. We want to provide students opportunities to celebrate their learning in authentic ways. After all, written words—these relics of our thinking, these works of art—are meant to be shared.

Chapter Summary

In the workshopping classroom, writing and researching emerge naturally from reading, and students engage in both writing as process and writing as product. Students write throughout a focus unit, clarifying their meaning-making during read-alouds, independent reading, shared reading, close reading, readers theater, book clubs, Socratic circles, and mini-lessons. Students also write in response to a unit focus and/or essential questions at the conclusion of a unit, creating a culminating narrative, informative/explanatory (e.g., list, summary, description, process, definition, compare–contrast, classification, cause–effect, and problem–solution), argumentative, literary, multigenre, or I-Search paper or project to demonstrate their thinking and meet the CCR anchor standards for writing. Workshopping teachers support the writing process through a variety of workshop structures, including mentor texts, writing plans, independent writing, writing circles, craft mini-lessons, and publishing opportunities. Each of these pieces fits together to form the whole of a writing workshop, which extends naturally from the reading workshop.

8

Workshopping as a Process

Think of what you can do with that there is.

—ERNEST HEMINGWAY, *The Old Man and the Sea*

Workshopping the canon requires a great deal of thinking and planning, and this chapter explains how to shape the curriculum and classroom using workshopping as a process. When we organize the workshop, we consider how structures such as read-alouds, independent reading, response engagements, shared and close reading, readers theater, book clubs, Socratic circles, mini-lessons, mentor texts, writing plans, independent writing, writing circles, and publishing connect with one another and form a cohesive and holistic reading and writing experience. We add texts to the workshop, matching what students and the teacher are doing with what the students and the teacher are reading. We create assignments that motivate students to take part in a reading mini-lesson or book club conversation. We derive standards and objectives from national, state, or district expectations as well as from student engagement with the structures, strategies, and texts encountered during the workshop. The final stage of workshopping involves creating a unit calendar. This visual mapping of days helps teachers and students see the connections between workshop structures.

This chapter describes and demonstrates the reciprocal processes of organizing the workshop structures, adding texts to the workshop, devising assignments for students, meeting standards and objectives, and creating a unit calendar using an example drawn from the canon. Workshopping is a process that shows teachers how to bring order to "that there is."

How to Workshop as a Process

Developing, implementing, and facilitating a workshop requires a great deal of preparation. Teachers actually begin the workshopping process as they find a unit focus, ask essential questions, and collect diverse texts, as introduced in Chapter 1. While Chapters 2–7 described the reading and writing workshop structures and strategies used to workshop the canon, these structures and strategies now need to be arranged in such a way as to bring order to the workshop experience for students and the teacher.

Organizing the workshop structures involves considering how read-aloud, readers theater, or independent writing connect with one another. We want structures to fit together like a puzzle, forming a cohesive and holistic picture of classroom literature and literacy experience. Will a read-aloud of a particular text lead into a reading mini-lesson during which students construct mental images? Will book clubs evolve naturally from independent reading? Will a literary close reading follow?

What will students read during a shared reading experience? While we have already collected a wide variety of texts, *adding texts to the workshop* involves specifically matching what the students and the teacher are doing with what the students and the teacher are reading. For example, what will the teacher read aloud as she provides a reading mini-lesson or facilitates a response engagement? Which text will students read independently and discuss with their book clubs?

How will students demonstrate their involvement during a literary mini-lesson or participation during a book club conversation? When *devising assignments for students*, teachers create classwork that motivates students to engage in a language close reading or take part in a Socratic circle, ensuring that assignments encourage response and promote comprehension through authentic reading and writing experiences.

Meeting standards and objectives is one of the final processes when workshopping the canon, as these criteria derive not only from national, state, or district guidelines but also from the texts, structures, and strategies encountered during the workshop.

The workshopping process concludes with *creating a unit calendar*. This visual mapping of days helps teachers and students see the connections between workshop structures and frees everyone to live the workshop process.

The following section demonstrates the process of workshopping the canon, including how to organize the workshop structures, add texts to the workshop, devise assignments for students, meet standards and objectives, and create a unit calendar (using *Beowulf* as a core text and heroes as a unit focus). Narratives of teachers describing their workshopping process with a variety of other canonical texts follow. The chapter concludes with questions and guidance for teachers to consider as they workshop their own classroom and curriculum.

Organizing the Workshop Structures

Once teachers have decided on a core text, unit focus, essential questions, and diverse texts, it is time to select and organize the reading and writing workshop structures and strategies to be included. For example, knowing that I want to spend about four weeks on a unit including *Beowulf*, realizing that I will not be able to include every component of a reading and writing workshop, and accepting that depth is better than breadth, I opt to design a reading workshop that allows time for read-alouds, shared reading, independent reading, book clubs, reading mini-lessons, response engagements, vocabulary mini-lessons, and literary mini-lessons.

Organizing the writing workshop requires me to think backwards. I want some sort of culminating project that includes writing, relates to the unit focus on heroes, and leads students to make connections across texts and ideas. Once I decide students will write a narrative, the writing workshop will include mentor texts, writing plans, independent writing, craft mini-lessons, writing circles, and publishing.

After making these larger decisions concerning the components of reading and writing workshop to be included in this unit, a teacher next considers how the workshop structures might connect with or expand from one another. We want one structure and engagement to grow naturally and authentically from another. For example, a read-aloud of *Beowulf* can provide a wonderfully rich springboard for literary discussion, strategic teaching, or word study. We can combine read-alouds with a variety of mini-lessons. In doing so, we will engage in shared reading as students follow along with their own copies of the poem, noting some of the characteristics of Anglo Saxon poetry, such as caesura, alliteration, and kennings. Together, we might also note challenging vocabulary and engage in word study.

I could also utilize the read-aloud as a means of involving students in reading mini-lessons, modeling my reading process for students while reading aloud to them. As the Anglo Saxon poem contains much vivid imagery, I opt to design reading mini-lessons around visualization. Moving from reading aloud to a language close reading will help students read like writers, note new vocabulary, and allow for a craft mini-lesson focused on imagery. But I need to be careful. My zeal for literary analysis and strategic teaching could distract students from the simple pleasure of the read-aloud experience. I also want to allow time for those purely aesthetic moments when students are encouraged to take pleasure in the language experience. Response engagements will nurture student transaction with the text.

So far I have determined how the read-aloud, shared reading, literary minilessons, reading mini-lessons, vocabulary mini-lessons, craft mini-lessons, and response engagements will relate to one another within the larger workshop frame. I still need to decide how I will incorporate independent reading, book clubs, independent writing, writing circles, and publishing.

As mentioned in earlier chapters, students will read a variety of different genres at the same time they are reading *Beowulf*. Together, we will unpack the characteristics of an epic hero and consider heroes in modern-day society. Students will make selections from informational articles and comic books. They will consider *Beowulf* from a different point of view and experience an epic from a different culture. Students will select a biography, autobiography, or memoir about a hero. They will read independently during class and discuss these works within book clubs. Time will be allotted for independent writing as students draft narratives and work on book club projects. There will be opportunities for sharing ideas and drafts in writing circles and teacher conferences, and finished papers and projects will be posted and shared.

Adding Texts to the Workshop

A workshopping teacher has to decide how the texts will be paired with the workshop structures. For example, I mentioned above that I want to include read-alouds and shared reading. But which literary work will I read aloud to students and use as a springboard for literary, reading, vocabulary, and craft mini-lessons? As *Beowulf* and the *Mwindo Epic* were passed orally from generation to generation, it makes perfect sense for these texts to be read aloud. They are difficult for students to read alone, and reading them together allows me to model fluent reading, introduce literary elements, teach reading strategies, explain difficult vocabulary, and offer craft lessons along the way.

Students will read more accessible texts independently. They will read informational texts (e.g., newspaper and magazine articles about modern day heroes) and comic books about superheroes. They will select a biography, autobiography, or memoir heroic in theme. How-to mini-lessons will be provided on the book club process as students read and discuss these texts during book club meetings. Students will watch an epic movie of their choice.

Devising Assignments for Students

How will students demonstrate their involvement during a mini-lesson or participation during a book club conversation? When devising assignments for students, teachers consider how we are affirming student response, comprehension, or participation during the workshop structures and strategies. We create assignments that motivate students to engage in a reading mini-lesson or take part in a book club conversation. And we want to provide both formative and summative feedback to students about these assignments.

For this unit, students will keep evidence of their participation during mini-lessons and response engagements in a print or online binder (see Appendix D), which represents a certain number of points. Homework assignments including the movie response sheet are also worth points (see Appendix E). Participation in book clubs comprises points for this unit too (see Appendix F). Participation in the writing circle counts as points. As I like to balance a test grade with a project grade, the unit test (see Appendix G) and book club project are worth similar points. The culminating written narrative is worth points as well (see Appendix H). Sample descriptions of all of these assignments are included in the appendixes.

Meeting Standards and Objectives

Undoubtedly, standards and objectives will vary, depending on the unit, and these will be derived from national, state, and district guidelines as well as from student engagement with the structures, strategies, and texts encountered during the workshop. Through this unit, many CCR anchor standards (National Governors Association, 2010) for reading, speaking and listening, writing, and language are met (see Figure 8.1).

As for simplified objectives for this unit, students will:

- define *hero* in the context of literature and society;
- visualize text to increase comprehension and consider the relationship between visualization and imagery;
- compare and contrast qualities of an epic hero as presented through varied media;
- read independently for a sustained period of time;
- respond to texts, making personal and societal connections;
- reflect critically on responses to text and media;

Reading

Key Ideas and Details

2. Determine central ideas or themes of a text and analyze their development.

Craft and Structure

4. Interpret words and phrases as they are used in a text, including determining technical, connotative, and figurative meanings, and analyze how specific words choices shape meaning or tone.
6. Assess how point of view or purpose shapes the content and style of a text.

Integration of Knowledge and Ideas

7. Integrate and evaluate content presented in diverse media and formats, including visually and quantitatively, as well as in words.
9. Analyze how two or more texts address similar themes or topics in order to build knowledge or to compare the approaches the authors take.

Range of Reading and Level of Text Complexity

10. Read and comprehend complex literary and informational texts independently and proficiently.

Speaking and Listening

Comprehension and Collaboration

1. Prepare for and participate effectively in a range of conversations and collaborations with diverse partners, building on others' ideas and expressing their own clearly and persuasively.
2. Integrate and evaluate information presented in diverse media and formats, including visually, quantitatively, and orally.

Presentation of Knowledge and Ideas

5. Make strategic use of digital media and visual displays of data to express information and enhance understanding of presentations.

Writing

Text Types and Purposes

3. Write narratives to develop real or imagined experiences or events using effective technique, well-chosen details, and well-structured event sequences.

Production and Distribution of Writing

4. Produce clear and coherent writing in which the development, organization, and style are appropriate to task, purpose, and audience.
5. Develop and strengthen writing as needed by planning, revising, editing, rewriting, or trying a new approach.
6. Use technology, including the Internet, to produce and publish writing and to interact and collaborate with others.

Range of Writing

10. Write routinely over extended time frames (time for research, reflection, and revision) and shorter time frames (a single sitting or a day or two) for a range of tasks, purposes, and audiences.

Language

Conventions of Standard English

1. Demonstrate command of the conventions of standard English grammar and usage when writing or speaking.
2. Demonstrate command of the conventions of standard English capitalization, punctuation, and spelling when writing.

Vocabulary Acquisition and Use

4. Determine or clarify the meaning of unknown and multiple-meaning words and phrases by using context clues, analyzing meaningful word parts, and consulting general and specialized reference materials, as appropriate.
5. Demonstrate understanding of figurative language, word relationships, and nuances in word meanings.

FIGURE 8.1. CCR anchor standards for *heroes* focus unit.

- work collaboratively as a group member;
- explore characteristics of Anglo Saxon poetry;
- discuss characteristics of an epic and epic hero;
- consider point of view in literature;
- identify and define new vocabulary in the context of reading; and
- write a narrative.

Creating a Unit Calendar

Once I have a focus determined; essential questions asked; the core and supporting texts selected; the workshop structures organized; the texts matched with structures; the assignments aligned with structures, standards, objectives; and the standards and objectives met through structures and assignments, I conclude the workshopping process by creating a unit calendar, to help everyone see the connections among the workshop structures. As an example, I have outlined a four-week *heroes* unit as a means to prompt your own thinking around workshopping the classroom curriculum. While some of us have forty-four-minute class periods that meet every day, others have ninety-minute classes that meet every other day or meet only for a single semester. For the purposes of description, a *day* in this calendar (see Figure 8.2) represents a sixty-minute class period.

Now that we share a common understanding of the process of workshopping the canon, it is time to translate this idea into classroom realities. The remainder of this chapter shares stories of teachers workshopping the canon. They detail their classroom teaching, making the often invisible and always messy processes of planning visible to encourage others. These units are provided as examples to springboard your own curricular conversations about how best to interweave reading and writing workshop with the canon.

Workshopping *Romeo and Juliet* (Jessica's Classroom)

As discussed in Chapter 1, Jessica and I implemented a reading and writing workshop around the cornerstone classical text *Romeo and Juliet*. Our unit focus was ill-fated love, so we began by discussing unfortunate relationships. We considered star-crossed lovers in movies and on television. We listened to songs such as Taylor Swift's "Love Story" and We the Kings' "Check Yes Juliet" to introduce the unit focus. To prompt higher levels of critical thinking across texts,

Monday	Tuesday	Wednesday	Thursday	Friday
• Introduce unit focus • Watch movie trailers of epics and heroes • Show varied images of heroes as depicted through diverse media, including books, film, TV, graphics, comic books, and video games • Show images of historical and current heroes from around the world • Discuss essential questions: What defines a hero? What are heroic actions? • Read aloud short story (from *The Struggle to be Strong: True Stories by Teens about Overcoming Tough Times*) • Reading mini-lesson (making connections) • Discuss essential questions again: What defines a hero? What are heroic actions? • How-to mini-lesson (classwork binder)	• Introduce newspaper and magazine articles about heroes • Independent reading • Response engagement • How-to mini-lesson (book/article clubs) • Book/article club meeting (groups based on article choice) • Book/article clubs share	• Literary mini-lesson (historical background of *Beowulf*) • Shared strategic reading (*Beowulf*) • Reading mini-lesson (visualization) • Literary mini-lesson (imagery) • Independent reading (*Beowulf*)	• Close reading (*Beowulf*) • Literary mini-lesson (characteristics of Anglo Saxon poetry) • Vocabulary mini-lesson • Read aloud (*Beowulf*)	• Close language reading (*Beowulf*) • Vocabulary mini-lesson • Literary mini-lesson (epic, epic hero) • How-to mini-lesson (movie response sheet)
• Literary mini-lesson (point of view) • Read aloud (from *Grendel*) • Response engagement	• How-to mini-lesson (how to read a graphic) • Independent reading (choice of *Batman, Superman, Wonder Woman, Spider-Man, Captain America, X-Men, Wolverine, Hulk, The New Avengers, Justice League* comics) • Response engagement	• Discuss movie response sheets • Book pass (biographies, autobiographies, and memoirs of heroes) • Independent reading • How-to mini-lesson (response journal in classwork binder or response blog)	• Independent reading (biographies, autobiographies, and memoirs of heroes) • Response journal or blog • Book club meeting	• Literary mini-lesson (historical/cultural background of the *Mwindo Epic*) • Read aloud (from the *Mwindo Epic*) • Literary mini-lesson (epic, epic hero) • Independent reading (biographies, autobiographies, and memoirs of heroes)

FIGURE 8.2. Unit calendar for *Beowulf*.

continued on next page

FIGURE 8.2. Continued.

Monday	Tuesday	Wednesday	Thursday	Friday
	• Book/comic club meeting (groups based on comic choice) • Critical mini-lesson (what shapes our response to heroic images) • Discuss essential questions again: What defines a hero? What are heroic actions?			
• Independent reading (biographies, autobiographies, and memoirs of heroes) • Response journal or blog • How-to mini-lesson (book club project) • Book club project planning	• Independent reading (biographies, autobiographies, and memoirs of heroes) • Response journal or blog • Book club project planning	• Unit test review • Book club project planning	• Unit test • Book club project planning	• Present book club projects
• Close reading (mentor narrative text) • How-to mini-lesson (heroic narrative essay) • Writing plans	• Writing plans or independent writing • Craft mini-lesson (show-don't-tell, figurative and sensory language) • How-to mini-lesson (writing circle and teacher conferences) • Writing circles and teacher conferences	• Close reading (mentor narrative text) • Independent writing • Writing circles and teacher conferences	• Craft mini-lesson (dialogue, sentence structure) • Independent writing • Writing circles and teacher conferences	• Publishing writing (heroic narrative essay)

we asked the following essential questions: "Are some relationships more ill-fated than others?" and "To what extent are Romeo and Juliet victims of fate or their own poor decisions?"

After exploring the unit focus and establishing essential questions, we introduced students to the supplementary texts. We purposefully selected more contemporary and accessible genres that complemented the canonical text and expanded the unit focus. We introduced a variety of YA novels through book talks and book passes. Eventually, students voted on their top three choices, selecting among John Green's *The Fault in Our Stars*, Simon Elkeles's *Perfect*

Chemistry, Ally Condie's *Matched*, Walter Dean Myers's *Street Love*, Mary E. Pearson's *Scribbler of Dreams*, Gordon Korman's *Son of the Mob*, Jacqueline Woodson's *If You Come Softly*, and Sharon Draper's *Romiette and Julio*. Students were placed in book clubs based on their choices, with some consideration given to student personalities and reading abilities.

Once we introduced the unit focus and diverse texts, the reading workshop took on a mostly predictable structure. Barring field trips and mandated testing, students engaged in shared reading and close reading of Shakespeare's play three days a week. Sometimes, students read independently for homework. Jessica conducted literary mini-lessons on iambic pentameter, blank verse, puns, and paradox. To help students overcome some of their anxiety about Shakespeare's language, she showed a TEDx talk by British hip-hop artist Akala (TEDx Talks, 2011). Through his talk, students were able to make connections between modern hip-hop artists like JAY-Z, Eminem, and the Wu-Tang Clan to Shakespeare, both in terms of subject matter and rhythm. Following a craft mini-lesson, students rewrote the Prologue using modern-day language and situations (Mast, 2002). To help students visualize, Jessica showed snippets of various film adaptations and taped performances of the play. Students formed tableaux in response to certain scenes. They also drew body biographies, to create visual and artistic representations of characters. Additional literary mini-lessons introduced foils, soliloquys, imagery, and figurative language; these were followed by close readings of key scenes, highlighting the subject matter of each mini-lesson. Jessica used a wide variety of methods to engage students with both the content and language of the play.

On alternate days, we switched texts and focused on YA novels. Students and teachers read independently, making themselves comfortable along the walls or squabbling over the beanbags. Sometimes, reading conferences were held. After reading, Mary prodded personal connections, helping students recall experiences, elicit associations, and prompt reactions to what they were reading. These were recorded in a response journal. As responses were shared, the interpretive community grew. A mini-lesson would follow, focusing either on reading strategies (e.g., visualization, questions, predictions), literary analysis (e.g., story elements, figurative language), or author's craft (e.g., syntax, style). Students then met within book clubs, using the ideas and products of mini-lessons to move conversation along. If time allowed, each group would briefly share what they talked about. Students reflected on their book club experiences in writing.

Writing workshops evolved from the reading workshops as students wrote in response to the unit focus and novels read. Approximately two weeks into the unit, they began writing a multigenre paper that demonstrated their thinking about *Romeo and Juliet* as well as their book club novel, choosing an idea that bound the two texts and different genres together into a coherent paper. Along with a title, table of contents, and introduction, students created six to nine different informational/explanatory formats, including lists, summary, description, process description, comparison–contrast, cause–effect, and definition, in response to both *Romeo and Juliet* and their YA novel. On the last day, students wrote a reflection on their writing process.

As workshop teachers, we supported student writing in a variety of ways. We provided mini-lessons on different genres, including models of craft. We afforded time and technology for writing. We offered feedback on drafts of varied genres written for homework. Students also met with their book clubs (also known as writing circles) to share drafts and gain feedback. When finished, students published their final copies and thereby shared with classmates.

Workshopping *Animal Farm* (Kayla's Classroom)

George Orwell's *Animal Farm* is a canonical text that is required reading within the district that I teach. Therefore, it was important to workshop this novel, to make it more intriguing and relatable to my ninth-grade students. So I decided to focus a unit around the idea that absolute power corrupts absolutely. Teenagers relate to this idea because many of them feel powerless and controlled by parents, teachers, and other adults. They also have studied the Holocaust in history class and have background knowledge of historical leaders who have used and abused power.

Tied to the unit focus are essential questions. These essential questions relate the core text to all of the additional texts throughout the unit. "How does power or lack of power affect individuals?" encouraged students to think about the ways in which power affects individuals who hold and do not hold power. "What is the role of an individual in his/her society?" prompted students to think about characters and their own role in society. Finally, "How does propaganda influence the actions of an individual?" allowed students to critique characters in the texts and consider how persuasion can be used to manipulate others. This essential question also helped them discover how everyday propaganda affects them.

I began this unit asking students to visualize some of the beliefs they hold. I placed signs with the texts "strongly agree," "somewhat agree," "somewhat disagree," and "strongly disagree" in the four corners of the classroom. I told students that I was going to read a statement to them. They then had to move to the sign they felt expressed their belief in relation to the statement. For example,

I read the statements "Children should always listen to their parents," "The government usually does what is best for the most people," "You should always believe everything that you are told," "All humans are equal," and so on. After each statement, I called on two people from each sign to explain why they responded the way that they did. This opinion survey set the tone for many of the concepts students would uncover in their shared and close reading of *Animal Farm*.

Following this engagement, we discussed the unit focus and essential questions. Then I introduced students to their book club texts, using book passes and book trailers for each of the titles. Students voted on their top four choices. I arranged students into book clubs based on their choices and personalities. Once students were placed into book clubs, they created their norms and reading schedules. Book clubs met every Friday during this unit.

The next day, I read aloud the picture book *Bossy Bear* by David Horvath. As I read, I asked students to pay close attention to Bossy Bear's actions. After I finished reading, I asked the students to write in their reader response journals, describing how Bossy Bear abused his power. I promoted personal response: "Have you ever known anyone who has abused his/her power in some way?" "Have you ever abused your power? Why? What happened?" We then held a class discussion, and students shared their responses. Students kept journals for the entire unit, responding to numerous texts and response engagements.

Later, I conducted a literary mini-lesson on the Russian Revolution of 1917, introducing the key figures. Students made flashcards that paired the historical figure with the appropriate character in the novel. Once the historical context was set, the reading workshop took on a predictable structure. Students engaged in shared and close reading of *Animal Farm*, two to three days a week. They would read independently their YA novels for homework. Every Friday, students met with their book clubs to discuss their YA novels.

I taught a variety of reading mini-lessons throughout the unit, guiding students to make connections, visualize, and question. I taught craft mini-lessons on the rhetorical triangle (ethos, pathos, logos) and propaganda. Literary mini-lessons were focused around allegory and theme, and were followed by close readings of the text highlighting the subject matter of the mini-lesson. For example, after I taught the rhetorical triangle, students conducted a close reading of Old Major's speech, highlighting and identifying pathos, ethos, and logos. How-to, reading, and literary mini-lessons were also taught each week, before students' book club meetings. This way, students had notes to share during conversations. They also used their responses in their reader response journals to foster conversations with their book clubs.

The writing workshop emerged from the reading workshop. Three weeks into the unit, students were given a choice of either working in a group or independently to complete a culminating project. They could create a propaganda poster, political speech, and propaganda commercial in a group, or they could individually create a fictional protest/revolution project and write a manifesto, create a handout, and gather props for their protest. These projects utilized a variety of informational/explanatory text structures. During the last two weeks of the unit, students constructed an argumentative essay in response to one of six provided prompts. Their essay response had to use textual examples from *Animal Farm*, their YA novel, and two other texts read in class.

As a workshop teacher, I supported student writing in a variety of ways. Primarily, I used mentor texts for students to refer to during their writing process. I provided students with feedback on drafts. For their final argumentative paper, I had one-on-one conferences with students. They also provided one another with peer feedback in their book club/writing circles, and they shared their projects and essays with classmates. They were also provided the opportunity to submit their writing to *Teen Ink* for publication.

Workshopping *Lord of the Flies* (Nicole's Classroom)

William Golding's classic novel *Lord of the Flies* presents an opportunity to examine the complexity of humanity, and why we are drawn to collective experience over individual existence. Since the collective experience requires leadership to maintain order, the novel provides an entry into a unit focus on the difference between power and control of a group, and what kind of leaders gravitate toward each particular method of influence. This focus is organized around three essential questions: "What is an individual's responsibility to a community?," "Do individuals control groups, or do groups control individuals?," and "How do fear and desire for acceptance influence human behavior?"

To answer these questions, we explored multiple texts. First, I wanted students to understand what it is to move beyond the comforts of society and to consider how quickly a person might be forced to cast off the bounds of social norms in order to survive. So we began with reading the nonfiction *I Had to Survive* by Roberto Canessa, about the 1972 Andes plane crash, and a powerful example of the trials that exist that might push a human to do something he or she never thought himself or herself capable of doing. This work offers insight into the psychology of loneliness, despair, and the drive for survival. In many ways, the text helps provide an emotional context for what otherwise might seem arbitrary actions of the boys in the next text, *Lord of the Flies*.

As for the structure of our workshop, once students were introduced to the unit focus, essential questions, and *I Had to Survive*, they continued reading this work independently; time was allotted, three days per week, for silent, sustained reading, and students were asked to read for homework as well. As a class, we share and close read *Lord of the Flies*. Other texts were introduced throughout the unit. Richard Connell's "The Most Dangerous Game" provided students with a juxtaposition, as this short story focuses not on what people must do outside the bounds of social norms, but instead on what they want to do (i.e., as the antagonist of the story intentionally hunts humans). This provided a contrast that springboarded discussions about the difference between Jack and the others of his group as he has chosen a path not out of necessity but out of desire. Jack, the dark foil to the protagonist Ralph, prods a complex look at a leader who wishes to use his influence for his own animalistic gratifications. Poetry, by its very nature, easily taps into the emotional pulse of this idea, and students found rich discussions in other comparison texts, including "In a Dark Time" by Theodore Roethke and "Sympathy for the Devil" by the Rolling Stones, which both deal with the darker nature of man and the impulse to explore that nature.

In addition to the intensive discussions held in class, I structured a Socratic circle about midway through the unit. Following a how-to mini-lesson on questioning, students drafted questions on index cards in response to texts read before they left class. I read through the questions overnight, providing feedback and guiding students to ask open-ended, thought-provoking, and clear questions. The next day, I gave the index cards back, offered a brief review how-to mini-lesson about our guidelines for Socratic circles, and we were off.

We spent a great deal of time studying the craft of *Lord of the Flies*. I emphasize with students that, if literature presents windows and mirrors, we need to take the time to unpack how this is done, in an effort to apply those insights to other areas of life. Noticing and noting craft is exactly that. So I taught a variety of craft mini-lessons and encouraged language close reading.

Similarly, we spent a day noticing imagery. First, I taught a literary mini-lesson and then facilitated a literary close reading, instructing students to:

- Find a passage that contains imagery and write it down on a sheet of paper.

- Highlight/underline/note the descriptive phrases in the passage.

- Below the passage, explain how you knew it was imagery, and ask yourself, "Why did the author use this imagery, these descriptive phrases, instead of something else?" Examine your thoughts in a short paragraph.

- Repeat this process three times and be ready to discuss your results.

Our vocabulary mini-lessons focused on the authors' word choices. Our vocabulary work is also in hopes of cross-application. We spent time creating word maps, finding examples of the word in other texts, and creating image/connotation streams that are posted to our ongoing Google Site that students can reference at all times.

The culminating assignment for this unit was a written literary argument, answering one of the essential questions: "What is an individual's responsibility to a community?," "Do individuals control groups, or do groups control individuals?," or "How do fear and desire for acceptance influence human behavior?" Students were asked to collect evidence from a variety of texts read throughout the unit. They were supported in their process during writing workshop as we studied mentor texts, planned for writing, drafted, revised, conferenced, and edited.

Workshopping Your Classroom and Curriculum

> She had not known the weight until she felt the freedom.
> —Nathaniel Hawthorne, *The Scarlet Letter*

There is great weight that comes with teaching the canon, but workshopping frees us to bridge the divide between literature and literacy. Through reading and writing workshop structures and strategies, teachers can interweave authentic reading and writing processes, increase student comprehension and motivation, reach diverse learners, and foster diverse perspectives.

In this final chapter, I have explained how to shape the classroom and curriculum using workshopping as a process. Three teachers have shared their workshopping classrooms and curriculum. I now encourage you to consider the following as you begin the process of workshopping the canon:

- What is a core canonical text you want to teach?
- Decide on a focus for a unit of study, including this core text.
- Ask essential questions.
- List other genres to supplement the core text and support the unit focus.
- What structures and strategies of the reading and writing workshop do you want to include?
- How will you organize the structures and strategies?
- Which texts will you partner with workshop structures and strategies?

- What assignments can you design that will affirm student comprehension and participation when workshopping?

- What standards and objectives will you meet?

- Create a unit calendar.

Chapter Summary

Teachers actually begin the workshopping process as they find a unit focus, ask essential questions, and collect diverse text, as introduced in Chapter 1. While Chapters 2–7 describe the reading and writing workshop structures and strategies used to workshop the canon, these now need to be arranged in such a way as to bring order to the workshop experience for the students and the teacher.

This chapter describes the reciprocal processes of organizing the workshop structures, adding texts to the workshop, devising assignments for students, meeting standards and objectives, and creating a unit calendar using *Beowulf* as a core text and heroes as a unit focus. Stories of teachers workshopping a variety of other canonical texts, including *Romeo and Juliet, Animal Farm,* and *Lord of the Flies,* follow. The chapter concludes with questions and guidance for teachers to consider as they workshop their own classroom and curriculum.

Appendixes

Appendix A

Canonical Texts with Sample Unit Foci and Essential Questions

Canonical Text	Sample Unit Focus	Sample Essential Question
To Kill a Mockingbird	Justice	Is social justice attainable?
Fahrenheit 451 or *1984*	Freedom of thought, speech, and expression	What are the effects of censoring thoughts, speech, language, and expression?
Romeo and Juliet	Ill-fated love	What is the relationship between love and fate?
Hamlet	Making decisions	How much control do we have over our choices and actions?
Julius Caesar or *Animal Farm*	Power and corruption	Does power lead to corruption?
The Odyssey	Journey	What is more important, the journey or destination?
Beowulf	Heroes	What defines a hero and heroic action?
Macbeth or *Dr. Faustus*	Dark side of ambition	What is the dark side of ambition?
The Crucible or *The Scarlet Letter*	Persecution	How and why do we persecute others?
Lord of the Flies	Survival	What does it take to survive?
1984 or *Brave New World* or *Fahrenheit 451*	Dystopia/utopia	Is utopia possible?
The Great Gatsby or *A Raisin in the Sun*	American dream	Is the American dream equally accessible?
Night or *The Diary of a Young Girl*	Resilience	What hope, if any, may be found in times of hopelessness?

Appendix B

Canonical Texts with Sample Unit Foci, Essential Questions, and Supplementary Texts

Canonical Text	Sample Unit Focus	Sample Essential Question	Sample Supplementary Texts
To Kill a Mockingbird	Justice	Is social justice attainable?	**YA Novels** · Chris Crowe, *Mississippi Trial, 1955* · Karen Hesse, *Witness* · Susan Carol McCarthy, *Lay that Trumpet in Our Hands* · Mildred D. Taylor, *Roll of Thunder, Hear My Cry* · Christopher Paul Curtis, *The Watsons Go to Birmingham, 1963* · Cynthia Kadohata, *Kira-Kira* · Sue Monk Kidd, *The Secret Life of Bees* · Lorene Cary, *Black Ice* **Short Stories** · James Hurst, "The Scarlet Ibis" · Alice Walker, "The Flowers" **Informational Texts** · Martin Luther King Jr., "I Have a Dream" · Sara Corbett, "A Prom Divided," www.nytimes.com · Mary Mebane, "The Back of the Bus" · Trayvon Martin, www.nytimes.com/pages/topics · Matthew Shepard, www.nytimes.com/pages/topics · Brent Staples, "Black Men and Public Space" · Judy Brady, "I Want a Wife" · James Goodman, *Stories of Scottsboro* · Melba Pattillo Beals, *Warriors Don't Cry* **Picture Books** · Eve Bunting, *Smoky Night* · Deborah Wiles, *Freedom Summer* · Eve Bunting, *Terrible Things* · Becky Birtha, *Grandmama's Pride* **Poetry** · Edna St. Vincent Millay, "Justice Denied in Massachusetts" · Maya Angelou, "Still I Rise" and "Equality" · Langston Hughes, "Freedom" and "I, Too, Sing America" **Music** · The Black Eyed Peas, "Where is the Love?" · Ben Harper and Jack Johnson, "My Own Two Hands" · Bob Marley, "Buffalo Soldier" · OutKast, "Rosa Parks" · Aretha Franklin, "Think"

Canonical Text	Sample Unit Focus	Sample Essential Question	Sample Supplementary Texts
			Art · Frederick C. Baldwin, *Freedom's March: Photographs of the Civil Rights Movement in Savannah* Movies · *Freedom Writers* · *Pleasantville* Graphic Novels · Marshall Poe and Ellen Lindner, *Little Rock Nine*
Fahrenheit 451 or *1984*	Freedom of thought, speech, and expression	What are the effects of censoring thoughts, speech, language, and expression?	YA Novels · M. T. Anderson, *Feed* · Scott Westerfeld, *Uglies* · Laurie Halse Anderson, *Speak* · Avi, *Nothing But the Truth* · Robert Cormier, *The Chocolate War* · Rodman Philbrick, *The Last Book in the Universe* · Lois Lowry, *The Giver* Short Stories · Kurt Vonnegut, "Harrison Bergeron" · Ray Bradbury, "Usher II" · Luisa Valenzuela, "The Censors" Informational Texts · U.S. Constitution, First Amendment · Jonathan Kozol, "The Human Cost of an Illiterate Society" · George Orwell, "Politics and the English Language" · McClatchy-Tribune News Service, "Should Snowden Get a Freedom Medal or Jail Time?," https://newsela.com/ · Kirk Johnson, "Today's Kids Are, Like, Killing the English Language" · Floyd Abrams, "Save Free Speech" · Brock Read, "Can Wikipedia Ever Make the Grade?" · Richard Rodriguez, "Private Language, Public Language" · *Common Sense, The Rights of Man, and Other Essential Writings of Thomas Paine* · Frederick Douglass, "Learning to Read and Write" · Jonathan Dame, "Will Employers Still Ask for Facebook Passwords in 2014?," www.usa.com · "What's Wrong with Public Video Surveillance?," https://www.aclu.org/ · Jaime Sarrio, "Tennessee Teen Expelled for Facebook Posting," www.usa.com · "Banned and Challenged Books," www.ala.org · Internet Censorship, www.huffingtonpost.com · Student Press Law Center, www.splc.org

Canonical Text	Sample Unit Focus	Sample Essential Question	Sample Supplementary Texts
			Picture Books · Toni Morrison, *The Big Box* · Paul Buckley and Kate Buckley, *Amy Belligera and the Fireflies* **Poetry** · Langston Hughes, "Freedom's Plow" · Sylvia Chidi, "Freedom is Walking" · Stephen Crane, "Think As I Think" · Jeffrey McDaniel, "The Quiet World" **Music** · Muse, "Uprising" · 2 Live Crew, "Banned in the USA" · Green Day, "American Idiot" **Art** · Norman Rockwell, *Freedom of Speech* **TV** · *The Twilight Zone*, "Number 12 Looks Just Like You" **Movies** · *WALL-E* · *Idiocracy*
Romeo and Juliet	Ill-fated love	What is the relationship between love and fate?	**YA Novels** · Ally Condie, *Matched* · Simone Elkeles, *Perfect Chemistry* · John Green, *The Fault in Our Stars* · Rainbow Rowell, *Eleanor & Park* · Sabaa Tahir, *An Ember in the Ashes* · Gayle Forman, *Just One Day* · Sharon M. Draper, *Romiette and Julio* · Gordon Korman, *Son of the Mob* · Jamie Ford, *Hotel on the Corner of Bitter and Sweet* · Stephenie Meyer, *Twilight* · Walter Dean Myers, *Street Love* · Mary E. Pearson, *Scribbler of Dreams* · Jerry Spinelli, *Stargirl* · Jacqueline Woodson, *If You Come Softly* **Short Stories** · Walter Dean Myers, "Kitty and Mack: A Love Story" **Informational Texts** · Matthew Price, "Star-Crossed Lovers Quit West Bank," http://news.bbc.co.uk/ · Amanda Foreman, "A History of Star-Crossed Lovers," www.wsj.com · Mike Krever, "Afghanistan's Romeo and Juliet: Defying Religion and Culture for Love," www.cnn.com

Canonical Text	Sample Unit Focus	Sample Essential Question	Sample Supplementary Texts
			· Laura Tangley, "A Pair of Star-crossed Love Bugs," www.sciencenews.org · Mike Harden, "O Romeo, O, Like Wow," www.legendsmagazine.net/75/oromeo.htm Picture Books · James Howe and Chris Raschka, *Otter and Odder* Poetry · Ella Wheeler Wilcox, "The Winds of Fate" and "Fate and I" · William Blake, "Love's Secret" · Thomas Moore, "At the Mid Hour of Night" · Edgar Allan Poe, "Annabel Lee" · Dante Gabriel Rossetti, "Severed Selves" Music · We the Kings, "Check Yes Juliet" · Taylor Swift, "Love Story" · MAGIC!, "Rude" · Gavin DeGraw, "We Belong Together" · The Killers (original, Dire Straits), "Romeo and Juliet" Art · Auguste Rodin, *The Kiss* · Frank Dicksee, *Romeo and Juliet* Movies · *Titanic* · *High School Musical* · *Star Wars: Episode II — Attack of the Clones* · *Valley Girl*
Hamlet	Making decisions	How much control do we have over our choices and actions?	YA Novels · Sharon M. Draper, *Tears of a Tiger* · Robert Cormier, *The Chocolate War* · Walter Dean Myers, *Monster* · Paul Fleischman, *Whirligig* · Jan Cheripko, *Imitate the Tiger* · Angela Johnson, *The First Part Last* · Joyce McDonald, *Swallowing Stones* · Matt Haig, *The Dead Fathers Club* · Lisa Fiedler, *Dating Hamlet: Ophelia's Story* Short Stories · Donald Gallo, *No Easy Answers: Short Stories about Teenagers Making Tough Choices* · Edgar Allan Poe, "The Cask of Amontillado" Informational Texts · Richard Wright, "The Rights to the Streets of Memphis" · George Orwell, "Shooting an Elephant" · Amanda Leigh Mascarelli, "The Teenage Brain," www.sciencenewsforstudents.org

Canonical Text	Sample Unit Focus	Sample Essential Question	Sample Supplementary Texts
			· Danica Davidson, "Why Do Teenagers Make Bad Choices? One Word: Science," www.mtv.com · Tara Parker-Pope, "Teenagers, Friends, and Bad Decisions," https://well.blogs.nytimes.com/ Picture Books · Eve Bunting, *Riding the Tiger* · Barney Saltzberg, *Stanley and the Class Pet* · Victoria Kann and Elizabeth Kann, *Purplicious* · Maya Angelou, *Life Doesn't Frighten Me* · Marybeth Lobiecki and David Diaz, *Just One Flick of a Finger* Poetry · Robert Frost, "The Road Not Taken" · T. S. Eliot, "The Love Song of J. Alfred Prufrock" · Ella Wheeler Wilcox, "The Winds of Fate" · Stephen Crane, "Think As I Think" Music · George Jones, "Choices" · Uriah Heep, "Choices" · The Clash, "Should I Stay or Should I Go?" · Brian McKnight, "Shoulda Coulda Woulda" · Lee Ann Womack, "I Hope You Dance" Art · M. C. Escher, *Ascending and Descending* · M. C. Escher, *Relativity* · Don W. Larson, *Indecision* TV · *One Bad Choice* Movies · *How to Make Better Decisions*
Julius Caesar or *Animal Farm*	Power and corruption	Does power lead to corruption?	YA Novels · Todd Strasser, *The Wave* · Alex Flinn, *Breaking Point* · Sharon Draper, *Battle of Jericho* · Lois Duncan, *Killing Mr. Griffin* · Gail Giles, *Shattering Glass* · Adele Griffin, *Amandine* · Joyce McDonald, *Shadow People* · Robert Cormier, *The Chocolate War* Short Stories · Richard Peck, "Priscilla and the Wimps" · Gloria D. Miklowitz, "Confession" · Will Weaver, "The Photograph"

Canonical Text	Sample Unit Focus	Sample Essential Question	Sample Supplementary Texts
			Informational Texts · Stanley Milgram, "The Perils of Obedience" · Christopher Shea, "Why Power Corrupts," www.smithsonianmag.com · Nelson D. Schwartz, "Bribes and Punishment," www.nytimes.com Picture Books · Eve Bunting, *Riding the Tiger* · Stanley Tookie Williams, *Gangs and the Abuse of Power* · Victoria Kann and Elizabeth Kann, *Purplicious* · Dr. Seuss, *The Sneetches and Other Stories* and *Yertle the Turtle and Other Stories* · Barney Saltzberg, *Stanley and the Class Pet* Poetry · George MacDonald, "Power" · Francis Duggan, "To Have Power Over Others" · Emily Dickinson, "I Took Power in My Hand" · Lonnie Hicks, "All Power" · Carl Sandburg, "The Government" Music · The Alarm, "Corridors of Power" · Susan Vega, "The Queen and the Soldier" · Dead Brain Cells, "Power and Corruption" Movies · *All the King's Men* · *The Last King of Scotland* · *Star Wars: Episode III—Revenge of the Sith* · *Point of Order* · *All the President's Men* · *Enron: The Smartest Guys in the Room*
The Odyssey	Journey	What is more important, the journey or destination?	YA Novels · Peter E. Morgan, *Running Out of Summer* · Lauren Barnholdt, *Two-Way Street* · Christopher Paul Curtis, *Bud, Not Buddy* · Tanita S. Davis, *Mare's War* · Mary E. Pearson, *The Miles Between* · Cheryl Strayed, *Wild: From Lost to Found on the Pacific Crest Trail* · Adam Rapp, *Punkzilla* · Yann Martel, *The Life of Pi* · Rick Riordan, *The Lightning Thief* · Siobhan Dowd, *Solace of the Road* · Paul Fleischman, *Whirligig* · Elisa Carbone, *Stealing Freedom* · Sharon Creech, *Walk Two Moons*

Canonical Text	Sample Unit Focus	Sample Essential Question	Sample Supplementary Texts
			Short Stories · Eudora Welty, "A Worn Path" · Joyce Carol Oates, "The Journey" · David Iglehart, "An Indian Odyssey" · Donald R. Gallo, *Destination Unexpected* Informational Texts · Sonia Nazario, *Enrique's Journey* (The Young Adult Adaptation) · Jon Krakauer, *Into the Wild* · Jon Krakauer, *Into Thin Air* · Caroline Alexander, "Back From War, but Not Really Home," www.nytimes.com · Wilfred Thesiger, *Arabian Sands* · Edmund Hillary, *High Adventure* · Meriwether Lewis and William Clark, *The Journals of Lewis and Clark* Picture Books · Aaron Becker, *Journey* · Mary Holmes, *A Giraffe Goes to Paris* · Maurice Sendak, *Where the Wild Things Are* · Tammy Yee, *Baby Honu's Incredible Journey* · William Grill, *Shackleton's Journey* Poetry · Robert Frost, "The Road Not Taken" · Walt Whitman, "Song of the Open Road" · Mary Oliver, "The Journey" · Edna St. Vincent Millay, "An Ancient Gesture" Music · Whitesnake, "Here I Go Again" · Symphony X, *The Odyssey* · Tom Petty, "Runnin' Down a Dream" · Fun, "Carry On" · The Script, "Hall of Fame" Video Game · *Journey* Movies · *Finding Nemo* · *O Brother, Where Art Thou?* · *Shrek* · *Homeward Bound: The Incredible Journey*

Canonical Text	Sample Unit Focus	Sample Essential Question	Sample Supplementary Texts
Beowulf	Heroes	What defines a hero and heroic action?	**YA Novels** · Robert Cormier, *Heroes* · Mike Lupica, *Hero* · S. L. Rottman, *Hero* · Graham McNamee, *Acceleration* · Gary Paulsen, *Soldier's Heart: Being the Story of the Enlistment and Due Service of the Boy Charley Goddard in the First Minnesota Volunteers* · Walter Dean Myers, *Fallen Angels* · Cassandra Clare, *The City of Bones* · Michael Crichton, *Eaters of the Dead* · John Gardner, *Grendel* **Short Stories** · Sue Ragland, "The Hero" · Al Desetta and Sybil Wolin, *The Struggle to be Strong: True Stories by Teens About Overcoming Tough Times* · Jonathan Diaz, *True Heroes: A Treasury of Modern-Day Fairy Tales Written by Best-Selling Authors* · Diane Higdon, *Uncommon Heroes: Inspiring Stories of Ordinary People Who Changed Communities through Unity* **Informational Texts** · Malala Yousafzai, *I Am Malala: The Girl Who Stood Up for Education and Was Shot by the Taliban* · Michele Langevine Leiby, "Malala Yousafzai: From a Schoolgirl to a Nobel Peace Prize Winner," www.washingtonpost.com · Victoria Pynchon, "September 11 and the Heroes of Flight 93," www.forbes.com · Arthur Kanegis, "New Heroes for a New Age," www.medialit.org · Mike Bellah, "Where Have All the Heroes Gone?," www.bestyears.com · William Kamkwamba and Bryan Mealer, *The Boy Who Harnessed the Wind: Creating Currents of Electricity and Hope* · Chris Kyle, with Scott McEwen and Jim DeFelice, *American Sniper: The Autobiography of the Most Lethal Sniper in U.S. Military History* · Ji-li Jiang, *Red Scarf Girl: A Memoir of the Cultural Revolution* · Bruce H. Norton, *Encyclopedia of American War Heroes* **Picture Books** · Nikki Rogers, *A Hero Is—* · Ken Mochizuki, *Heroes* · William J. Bennett, *The Children's Book of Heroes* **Poetry** · Wilfred Owen, "Dulce et Decorum Est" · Siegfried Sassoon, "The Hero" · A. E. Stallings, "Fairy-Tale Logic" · Lewis Carroll, "Jabberwocky"

Canonical Text	Sample Unit Focus	Sample Essential Question	Sample Supplementary Texts
			Music · Mariah Carey, "Hero" · Chad Kroeger and Josey Scott, "Hero" · Kiss, "A World Without Heroes" · Idina Menzel, "A Hero Comes Home" · Skillet, "Hero" · Amon Amarth, "Runes to My Memory" TV · *Heroes* Movies · *Shrek* · *Gandhi* · *Life is Beautiful* · *Apollo 13* · *The Matrix* · *The Incredibles* Comics · *Batman* · *Superman* · *Wonder Woman* · *Spider-Man* · *Captain America* · *X-Men* · *Wolverine* · *Hulk* · *New Avengers* · *Justice League* Graphic Novels · *Watchmen*
Macbeth or Doctor Faustus	Dark side of ambition	What is the dark side of ambition?	YA Novels · Daniel Nayeri and Dina Nayeri, *Another Faust* · Thalia Kalkipsakis, *Silhouette* · Robert Cormier, *The Chocolate War* · Kate Brian, *Ambition* · Caroline B. Cooney, *Enter Three Witches* · Kate Brian, *Private* Short Stories · Guy de Maupassant, "The Orphan" · Guy de Maupassant, "The Necklace" · Washington Irving, "The Devil and Tom Walker" Informational Texts · Daniel Goleman, "Why Records Fail," www.nytimes.com · Eric Schlosser, "Why McDonald's Fries Taste So Good" · Malcolm Gladwell, "Examined Life," www.newyorker.com · Walter Mosley, "Get Happy," www.thenation.com

Canonical Text	Sample Unit Focus	Sample Essential Question	Sample Supplementary Texts
			· Jere Longman, "Jealousy on Ice," www.nytimes.com · Anne Lang and Kristen Mascia, "The Texas Cheerleader Case: A Daughter's Painful Journey," http://people.com/ · Julia Brucculieri, "Robin Thicke Finally Speaks About 'Blurred Lines' Lawsuit," www.huffingtonpost.com · Steve Forbes and John Prevas, "Ego and Ambition," www.forbes.com · Seth Borenstein, "Technology's Disasters Share Long Trail of Hubris," www.nbcnews.com Picture Books · Dr. Seuss, *Yertle the Turtle and Other Stories* · Laura Joffe Numeroff and Felicia Bond, *If You Give a Mouse a Cookie* · Mini Grey, *Egg Drop* Poetry · Anne Sexton, "The Ambition Bird" · Robert Herrick, "Ambition" · Robert Frost, "Fire and Ice" · Percy Bysshe Shelley, "Ozymandias" Music · Queen, "I Want it All" · Procul Harum, "The Wall Street Blues" · Three Days Grace, "Animal I Have Become" TV · *House of Cards* Movies · *Wall Street: Money Never Sleeps* · *The Social Network* Play · David Mamet, *Glengarry Glen Ross* Podcast · Charlie Hoehn, *The Dark Side of Ambition with Charlie Hoehn*, https://unmistakablecreative.com/
The Crucible or *The Scarlet Letter*	Persecution	How and why do we persecute others?	YA Novels · Randa Abdel-Fattah, *Does My Head Look Big in This?* · Hillary Jordan, *When She Woke* · Jay Asher, *13 Reasons Why* · Celia Rees, *Witch Child* · Sara Zarr, *Story of a Girl* · Laurie Halse Anderson, *Speak* · Laura Ruby, *Good Girls* · Mitzi Miller and Denene Millner, *Hotlanta* · Sharon Flake, *The Skin I'm In* · M. E. Kerr, *Deliver Us from Evie*

Canonical Text	Sample Unit Focus	Sample Essential Question	Sample Supplementary Texts
			Short Stories · Guy de Maupassant, "Piece of String" · James Thurber, "The Very Proper Gander" · Bruce Coville, "Am I Blue?" · Nancy Garden, "Parents Night" · Nathaniel Hawthorne, "Young Goodman Brown" · Flannery O'Connor, "Good County People" **Informational Texts** · David Scharfenberg, "County Ad Put Spotlight on Parents Who Owe Child Support," www.nytimes.com · Harry Ferguson, "'Manzanar Nice Place—It Better than Hollywood'" · Arthur Miller, "Are You Now Or Were You Ever" · Harry S. Truman, Executive Order 9835 ("Loyalty Order") · Mark Twain, "The Disgraceful Persecution of a Boy" **Picture Books** · Eve Bunting, *Terrible Things* · Hans Christian Andersen, Stefan Czernecki (Illus.), and Mus White (Trans.), *For Sure! For Sure!* · Miriam Nerlove, *Flowers on the Wall* · Karen Gedig Burnett, *If the World Were Blind. . .: A Book about Judgment and Prejudice* **Poetry** · Margaret Atwood, "Half-Hanged Mary" · Langston Hughes, "Still Here" · Maya Angelou, "Still I Rise" · Martin Niemöller, "First They Came for the Socialists" **Music** · Rush, "Witch Hunt" · Bob Marley, "Judge Not" · Sly and the Family Stone, "Everyday People" · Misfits, "Witch Hunt" · Bruce Springsteen, "Devils and Dust" · Five Man Electrical Band, "Sign" · The Smiths, "Barbarism Begins at Home" · Billy Joel, "We Didn't Start the Fire" **YouTube** · Jeff Nagel, *Dog Shaming Highlights 2012* · Cactuar678, *Monty Python "She's a Witch"* **Movies** · *Pleasantville* · *Good Night, and Good Luck* · *The Matthew Shepard Story* · *Schindler's List* **Play** · Eugène Ionesco, *The Rhinoceros*

Canonical Text	Sample Unit Focus	Sample Essential Question	Sample Supplementary Texts
Lord of the Flies	Survival	What does it take to survive?	**YA Novels** · Michael Grant, *Gone* · Will Hobbs, *Downriver* · Gary Paulsen, *Hatchet* · Cynthia Voigt, *Homecoming* · Laurie Halse Anderson, *Fever, 1793* · Kass Morgan, *The 100* · Libba Bray, *Beauty Queens* · Rick Yancey, *The Fifth Wave* · Max Brooks, *World War Z: An Oral History of the Zombie War* · Michael Harmon, *Skate* · Terry Hokenson, *The Winter Road* · Ann Jaramillo, *La Linea* · John Marsden, *Tomorrow, When the War Began* · Suzanne Collins, *The Hunger Games* · Linda Sue Park, *A Long Walk to Water* · Andrew Klavan, *If We Survive* · Jean Hegland, *Into the Forest* **Short Stories** · Jack London, "To Build a Fire" · Stephen Crane, "The Open Boat" · Richard Connell, "The Most Dangerous Game" · John Floyd, "Survival" · Arthur Gordon, "The Sea Devil" · Gerald Hausman, *Castaways: Stories of Survival* **Informational Texts** · Jon Krakauer, *Into the Wild* · Jon Krakauer, *Into Thin Air* · Alfred Lansing, *Endurance: Shackleton's Incredible Voyage* · Piers Paul Read, *Alive: The Story of the Andes Survivors* · Ishmael Beah, *A Long Way Gone: Memoirs of a Boy Soldier* · Laura Hillenbrand, *Unbroken: A World War II Story of Survival, Resilience, and Redemption* · Aron Ralston, *Between a Rock and a Hard Place* · Steven Callahan, *Adrift: Seventy-Six Days Lost at Sea* · Jeanna Bryner, "Modern Humans Retain Caveman's Survival Instincts," www.livescience.com · Nancy F. Koehn, "Leadership Lessons from the Shackleton Expedition," www.nytimes.com · Alex Hannaford, "127 Hours: Aron Ralston's Story of Survival," www.telegraph.co.uk · Hector Tobar, "33 Miners, Buried Alive for 69 Days: This is Their Remarkable Survival Story," www.rd.com · "Four True Stories of Survival," www.fieldandstream.com **Picture Books** · Kirby Larson and Mary Nethery, *Two Bobbies: A True Story of Hurricane Katrina, Friendship, and Survival* · Sheila Burnford, *The Incredible Journey* · Lola M. Schaefer, *Arrowhawk: A True Survival Story* · Marilyn Nelson, *Snook Alone* · Robyn Belton, *Herbert: The True Story of a Brave Sea Dog*

Canonical Text	Sample Unit Focus	Sample Essential Question	Sample Supplementary Texts
			Poetry · Siegfried Sassoon, "Survivors" · Primo Levi, "The Survivor" · Theodore Roethke, "In a Dark Time" Music · Survivor, "Eye of the Tiger" · Rachel Platten, "Fight Song" · The Script, "Hall of Fame" · Kelly Clarkson, "Stronger" · Destiny's Child, "Survivor" · Iron Maiden, "Lord of the Flies" TED Talk · Hyeonseo Lee, "A Story of Survival, Resilience, and Hope" TV · *Jericho* · *Falling Skies* · *The Colony* · *Lost* · *Out of the Wild* · *Ray Mears' Extreme Survival* · *Man vs. Wild* Movies · *Everest* · *Eight Below* · *Cast Away* · *127 Hours* · *Alive* · *The Impossible* · *Hours*
1984 or *Brave New World* or *Fahrenheit 451*	Dystopia/utopia	Is utopia possible?	YA Novels · Paolo Bacigalupi, *Ship Breaker* · Ernest Cline, *Ready Player One* · Suzanne Collins, *The Hunger Games* · Nancy Farmer, *The House of the Scorpion* · Marie Lu, *Legend* · Gemma Malley, *The Declaration* · Veronica Roth, *Divergent* · Suzanne Weyn, *The Bar Code Tattoo* · Cory Doctorow, *Little Brother* · Francine Prose, *After* · Lauren Oliver, *Delirium* · Margaret Peterson Haddix, *Among the Hidden* · Lois Lowry, *The Giver* · Meagan Spooner, *Skylark* · Neal Shusterman, *Unwind* · Scott Westerfeld, *The Uglies*

Canonical Text	Sample Unit Focus	Sample Essential Question	Sample Supplementary Texts
			Short Stories · Kurt Vonnegut, "Harrison Bergeron" · Ray Bradbury, "The Pedestrian" · Ursula K. Le Guin, "The Ones Who Walk Away from Omelas" Informational Texts · Thomas More, *Utopia* · Rory Cellan-Jones, "First Human 'Infected with Computer Virus,'" www.bbc.co.uk · Megan Geuss, "Facebook Facial Recognition: Its Quiet Rise and Dangerous Future," www.pcworld.com · Adam Liptak, "Court Case Asks if 'Big Brother' is Spelled GPS," www.nytimes.com · Clive Thompson, "Brave New World of Digital Intimacy," www.nytimes.com Picture Books · Dr. Seuss, *The Lorax* Poetry · T. S. Eliot, "The Waste Land" · Percy Bysshe Shelley, "Ozymandias" Music · John Lennon, "Imagine" · Pennywise, "Land of the Free?" · Oingo Boingo, "Perfect System" · Lockdown, "Thrice" · Rage Against the Machine, "Testify" Art · Thomas Cole, "The Course of Empire" series TV/Movies · *The Island* · *Minority Report* · *Gattaca* · *The Village* Graphic Novels · *V for Vendetta* · *Watchmen*
The Great Gatsby or *A Raisin in the Sun*	American dream	Is the American dream attainable, and, if so, is it equally accessible?	YA Novels · Sherman Alexie, *The Absolutely True Diary of a Part-Time Indian* · Sara Benincasa, *Great* · Sandra Cisneros, *The House on Mango Street* · S. E. Hinton, *The Outsiders* · Sampson Davis and George Jenkins, *The Pact* · Gordon Korman, *Jake, Reinvented* · Gary Soto, *Jesse* · Mildred D. Taylor, *Roll of Thunder, Hear My Cry*

Canonical Text	Sample Unit Focus	Sample Essential Question	Sample Supplementary Texts
			Short Stories · Katherine Mansfield, "Bliss" · James Baldwin, "Sonny's Blues" **Informational Texts** · Lorie Johnson, "The American Dream Does Not Exist," ic.galegroup.com · Marie Myung-Ok Lee, "I Was an 'Anchor Baby'" · Eric Liu, "A Chinaman's Chance: Reflections on the American Dream" · Michael Lewis, "The Ballad of Big Mike," www.nytimes.com · Sandra Cisneros, "Straw into Gold: The Metamorphosis of the Everyday" · Martin Luther King Jr., "I Have a Dream" · United States Declaration of Independence · Anzia Yezierska, "America and I" **Picture Books** · Linda Jacobs Altman, *Amelia's Road* · Avi, *Silent Movie* · Faith Ringgold, *Tar Beach* · Walter Dean Myers, *We Are America: A Tribute from the Heart* **Poetry** · Langston Hughes, "Let America Be America Again" · Langston Hughes, "A Dream Deferred" · Langston Hughes, "Mother to Son" · Tupac Shakur, "The Rose that Grew from Concrete" · Ricardo Sanchez, "I Yearn" · Walt Whitman, "I Hear America Singing" · Pat Mora, "Legal Alien" **Music** · Lorde, "Royals" · Madonna, "American Life" · James Brown, "Living in America" · Miley Cyrus, "The Climb" **Art** · Dorothea Lange, *Migrant Mother* · Grant Wood, *American Gothic* · Norman Rockwell, *Freedom from Want* **Movies** · *The Pursuit of Happyness* · *An American Tail* · *The Social Network* **Plays** · Lin-Manuel Miranda, *Hamilton* · Tennessee Williams, *The Glass Menagerie* · Arthur Miller, *Death of a Salesman*

Canonical Text	Sample Unit Focus	Sample Essential Question	Sample Supplementary Texts
Night or *The Diary of a Young Girl*	Resilience	What hope, if any, may be found in times of hopelessness?	**YA Novels** · Julia Alvarez, *Return to Sender* · Sharon Draper, *Copper Sun* · Sharon Draper, *Fire from the Rock* · Louise Erdrich, *The Birchbark House* · Sharon Flake, *The Skin I'm In* · Khalid Hosseini, *And the Mountains Echoed* · Jeanne Wakatsuki Houston and James D. Houston, *Farewell to Manzanar* · Bodie Thoene and Brock Thoene, *Warsaw Requiem* and *Danzig Passage* (two books of note within a series) **Short Stories** · Bruce A. Glasrud and Laurie Champion, *The African American West: A Century of Short Stories* · Pat McNees, *Contemporary Latin American Short Stories* · Linda Schermer Raphael and Marc Lee Raphael, *When Night Fell: An Anthology of Holocaust Short Stories* **Informational Texts** · Corrie ten Boom, *The Hiding Place* · Dee Brown, *Bury My Heart at Wounded Knee: An Indian History of the American West* · (excerpts) Erik Bruun and Jay Crosby, *The American Experience: The History and Culture of the United States through Speeches, Letters, Essays, Poems, Editorials, Songs, and Stories* · Sonia Nazario, *Enrique's Journey* (The Young Adult Adaptation) · Doreen Rappaport, *Beyond Courage: The Untold Story of Jewish Resistance during the Holocaust* · Esmeralda Santiago, *When I Was Puerto Rican: A Memoir* **Picture Books** · Laetitia Devernay, *The Conductor* · Ai-Ling Louie, *Yeh-Shen: A Cinderella Story from China* · Patricia Polacco, *January's Sparrow* · Ruth Vander Zee, *Erika's Story* **Poetry** · Lori Carlson, *Red Hot Salsa: Bilingual Poems on Being Young and Latino in the United States* · Hayan Charara, *Inclined to Speak : An Anthology of Contemporary Arab American Poetry* · Kenneth Rosen, *Voices of the Rainbow: Contemporary Poetry by Native Americans* · Mark Eleveld, *The Spoken Word Revolution: Slam, Hip Hop & the Poetry of a New Generation* **Music** · Władysław Szpilman, Andrzej Szpilman, Janusz Olejniczak, and Wojciech Kilar, *The Pianist* (Original Motion Picture Sound Track)

Canonical Text	Sample Unit Focus	Sample Essential Question	Sample Supplementary Texts
			· Various artists, *Soundtrack For a Revolution* · Marvin Sapp, "Never Would Have Made It" · Various artists, *Rolas de Aztlán: Songs of the Chicano Movement* Art · Paul Botello, *Muro que Habla, Canta y Grita* · Aaron Douglas, *Rebirth* · Gustav Klimt, *The Woman in Gold* · Max D. Standley, *The Trail of Tears* Movies · *Among the Righteous: Lost Stories from the Holocaust in Arab Lands* · *We Shall Remain: America through Native Eyes* · *The Island on Bird Street* · *Bella* · *American Experience: Freedom Riders* · *God Grew Tired of Us* · *Latino Americans* (documentary) · *Friendship in Vienna* Graphic Novels · Matt Dembicki, *Trickster: Native American Tales, A Graphic Collection* · Ryan Inzana, *Ichiro* · Tom Pumplun and Lance Tooks, *African-American Classics (Graphic Classics Vol. 22)* · Marjane Satrapi, *The Complete Persepolis* · Kiyoshi Konno, *Che Guevara: A Manga Biography* · Art Spiegelman, *Maus*

Appendix C

Reading Survey

1. Describe yourself as a reader: What kind of reader are you?

2. What have you read lately? List all of the things (book, story, article, poem, website, etc.) that you remember reading in the last few months—use the back of this page if you need to.

3. How do you decide what you'll read?

4. Who are your favorite authors? (If you can't think of an author's name, list the title of a book they've written.)

5. Do you prefer reading fiction or nonfiction? Books that seem real or books about fantasy worlds? Short books or long ones? Science fiction, mystery, action/adventure, romance, or urban lit? Do you like stories that are happy or sad? Romantic or scary? Books about historical events or books about teen issues?

6. Have you ever read the same thing (book, story, article, poem, etc.) over and over again? Why? What was it (book, story, article, poem, etc.)?

7. What do you like most of all to read?

8. What do you read routinely (every day or every week)?

9. What is the most difficult thing you have ever had to read? What made it so difficult?

10. What are you good at as a reader? What do you know how to do?

11. What would you like to do to be better as a reader?

12. When and where do you read?

Appendix D

Classwork/Online Binder

Either purchase a three-ring binder or create an online equivalent using Live-Binders (www.livebinders.com), Wix, or Google Docs. Create tabs or links for different units of study. The first unit is called "Beowulf: A Hero among Us." Within each unit, there will be subsections or additional links. This particular unit will have the following tabs/links:

- reading mini-lessons;
- word study;
- literary mini-lessons;
- response journal.

Place all of your writing from class in the appropriate section of the binder. For example, during or after a reading mini-lesson on visualization, place your drawings in the binder's *reading mini-lessons* section. In the *word study* section, include all work pertaining to new vocabulary. The *response journal* section should include writing you do that demonstrates your transaction with what you are reading. Often, these responses will be prompted by response engagements in class.

Each entry needs to have an appropriate heading. Reading mini-lessons should include the title of what you are reading as well as the strategy you are using; word study should include the title and pages of the work from which the words are taken; responses should include the title and pages of the work and the name of the engagement prompting response.

This binder is worth twenty points toward your final unit grade. It will be evaluated using the following criteria:

- Completeness—Are the required number of entries for the unit included? Are the entries sufficient in length to demonstrate effort?
- Organization—Does the binder include the necessary divisions? Are entries appropriately labeled?
- Quality—Do the entries in the binder demonstrate effort as well as understanding of the mini-lesson, vocabulary, and text?

Appendix E

Movie Response Sheet[1]

Select an epic to watch (you can find many recommendations online). Epics come in many forms—western, biblical, war, science fiction, fantasy, and so on. I will be showing an epic during lunch over the next three days in my classroom; see me if you need a pass. After you have watched the movie, answer the following questions. Feel free to talk with others as you do so.

List the title of the movie you watched:

Explain why you think this movie is an epic:

Describe how the hero is portrayed in your movie. What tests of courage does he/she undergo? What messages about the image of a hero are communicated through the movie? How and why?

Is the image of the hero conveyed by the movie you watched similar or different from the image revealed in *Beowulf*? How so?

How does the image of the hero in this movie compare to other cultural images of the hero, such as those in other movies, in songs, in games, or on TV?

What are the ramifications of this image of a hero? Is there something we need to do about the cultural representation of the hero in our society? If so, what can we do about it?

---

1. This Movie Response Sheet was adapted from Wilhelm (2004), p. 125.

Appendix F

Book Club Project

Over the past week, you have had the opportunity to meet with your book club and discuss your reading. Now you are challenged to answer the unit essential question: What defines a hero and heroic action? Think about this question as a group, and then design a project that answers the question. Select a medium through which to relay your thinking. No posters or collages, please—let's think more creatively. Your response can take many forms:

- musical (e.g., create a sound track or write and perform a song that answers the questions);
- artistic (e.g., create a comic book or picture book that answers the questions);
- technological (e.g., create a website, WebQuest, Wix, Google Docs, Prezi, or Instagram item that answers the questions);
- linguistic (e.g., write a poem, play, or talk show that answers the questions);
- dramatic (e.g., perform a play or make a movie that answers the questions);
- kinesthetic (perform a mime or dance that answers the questions);
- mathematical (e.g., create a game or series of equations that answers the questions);
- a combination of the above;
- any other way you can think of to answer the questions (but check with me first).

An individual reflection of two typed pages must accompany this project. Consider the following as you reflect:

- Explain your project. How does it answer the question of what defines a hero and heroic action?
- Why did you choose to answer the question in this way?
- How was your project inspired by class readings or engagements?
- Why did you choose this medium to reveal the answer to the question?
- Share the process of your project: How did you go about creating this response?
- What was your contribution to this project? Be specific.
- What do you like best about your project?
- What would you want to change about your project?
- What do you want your classmates to think about as they watch the presentation of your project?

This project is worth twenty-five points. A rubric for grading is as follows:

- Preparation—Did you use the time provided in class to work on this project? Does the project demonstrate effort and time commitment outside of class?

- Content—Does the project answer the question of what defines a hero and heroic action? Does the content demonstrate depth and insight, and does it draw from class readings?

- Creativity—Does the project express original response? Is the response revealed through aesthetic means?

- Reflection—Is the reflection of adequate length? Does the reflection answer the queries above? Is the reflection written in an appropriate style and does it demonstrate proper grammatical structure?

- Presentation—Did you remain within the five-minute presentation time limit? Was your presentation well planned and rehearsed?

Appendix G

Beowulf: A Hero among Us—Unit Test

Write your responses to five of the following six questions in complete sentences and interesting paragraphs:

1. What is an epic? Why do you think *Beowulf* is an epic? What is a current example of an epic? What makes it so?

2. Why is Beowulf an epic hero? Compare his characteristics with that of the hero you read about in your biography, autobiography, or memoir. Whom do you prefer and why?

3. How did reading the informational articles, graphic novels, the *Mwindo Epic*, and heroic images deepen your understanding of heroes? Which of the above did you prefer reading and why?

4. Define and describe three characteristics of Anglo Saxon poetry as evidenced in *Beowulf*.

5. What is visualization? What strategies can help you visualize a text? Which of the strategies did you prefer and why? Explain how visualization aided your comprehension when reading during this unit. How is visualization related to imagery? Be sure to define and provide examples of imagery.

6. List and define five new vocabulary words you learned from reading in the course of this unit. Explain the context in which you discovered the words and the strategy(ies) that helped you learn these words.

Appendix H

Heroic Narrative Essay

Throughout this unit, we have read about heroes and heroic events. We have discussed the depiction of the hero in society and in the media and considered the characteristics of an epic hero across literature. Now it is your turn to tell a story.

Think about a personal experience that is in some way heroic. Remember that a hero does not have to wear a cape or know how to fly—heroic moments occur in everyday life. Remember your essential question for this unit: What defines a hero and heroic action? You do not have to have been the hero, but you should be personally associated with the experience. It does not have to have been especially dramatic or important, but it should be significant. You want to tell this story for a reason.

Journey through time. When and where does this story take place? Who are the characters? Is there a conflict (i.e., person versus. . . person, self, society, nature, supernatural, technology)? What are the events and actions leading up to the climax? What is the outcome? Is there a change or resolution? What are the beginning, middle, and end of your story? Carefully plan your sequence of events.

Write the story of this heroic experience in first or third person. Show, don't tell, what happened. Write descriptively, using action verbs, sensory language, and figurative language (e.g., metaphors, similes, personification). Vary your word choice and sentence structure. Include dialogue to move your story along. Make clear transitions between events and paragraphs. Use Standard English and adhere to grammatical conventions unless your dialogue or voice warrants otherwise. Make your audience (i.e., teacher and classmates) feel as though they are experiencing this heroic moment with you. Tell your story in three to four typed pages.

Your paper will be evaluated using the following criteria:
- content;
- organization;
- word choice;
- voice/style/tone;
- sentence fluency/structure;
- conventions.

We will design and discuss a more detailed grading rubric as we revise and edit our papers during writing workshop.

References

Afflerbach, P., Pearson, P. D., & Paris, S. G. (2008). Clarifying differences between reading skills and reading strategies. *The Reading Teacher, 61*(5), 364–73.

Allen, J. (1999). *Words, words, words: Teaching vocabulary in grades 4–12.* Portland, ME: Stenhouse.

Allen, J. (2000). *Yellow brick roads: Shared and guided paths to independent reading 4–12.* Portland, ME: Stenhouse.

Allen, J. (2007). *Inside words: Tools for teaching academic vocabulary grades 4–12.* Portland, ME: Stenhouse.

Allington, R. L. (1980). Teacher interruption behaviors during primary-grade oral reading. *Journal of Educational Psychology, 72*(3), 371–77.

Allington, R. L. (2001) *What really matters for struggling readers: Designing research-based programs.* New York: Longman.

Amer, A. A. (2003). Teaching EFL/ESL literature. *Reading Matrix: An International Online Journal, 3*(2), 63–73.

Anderson, J. (2005). *Mechanically inclined: Building grammar, usage, and style into writer's workshop.* Portland, ME: Stenhouse.

Anderson, J. (2007). *Everyday editing: Inviting students to develop skill and craft in writer's workshop.* Portland, ME: Stenhouse.

Anderson, R. C., Wilson, P. T., & Fielding, L. G. (1988). Growth in reading and how children spend their time outside of school. *Reading Research Quarterly, 23*(3), 285–303.

Applebee, A. N. (1993). *Literature in the secondary school: Studies of curriculum and instruction in the United States.* Urbana, IL: NCTE.

Applebee, A. N., Langer, J. A., Nystrand, M., & Gamoran, A. (2003). Discussion-based approaches to developing understanding: Classroom instruction and student performance in middle and high school English. *American Educational Research Journal, 40*(3), 685–730.

Ash, G. E., & Kuhn, M. R. (2006). Meaningful oral and silent reading in the elementary and middle school classroom: Breaking the round robin reading addiction. In T. Rasinski, C. Blachowicz, & K. Lems (Eds.), *Fluency instruction: Research-based best practices* (pp. 155–72). New York: Guilford.

Atwell, N. (1998). *In the middle: New understandings about writing, reading, and learning* (2nd ed.). Portsmouth, NH: Heinemann.

Baker, R. (1980). *So this is depravity*. New York: Congdon & Lattès.

Barker, A. P. (1989). A gradual approach to feminism in the American-literature classroom. *English Journal, 78*(6), 39–44.

Barnes, D. (1992). *From communication to curriculum* (2nd ed.). Portsmouth, NH: Boynton/Cook.

Barnes, D. (2008). Exploratory talk for learning. In N. Mercer & S. Hodgkinson (Eds.), *Exploring talk in school: Inspired by the work of Douglas Barnes* (pp. 1–16). Los Angeles: SAGE.

Bean, T. W., & Moni, K. (2003). Developing students' critical literacy: Exploring identity construction in young adult fiction. *Journal of Adolescent & Adult Literacy, 46*(8), 638–48.

Beck, I. L., McKeown, M. G., & Kucan, L. (2002). *Bringing words to life: Robust vocabulary instruction*. New York: Guilford.

Beers, K. (2003). *When kids can't read, what teachers can do: A guide for teachers, 6–12.* Portsmouth, NH: Heinemann.

Beers, K., & Probst, R. (1998). Classroom talk about literature or the social dimensions of a solitary act. *Voices from the Middle, 5*(2), 16–20.

Beers, K., & Probst, R. (2013). *Notice & note: Strategies for close reading*. Portsmouth, NH: Heinemann.

Bellack, A. A., Kliebard, H. M., Hyman, R. T., & Smith, F. L., Jr. (1993). *The language of the classroom*. New York: Teachers College.

Berke, J., & Woodland, R. (1995). *Twenty questions for the writer: A rhetoric with readings* (6th ed.). Fort Worth, TX: Harcourt Brace College.

Bidwell, S. M. (1990). Using drama to increase motivation, comprehension, and fluency. *Journal of Reading, 34*(1), 38–41.

Black, A., & Stave, A. M. (2007). *A comprehensive guide to readers theatre: Enhancing fluency and comprehension in middle school and beyond*. Newark, DE: International Reading Association.

Bloom, H. (1994). *The Western canon: The books and school of the ages*. New York: Harcourt Brace.

Blum, H. T., Lipsett, L. R., & Yocom, D. J. (2002). Literature circles: A tool for self-determination in one middle school inclusive classroom. *Remedial and Special Education, 23*(2), 99–108.

Blunt, J. (2004). You're beautiful. On *Back to Bedlam* [CD]. New York: Atlantic.

Boyle, P. K. (2000). In praise of reader-response: Validating student voices in the literature classroom. *Teaching English in the Two-Year College, 27*(3), 315–19.

Brooks, W., & Browne, S. (2012). Towards a culturally situated reader response theory. *Children's Literature in Education, 43*(1), 74–85.

Bruchac, J. (1987). *Survival this way: Interviews with American Indian poets*. Tucson, AZ: Sun Tracks; University of Arizona Press.

Burke, C. (1987). Burke reading interview modified for older readers. Retrieved from http://assessment.aurorak12.org/wp-content/uploads/sites/5/2011/01/Burke-Reading-Interview-Modified-for-Older-Readers.pdf

Cai, M. S. (2008). Transactional theory and the study of multicultural literature. *Language Arts, 85*(3), 212–20.

Calkins, L. M. (1994). *The art of teaching writing* (2nd ed.). Portsmouth, NH: Heinemann.

Cambourne, B. (1984). *Towards a reading–writing classroom*. Portsmouth, NH: Heinemann.

Carlisle, A. (2000). Reading logs: An application of reader-response theory in ELT. *ELT Journal: English Language Teachers Journal, 54*(1), 12–19.

College Entrance Examination Board. (2003). *The neglected "R": The need for a writing revolution* (Report of the National Commission on Writing in America's Schools and Colleges). Retrieved from http://www.collegeboard.com/prod_downloads/writing com/neglectedr.pdf

Conley, M. W. (2008). Cognitive strategy instruction for adolescents: What we know about the promise, what we don't know about the potential. *Harvard Educational Review, 78*(1), 84–106.

Copeland, M. (2005). *Socratic circles: Fostering critical and creative thinking in middle and high school*. Portland, ME: Stenhouse.

Daniels, H. (1994). *Literature circles: Voice and choice in the student-centered classroom*. Portland, ME: Stenhouse.

Daniels, H. (Writer). (2001). *Looking into literature circles* [DVD]. Portland, ME; Evanston, IL: Stenhouse; Plum Pictures, Inc.

Daniels, H. (2002). *Literature circles: Voice and choice in book clubs and reading groups* (2nd ed.). Portland, ME: Stenhouse.

Danoff, B., Harris, K. R., & Graham, S. (1993). Incorporating strategy instruction within the writing process in the regular classroom: Effects on the writing of students with and without learning disabilities. *Journal of Reading Behavior, 25*(3), 295–322.

De Temple, J., & Snow, C. E. (2003). Learning words from books. In A. van Kleeck, S. A. Stahl, & E. B. Bauer (Eds.), *On reading books to children: Parents and teachers* (pp. 16–36). Mahwah, NJ: Erlbaum.

Dionisio, M. (1989). Filling empty pockets: Remedial readers make meaning. *English Journal, 78*(1), 33–37.

Drucker, M. J. (2003). What reading teachers should know about ESL learners. *The Reading Teacher, 57*(1), 22–29.

Eeds, M., & Cockrum, W. A. (1985). Teaching word meanings by expanding schemata vs. dictionary work vs. reading in context. *Journal of Reading, 28*(6), 492–97.

Feng, S., & Powers, K. (2005). The short- and long-term effect of explicit grammar instruction on fifth graders' writing. *Reading Improvement, 42*(2), 67–72.

Fisher, D., & Frey, N. (2007). *Scaffolded writing instruction: Teaching with a gradual-release framework*. New York: Scholastic.

Fisher, D., & Frey, N. (2012). Close reading in elementary schools. *The Reading Teacher, 66*(3), 179–88.

Fisher, D., Frey, N., & Lapp, D. (2008). Shared readings: Modeling comprehension, vocabulary, text structures, and text features for older readers. *The Reading Teacher, 61*(7), 548–56.

Fletcher, R., & Portalupi, J. (2001). *Writing workshop: The essential guide*. Portsmouth, NH: Heinemann.

Fredricks, L. (2012). The benefits and challenges of culturally responsive EFL critical literature circles. *Journal of Adolescent & Adult Literacy, 55*(6), 494–504.

Gallagher, K. (2009). *Readicide: How schools are killing reading and what you can do about it*. Portland, ME: Stenhouse.

Gallas, K., Anton-Oldenburg, M., Ballenger, C., Beseler, C., Pappenheimer, R., & Swaim, J. (1996). Focus on research talking the talk and walking the walk: Researching oral language in the classroom. *Language Arts, 73*(8), 608–17.

Gaughan, J. (2003). From the secondary section: A dose of thematic teaching. *English Journal, 92*(5), 18–21.

Gilles, C. (2010). Making the most of talk. *Voices from the Middle, 18*(2), 9–15.

Goodlad, J. I. (1984). *A place called school: Prospects for the future*. New York: McGraw-Hill.

Goodson, F. T., & Goodson, L. A. (2005). You oughta use the periods and stuff to slow down: Reading fluency through oral interpretation of YA lit. *Voices from the Middle, 13*(2), 24–29.

Graham, S., & Hebert, M. (2010). *Writing to read: Evidence for how writing can improve reading*. Washington, DC: Alliance for Excellent Education.

Graves, D. H. (2003). *Writing: Teachers and children at work* (20th anniversary ed.). Portsmouth, NH: Heinemann. (Original work published 1983)

Greenleaf, C., Schoenbach, R., Cziko, C., & Mueller, F. (2001). Apprenticing adolescent readers to academic literacy. *Harvard Educational Review, 71*(1), 79–129.

Guthrie, J. T. (2004). Teaching for literacy engagement. *Journal of Literacy Research, 36*(1), 1–29.

Harste, J. C. (1978). Understanding the hypothesis: It's the teacher that makes the difference, Part II. *Reading Horizons, 18*(2), 89–98.

Herz, S., & Gallo, D. (2005). *From Hinton to Hamlet: Building bridges between young adult literature and the classics* (2nd ed.). Westport, CT: Greenwood.

Holdaway, D. (1979). *The foundations of literacy*. New York: Ashton Scholastic.

Hull, G. A., & Schultz, K. (2001). *School's out: Bringing out-of-school literacies with classroom practice*. New York: Teachers College.

Ivey, G. (1999). A multicase study in the middle school: Complexities among young adolescent readers. *Reading Research Quarterly, 34*(2), 172–92.

Jobe, R., & Dayton-Sakari, M. (1999). *Reluctant readers: Connecting students and books for successful reading experiences*. Markham, Ontario, Canada: Pembroke.

Johnson, H. (2000). "To stand up and say something": "Girls only" literature circles at the middle level. *New Advocate, 13*(4), 375–89.

Kaywell, J. F. (2000). *Adolescent literature as a complement to the classics*. Norwood, MA: Christopher-Gordon.

Keene, E. O. (2010). New horizons in comprehension. *Educational Leadership, 67*(6), 69–73.

Keene, E. O., & Zimmerman, S. (2013). Years later, comprehension strategies still at work. *The Reading Teacher, 66*(8), 601–6.

Knickerbocker, J., & Rycik, J. A. (2006). Reexamining literature study in the middle grades: A critical response framework. *American Secondary Education, 34*(3), 43–56.

Krashen, S. (1993). *The power of reading: Insights from the research*. Englewood, CO: Libraries Unlimited.

Langer, J. (1990). Understanding literature. *Language Arts, 67*(8), 812–16.

Lapp, D., & Fisher, D. (2009). It's all about the book: Motivating teens to read. *Journal of Adolescent & Adult Literacy, 52*(7), 556–61.

Latendresse, C. (2004). Literature circles: Meeting reading standards, making personal connections, and appreciating other interpretations. *Middle School Journal, 35*(3), 13–20.

Lause, J. (2004). Using reading workshop to inspire lifelong readers. *English Journal, 93*(5), 24–30.

Liaw, M. (2001). Exploring literary responses in an EFL classroom. *Foreign Language Annals, 34*(1), 35–45.

Ling, A. (1990). *Between worlds: Women writers of Chinese ancestry*. New York: Pergamon.

Livaudais, M. (1985). *A survey of secondary students' attitudes toward reading motivational activities* (Doctoral dissertation). University of Houston, Houston, Texas.

Long, T. W., & Gove, M. K. (2003). How engagement strategies and literature circles promote critical response in a fourth-grade, urban classroom. *The Reading Teacher, 57*(4), 350–61.

Macrorie, K. (1988). *The I-Search paper*. Portsmouth, NH: Boynton/Cook.

Marcell, B., DeCleene, J., & Juettner, M. R. (2010). Caution! Hard hat area! Comprehension under construction: Cementing a foundation of comprehension strategy usage that carries over to independent practice. *The Reading Teacher, 63*(8), 687–91.

Martinez, M., Roser, N., & Strecker, S. (1999). "I never thought I could be a star": A reader's theatre ticket to fluency. *The Reading Teacher, 52*(4), 326–34.

Mast, S. (2002). Copy change: Rewriting the prologue from Shakespeare's *Romeo and Juliet*. *The Quarterly, Spring,* 29. Retrieved from https://www.nwp.org/cs/public/download/nwp_file/452/Copy_Change.pdf?x-r=pcfile_d

McLaughlin, M., & DeVoogd, G. (2004). Critical literacy as comprehension: Expanding reader response. *Journal of Adolescent & Adult Literacy, 48*(1), 52–65.

McMahon, S. I. (2008). Matching instructional strategies to facets of comprehension. *Voices from the Middle, 15*(4), 9–15.

McMahon, S. I., & Raphael, T. E. (1997). *The book club connection: Literacy learning and classroom talk.* New York: Teachers College.

Milner, J. O., Milner, L. M., & Mitchell, J. F. (2012). *Bridging English* (5th ed.). Boston: Allyn & Bacon/Pearson Education.

Morrell, E. (2005). Critical English education. *English Education, 37*(4), 312–21.

Morrow, L. M., & Gambrell, L. B. (2002). Literature-based instruction in the early years. In S. B. Neuman & D. K. Dickinson (Eds.), *Handbook of early literacy research* (pp. 348–360). New York: Guilford.

Moyers, B. (1992, March 22). Old news and the new civil war. *The New York Times,* Editorial, p. E15.

Murray, D. (2004). *A writer teaches writing* (2nd ed.). Boston: Houghton Mifflin.

Myers, K. L. (1988). Twenty (better) questions. *English Journal, 77*(1), 64–65.

Nachowitz, M., & Brumer, N. (2014). Teaching the talk, not the text. *Voices from the Middle, 22*(1), 15–21.

National Center for Education Statistics. (2012). *The Nation's Report Card: Writing 2011* (NCES 2012-470). Retrieved from http://www.nationsreportcard.gov/writing_2011/writing_2011_report/

National Center for Education Statistics. (2013). *The Nation's Report Card: A First Look— 2013 Mathematics and Reading* (NCES 2014–451) Retrieved from https://nces.ed.gov/nationsreportcard/subject/publications/main2013/pdf/2014451.pdf

National Council of Teachers of English. (2007). *Adolescent literacy: A policy research brief.* Retrieved from http://www.ncte.org/library/NCTEFiles/Resources/Policy Research/AdolLitResearchBrief.pdf

National Endowment for the Arts. (2007). *To read or not to read: A question of national consequence* (Research report 47). Retrieved from https://www.arts.gov/sites/default/files/ToRead.pdf

National Endowment for the Arts. (2009). *Reading on the rise: A new chapter in American literacy.* Retrieved from https://www.arts.gov/sites/default/files/ReadingonRise.pdf

National Governors Association Center for Best Practices, Council of Chief State School Officers. (2010). *Common Core English language arts standards.* Retrieved from corestandards.orgNational Reading Panel. (2000). *Report of the National Reading Panel: Teaching children to read.* Washington, DC: National Institute of Child Health and Human Development.

Noden, H. R. (1999). *Image grammar: Using grammatical structures to teach writing*. Portsmouth, NH: Heinemann.

Nystrand, M., Gamoran, A., Kachur, R., & Prendergast, C. (1997). *Opening dialogue: Understanding the dynamics of language and learning in the English classroom*. New York: Teachers College.

Nystrand, M., Wu, L. L., Gamoran, A., Zeiser, S., & Long, D. A. (2003). Questions in time: Investigating the structure and dynamics of unfolding classroom discourse. *Discourse Processes, 35*(2), 135–98.

Oatley, K. (2011). In the minds of others. *Scientific American Mind, 22*(5), 62–67.

O'Donnell-Allen, C. (2006). *The book club companion: Fostering strategic readers in the secondary classroom*. Portsmouth, NH: Heinemann.

Opitz, M. F., Rasinski, T. V., & Bird, L. B. (1998). *Good-bye round robin: Twenty-five effective oral reading strategies*. Portsmouth, NH: Heinemann.

Organisation for Economic Co-operation and Development. (2013). Country note: United States. In *PISA 2012 results: What makes schools successful?* Retrieved from http://www.oecd.org/unitedstates/PISA-2012-results-US.pdf

Palmer, B. M., Codling, R. M., & Gambrell, L. B. (1994). In their own words: What elementary children have to say about motivation to read. *The Reading Teacher, 48*(2), 176–79.

Park, J. Y. (2012). A different kind of reading instruction: Using visualizing to bridge reading comprehension and critical literacy. *Journal of Adolescent & Adult Literacy, 55*(7), 629–40.

Patterson, T. H., & Crumpler, T. P. (2009). Slow transformation: Teacher research and shifting teacher practices. *Teacher Education Quarterly, 36*(3), 95–111.

Paul, T. (1996). *Patterns of reading practice*. Madison, WI: Institute for Academic Excellence.

Pearson, P. D., & Gallagher, M. C. (1983). The gradual release of responsibility model of instruction. *Contemporary Educational Psychology, 8*(3), 112–23.

Pressley, M. (2006). *Reading instruction that works: The case for balanced teaching* (3rd ed.). New York: Guilford.

Probst, R. E. (2004). *Response & analysis: Teaching literature in secondary schools* (2nd ed.). Portsmouth, NH: Heinemann.

Raphael, T. E., & Au, K. H. (2005). QAR: Enhancing comprehension and test taking across grades and content areas. *The Reading Teacher, 59*(3), 206–21.

Rasinski, T. V. (2003). *The fluent reader: Oral reading strategies for building word recognition, fluency, and comprehension*. New York: Scholastic.

Ray, K. W. (1999). *Wondrous words: Writers and writing in the elementary classroom*. Urbana, IL: NCTE.

Ray, K. W., & Laminack, L. L. (2001). *The writing workshop: Working through the hard parts (and they're all hard parts)*. Urbana, IL: NCTE.

Rayner, K., & Pollatsek, A. (1989). *The psychology of reading*. Englewood Cliffs, NJ: Prentice Hall.

Richison, J., Hernandez, A., & Carter, M. (2006). *Theme-sets for secondary students: How to scaffold core literature*. Portsmouth, NH: Heinemann.

Robb, L. (2012). *The smart writing handbook*. Portsmouth, NH: Firsthand.

Romano, T. (2000). *Blending genre, altering style: Writing multigenre papers*. Portsmouth, NH: Boynton/Cook.

Rosenblatt, L. M. (1994). *The reader, the text, the poem: The transactional theory of the literary work*. Carbondale: Southern Illinois University.

Rosenblatt, L. M. (1995). *Literature as exploration* (5th ed.). New York: Modern Language Association of America.

Rosenblatt, L. M. (2003). Literary theory. In J. Flood, D. Lapp, J. R. Squire, & J. M. Jensen (Eds.). *Handbook of research on teaching the English language arts* (pp. 58–61). New York: Macmillan.

Routman, R. (2003). *Reading essentials: The specifics you need to teach reading well*. Portsmouth, NH: Heinemann.

Rycik, J. A., & Irvin, J. L. (2005). *Teaching reading in the middle grades: Understanding and supporting literacy development*. Boston: Allyn & Bacon.

Sandman, A., & Gruhler, D. (2007). Reading is thinking: Connecting readers to text through literature circles. *International Journal of Learning, 13*(10), 105–14.

Serafini, F. (2001). *The reading workshop: Creating space for readers*. Portsmouth, NH: Heinemann.

Shepard, A. (2014). *Readers on stage*. Friday Harbor, WA: Shepard Publications.

Short, K. G., & Pierce, K. M. (1990). *Talking about books: Creating literate communities*. Portsmouth, NH: Heinemann.

Short, K. G., Tomlinson, C. M., Lynch-Brown, C. M., & Johnson, H. M. (2014). *Essentials of young adult literature*. New York: Pearson.

Smith, F. (1988). *Joining the literacy club: Further essays into education*. Portsmouth, NH: Heinemann.

Smith, M. W., Wilhelm, J. D., & Fredricksen, J. E. (2012). *Oh, yeah?! Putting argument to work both in school and out*. Portsmouth, NH: Heinemann.

Stahl, K. A. D. (2012). Complex text or frustration-level text: Using shared reading to bridge the difference. *The Reading Teacher, 66*(1), 47–51.

Stahl, S. A. (2003). What do we expect storybook reading to do? How storybook reading impacts word recognition. In A. van Kleeck, S. A. Stahl, & E. B. Bauer (Eds.), *On reading books to children: Parents and teachers* (pp. 363–83). Mahwah, NJ: Erlbaum.

Stanovich, K. E. (1980). Toward an interactive-compensatory model of individual differences in the development of reading fluency. *Reading Research Quarterly, 16*(1), 32–71.

Stanovich, K. E., Cunningham, A. E., & West, R. F. (1998). Literacy experiences and the shaping of cognition. In S. G. Paris & H. M. Wellman (Eds.), *Global prospects for education: Development, culture, and schooling* (pp. 253–88). Washington, DC: American Psychological Association.

Stevens, R. (1912). *The question as a measure of efficiency in instruction: A critical study of class-room practice*. New York: Teachers College.

Styslinger, M. E. (1999). Mars and Venus in my classroom: Men go to their caves and women talk during peer revision. *English Journal, 88*(3), 50–56.

Styslinger, M. E. (2004). Chasing the albatross: Gendering theory and reading with dual-voiced journals. *Journal of Adolescent & Adult Literacy, 47*(8), 628–37.

Styslinger, M. E., & Overstreet, J. (2014). Strengthening argumentative writing with speaking and listening (Socratic) circles. *Voices from the Middle, 22*(1), 58–62.

Styslinger, M. E., & Pollock, T. (2010). The chicken and the egg: Inviting response and talk through Socratic circles. *Voices from the Middle, 18*(2), 36–45.

Styslinger, M. E., Walker, N., & Lenker, T. (2014). Beyond the sticky note and Venn diagram: Comprehension strategies for 21st-century schools. *Voices from the Middle, 22*(2), 13–20.

Styslinger, M. E., & Whisenant, A. (2004). Crossing cultures with multi-voiced journals. *Voices from the Middle, 12*(1), 26–31.

Sumara, D. J. (2000). Researching complexity. *Journal of Literacy Research, 32*(2), 267–81.

Sweigart, W. (1991). Classroom talk, knowledge development, and writing. *Research in the Teaching of English, 25*(4), 469–96.

Swift, K. (1993). Try reading workshop in your classroom. *The Reading Teacher, 46*(5), 366–71.

Taba, H. (1967). *Teacher's handbook for elementary social studies*. Reading, MA: Addison-Wesley.

Taylor, B. M., Frye, B. J., & Maruyama, G. M. (1990). Time spent reading and reading growth. *American Educational Research Journal, 27*(2), 351–62.

TEDx Talks. (2011, December 7). *Hip-Hop & Shakespeare?* Akala at TEDxAldeburgh 2011 [Video file]. Retrieved from https://www.youtube.com/watch?v=DSbtkLA3GrY&list=RDDSbtkLA3GrY

Tovani, C. (2000). *I read it, but I don't get it: Comprehension strategies for adolescent readers*. Portland, ME: Stenhouse.

Tovani, C. (2004). *Do I really have to teach reading? Content comprehension, grades 6–12*. Portland, ME: Stenhouse.

Trelease, J. (2013). *The read-aloud handbook* (7th ed.). New York: Penguin Books.

Tucker, L. P. (2000). Liberating students through reader-response pedagogy in the introductory literature course. *Teaching English in the Two-Year College, 28*(2), 199–206.

Uthman, L. E. (2002). Readers' theatre: An approach to reading with more than a touch of drama. *Teaching PreK-8, 32*(6), 56–57.

Vopat, J. (2009). *Writing circles: Kids revolutionize workshop.* Portsmouth, NH: Heinemann.

Weaver, C. (2002). *Reading process & practice* (3rd ed.). Portsmouth, NH: Heinemann.

Wheatley, M. (2002). *Turning to one another: Simple conversations to restore hope to the future* (1st ed.). San Francisco: Berrett-Koehler.

Wilhelm, J. D. (1997). *"You gotta be the book": Teaching engaged and reflective reading with adolescents.* New York: Teachers College.

Wilhelm, J. D. (2004). *Reading is seeing: Learning to visualize scenes, characters, ideas, and text worlds to improve comprehension and reflective reading.* New York: Scholastic.

Wilhelm, J. D., Smith, M. W., & Fredricksen, J. E. (2012). *Get it done! Writing and analyzing informational texts to make things happen.* Portsmouth, NH: Heinemann.

Wu, Y., & Samuels, S. J. (2004). *How the amount of time spent on independent reading affects reading achievement: A response to the national reading panel.* Paper presented at the International Reading Association Conference, Reno, NV.

Index

Author

Mary E. Styslinger is an associate professor of English and literacy education at the University of South Carolina where she directs the Midlands Writing Project and has served as the secondary program coordinator. She is a past president of the South Carolina Council of Teachers of English and currently coedits *South Carolina English Teacher*. Her research interest includes interweaving literacy into the English curriculum and serving marginalized and at-risk youth; she has pub-lished articles in *English Journal, Voices from the Middle, Language Arts, Journal of Adolescent and Adult Literacy*, and *Kappan*. She is a coeditor of the recently published *Literacy behind Bars: Successful Reading and Writing Strategies for Use with Incarcerated Youth and Adults*.

This book was typeset in TheMix and Palatino by Barbara Frazier.

The typefaces used on the cover include Trajan Pro, New Century Schoolbook, Pea Lopi, and Pea Ashley Grace.

The book was printed on 50-lb. White Offset paper by Versa Press, Inc.